Corporeality:
Emergent Consciousness within its Spatial Dimensions

Consciousness, Literature & the Arts

39

General Editor:
Daniel Meyer-Dinkgräfe

Editorial Board:
Anna Bonshek, Per Brask, John Danvers,
William S. Haney II, Amy Ione,
Michael Mangan, Arthur Versluis,
Christopher Webster, Ralph Yarrow
Jade Rosina McCutcheon

Corporeality:
Emergent Consciousness within its Spatial Dimensions

Maya Nanitchkova Öztürk

Amsterdam - New York, NY 2014

Cover image: art manipulation by Umut İşbilir and Mina Öztürk (derived from iststockphoto-13008441).

Cover design by Aart Jan Bergshoeff.

ISBN: 978-90-420-3838-7
ISSN: 1573-2193
E-Book ISBN: 978-94-012-1083-6
E-book ISSN: 1879-6044

Contents

Acknowledgements

I wish to thank Mina and Halit, my closest, who have not only encouraged, listened, and questioned, but have cared for me and endured, faithfully, all the ups and downs throughout this process. I also thank my parents for extending, unconditionally, their love and trust.

I am deeply indebted to Professor Daniel Meyer-Dinkgräfe for his firm support of my academic efforts in many respects and over several years, and especially for his willingness to undertake the task of editing this book, and for his patience and kindness in guiding me through it.

Introduction

From elusive space to the generative potential of the corporeal
Space is a notoriously elusive matter, experientially and theoretically. Its theoretical elusiveness as physical presence from the vicinity of immediate experience, is rooted in the space-matter, and solid-void dichotomies through which built space comes to be conceptualized, and is entangled with the complexities of the various layers of experience it supports. Thus while constructing the physical framework with which life evolves, space might come forth rarely as the source of affect and feeling: its influences are subtle, and would tend to remain background and peripheral to intent and action.

The physical presence of built space is composite. It entails its object-like solid constitution by way of material elements and components (walls, floors, structural members, articulations, and decorative motifs), and the void that is brought about at the same time. Hence its depiction in theory oscillates among these two apparently different entities. Its appearance to phenomenal presence and, correspondingly, its functioning, socio-cultural role and meanings have come to be conceptualized and understood split along the duality of this constitution. Hence built space is understood both in terms of the fixity, permanence and the apparent immutability of its physical appearance as architectural form (object/figure/identity) in perception, and in relation to the less strict nature of the enclosed, or excluded void (space/spatiality)—construed as a field of action and experiences where a vast variety of purposes and activities unfold. While this dichotomy— solid/void, object/space, figure/field, vision/action—might appear too simplistic, it nevertheless points to the more obvious reasons for the persistent divergence of approaches to the study of built space. The notion of space lacks univocal definition, and, consequently, also a coherent conceptual framework at the basis of some more monolithic theorization.

In the broader realm of the humanities, discourse on space is a difficult territory, where each disciplinary field (philosophy, social theory, anthropology, spatial theory, geography, and architecture) develops its special perspective on space, along with the set of specified concepts through which to address the issues of correlations with space. That is to say that in the course of this specialization, the complex processes of ontological and social-cultural import that space embeds, come to be diffused to various disciplinary fields. Once allocated to a discipline, the focus shifts to the experiential processes themselves, and their explanation would tend to become associated with the factors and forces (social, political, ideological) characterizing the respective field, rather than with spatial circumstance. The discussion on space itself, too, is not simply allotted to different disciplines and subject to different perspectives, but enhances its inherent dichotomy. In this way aspects of space are taken up as separate concerns—such as its physical constitution as linked to perception, which is construed as distinct from space that is constitutive of social practice and experience. While this multiplicity would offer fertile grounds for the discourse on space, especially at the interstices, it has also fragmenting effects, maintaining the split in the notion of space itself, and, in this way, also leaving, potentially, unattended areas.

What these diverging perspectives and notions would share, is the emphasis on understanding space in terms of appearance and affordance as the prime areas for the correlation with space, and hence for the possibility of meaning formation. Yet the respective interpretations as to the effects of appearances and affordances would nevertheless come to be associated with different spatial and experiential realities. Hence while in some of these fields (such as architectural theory) built architectural space emerges in terms of its image, identity, and functional appropriateness, in others (such as sociology) it is posited as a field of activity, a background or framework of references, and as an area of intervention and constitution. The former perspective attends to the preconceived ideas which built space materializes and presents to perception, while the latter highlights the evolving life which it houses. In this way the two-fold presence of physical space extends into the discussion over built-space-as-designed-and-perceived versus experience-as-producing-and-appropriating-space. The former framework addresses the complexities of space as architectural form with respect to meaning formulation. In this way experiential components become submerged into perception, which, as a phase subsequent to experience, completes the process at a properly conscious reflective level and comes to stand for the whole process. Thus the physical space of form, becomes associated primarily with those aspects of space which are obvious, immutable, permanent, and representative—and allow safely separating the processes of interpretation of such effects of space into the special province of experience—perception. This object entity, then, can be observed, and its meanings deciphered. The process of correlation becomes one of mediation, and hence also supports explanation in the relatively passive terms of reception. It allows the prioritization of 'rational space'—i.e., its association with deterministic positions, transmitted knowledge frameworks, and an essentially 'constituted' subject. In this theoretical context the inquiry into immediate experience remains an under-explored latent possibility.

The latter perspective posits experience in terms of the active share of agency in the correlation, and highlights intent and intervention involved in transforming and producing space, which come to stand for the wholesome experience. As built space appears too permanent and, possibly, definitive to be pursued as genuinely productive, the correlations of the liberated autonomous subject take the form of evasion, resistance, opposition and re-formulation—all supported by the conception of space as 'open', in that it invites and allows transformation.

In theorizations of immediate experience itself, space retains a status of an omnipresent yet also tacit notion. With respect to the immediate, space, analogous to time, is being construed as already immediately present. That is to say that, for belonging to experience integrally, space comes to be taken as self-evident—the relation being too closely entangled to be examined analytically, or explicated. This self-evidence, though, does not implicate or establish that the possible import of the spatial is non-existent, or negligible. Rather, it renders material space with respect to immediate experience theoretically transparent.

The elusiveness of physical space at this level of theoretical inquiry reflects the elusiveness of material space, and the possible experience through it, from the registers of conscious awareness. Although prevalent and integral to all experience and present as the most tangible component vitalizing experience, in the process of experience space may be noticed rarely as a source. Its subtle influences are embedded in sense perception, evolve background and peripheral to other activity, and would remain, as such, deeper in the pre-conscious. They would tend to be fleeting and transitory, as the experiential borne through space, would shift towards and become assimilated in the complex mental processes related to intent and action which are closer to the threshold of conscious awareness. With respect to consciousness, this experiential elusiveness of the spatial can be understood in terms of the dominant nature of the experience that is action-centred, and would come to mobilise 'access consciousness'. As Burge (1997: 427-435) suggests, involvement in activities employs and relies on the operations of access consciousness which governs the abilities needed for action and foregrounds the workings of 'phenomenal consciousness' whose function is to ensure the continuity of sensation. In the light of this distinction among kinds and levels of consciousness, it can be understood that experience which evolves due to space would only figure as a vague awareness over the circumstances which trigger it.

This elusiveness of material space, the fragmentation of discourse on space and the diverging priorities of different disciplinary approaches, would suggest a discontinuity in the account of built physical space in particular: it is posited and studied predominantly in terms of perception. A systematic and detailed inquiry into the materiality of space with respect to lived experience, and in the vicinity of the body, would not be found readily as explicit direction of research in discourse on the 'lived'—body, and space, or in the larger frameworks engaging in experience. In view of the principles of continuity of sensibility and experience, this would point to a small but significant breach in the account of the physical presence of space—that which pertains to experience due to space.

Corporeality: discreet experience taking form

Building up on the profound insight that thinking experience in spatial terms does disclose the realities of our existence in a physical concreteness which its other dimension—time—does not offer (Massey 2005: 189), and relying on the intuition, that there is more to the experience 'with' space than is currently acknowledged, this book proposes an inquiry along a narrow incision that links up immediate experience and space, directly.

It will seek to re-construct, theoretically and methodologically, built architectural space in its corporeal presence and establish it in terms of a material shared framework, as it opens up to experience, with respect to the situated body. It holds that re-thinking physical space in terms of experience can help retrieve physical space from its latent self-evident states, and render it as an experientially consequential field which envelopes us incessantly, intimately, and immediately—a qualified matter with which we become. This will allow positing space at this level as a distinct area of research, re-articulate it as an empirical entity that can be analysed in terms of its unmediated effects, and examine the layer of space-body correlations—as a layer of vital processes integral to immediate experience. Approaching space in terms of experience is apt to provide new insights into the subtle bodily ways in which it works. Analysis of the spatial constructions and correlations in view of that experiential layer, then, would particularise certain special spatial underlying mechanisms, which allow understanding the productive capacities of space, and the operations of the experience in question in terms of their deeper internal structures. It would offer grounds for a conceptual reconsideration of experience through the material concreteness of its most tangible component—space. The experiential bearing and contents that become available in the course of such analysis, in turn, would offer glimpses on aspects of the ontological and socio-cultural import of the social realm through the perspective of immediate experience with space—i.e., it would disclose the constitutive potential embedded in the corporeality of space-body correlations.

Throughout, this book presents an inquiry into built architectural space and its generative potentialities with respect to emergent consciousness. It probes into a twilight zone of immediate experience—a zone of intimate reverberations between space and body, seeking to explore and establish these correlations as productive and authentic paths of grasping realities of the social and material world. It aims to bring to the foreground those bodily ways through which the situated agent would come to be affected, live with and appropriate its physical surrounds—phenomena that begin from without, evolve in terms of discreet pre-conscious, pre-contemplative mental events and processes. These belong to immediate corporeal experience, and are hence construed as both non-discursive and indeterminate. Yet, while they begin as events of phenomenal consciousness, these processes also build up the experiential material at the basis of bodily feeling and knowing, and in this way partake in the constitution of self/agency.

Inquiry in the proposed terms would offer insights into the links between the sensate aspects of social situatedness, and our human capacities in grasping these— i.e., into a cluster of experiential phenomena underlying the formulation of sensibilities enabling social togetherness—links that remain unattended on other accounts.

This inquiry proposes and entails a systematic re-conceptualization of built physical space in terms of experience. This rendition of space exceeds the definitive terms associated with space in the accustomed frameworks of 'perception', where space is seen as a separate, external, representational and objectified entity that is appreciated intellectually and interpreted. It differs also from those altogether suspect schemes where space is seen as separate, external entity exerting physical impact that is passively received, and the correlation is explicated in terms of causality—a process that is 'closed' and predictable. Instead, by shifting away from thinking space in terms of perception, and towards thinking the spatial as a dimension inherent in experience, it addresses a level of correlations, where space and body are merged, entwined, co-extensive, and experience emerges as a process which is felt, affective, corporeal, open-ended, and productive.

Altering the perspective on space allows bringing it forth as material presence and examining the ways in which it works—i.e., attains distinctiveness, presents possibilities for experience by proposing the specific circumstances of the contact. It opens up built architectural space to analytical inquiry—accessing the experiential (as distinct from the perceptual) and the phenomenal (as distinct from the purely visual, as well as the purely phenomenological). Such inquiry would complement accustomed perspectives on built space, which restrict its role to that of a frame and medium of meaning formulation in perception, with one that posits it as an equally shared, yet entirely corporeal and experiential framework. This would allow extending built architectural space as phenomenal physical presence into the realm of experience, and making a step towards recognizing space in its tangible non-representational materiality, and the capacities of this materiality to set us on the path of unique, explorative, irretrievable becoming.

As but one particular means towards such a re-construction, this current approach pursues the path of positing physical space as a dynamic constituent of experience in its own right. This offers grounds to explore the subtle ways in which spatial circumstance not only situates firmly within the 'here and now', but also conditions that 'here'—

i.e., discloses space in its capacity to trigger the experiential as active modality of becoming. Physical space emerges in its capacity to bring into presence the realities of our situatedness not only as inert static background, and not solely in terms of affordance. Rather, it exerts its activating and mobilizing effects by instating, simultaneously and at multiple levels, diverse spatial forces, mechanisms, and relations—space materializes and qualifies conditions. This perpetual configuring and re-configuring of spatial circumstance makes such conditions phenomenally available to the grasp through the body, influencing that which would be 'felt' and 'known'. By way of attending to its possible unmediated effects at multiple levels, material space can be understood in its workings with respect to the body, and recovered in its tangibility as a dimension integral to experience.

Validating the spatial dimension in its affective influence over the body and immediate experience depends on locating the inquiry at the level of the corporeal, and bringing concerns with the concrete correlations of bodies with the material realities of space foreground. It entails instituting the methodological means facilitating analysis of the physical constitution of concrete possibilities through which space and experience open up onto each other, and establishing these as material possibilities by which to infer that which emerges therein. At the level of the corporeal, physical space emerges in its palpable qualified presence as it surrounds, affects and suggests—it embeds our very existence, and in this way characterises and qualifies experience. Yet construing corporeality as the shared space-body realm—i.e., as the extension of the relation itself into its physical circumstances, does not implicate or presuppose that space and body become a unified whole. Rather, it sets the relation within the corporeal as grounds of the relation, and helps articulate the nature of that relation by way of involving space as an integral feature of the experiential continuum. It brings forth the relation as one of becoming, where engagement is direct, and unfolds, as yet, devoid of distance and intent—i.e., prior to moments which would presuppose processes of perceiving and hence rely on cognitive modality. At this level, and examined in the context and terms of the corporeal, the relation can be construed as founded on and evolving through the immediacy of direct encounter with sensate realities.

Involving the spatial dimension as integral to the experiential continuum allows attending to and explicating the relational nature of experience and becoming in a degree of specificity lacking in the abstract explanations of the larger philosophical frameworks. It allows exploring the processes of becoming in terms of a range of occurrences that pertain to the intimacy of direct acquaintance of the sensing body with concrete corporeal qualified space—i.e., within the circumstances and internal mechanisms through which experience evolves. It becomes possible to conceive of the correlations with space in their most productive phase—a phase which is quite distinct from the distanced and implicitly definitive cognitive modes of phenomenological perception, or the explicitly definitive claims of causality. Rather, the correlation emerges as embedded in bodily processes that are essentially explorative, improvisational, and hence also singular. Yet there would be also a crucial shared aspect: the tendency of vitality towards responsiveness. Within its spatial context the correlation can be understood as it becomes—based on a fundamental encounter with spatial circumstance and hence essentially open-ended. Yet it also can be analysed—for being founded in reverberation and entailing elements of correspondence, coherence and co-formation—with space.

Inquiry into space as integral dimension and constituent of experience offers insight into correlations with space at a deep level, where these correlations can be construed still as wholesome and in the making. It allows exploring that relation in its phase prior to action or intent, which would begin to chisel out sides and come to implicate space as distinct and apart from body. Rather, it brings into focus the relation in the phase of 'becoming with'—as it evolves within immediacy, devoid of distance—a phase where thresholds are permeable. Within the continuum of corporeality, this 'becoming' could be construed in its tangible twofold nature—the grasping of the self occurs within the specificities of the reality of the whole situation. What can be brought to the foreground in this close-up analysis of the corporeality of space-body relations, then, would pertain to that which emerges within the vital activity of correlating itself: a palpable-space-with-sensate-body. It would offer insight into the relation as it is felt, lived with, and possibly actualized—an actualization whereby the affective, cognitive and ethical embedded in the situation might come to be internalized.

Construing corporeality as the shared space-body realm—i.e., as the extension of the relation itself alters the vantage point through which to explore immediate experience: it captures the relation in its 'open' phase where circumstance (pertaining to space) and impulse (pertaining to the body) are not yet pulled apart. It is a co-extensive and material context which is being 'felt'—appreciated and acknowledged intuitively, prior even to reaching the threshold of awareness. It offers further aspects to attend to in understanding discrete experience—i.e., the particularly spatial and concretely bodily. It also allows construing of the correlation in a novel way: the corporeal correlation denoted in terms of this co-extensiveness differs from both the gravitational 'incorporation' of objects in space implicated in the deliberate directed ocular extensions of the phenomenological subject (Merleau-Ponty), and from the explorative instantiating extensions into space of the performing self (performance theory, theories of the performative). Prior to acts of purpose—perception or expression, the conception of corporeality allows thinking the relation as extending both ways. It opens up to a different understanding of the relations between body and space—one that is apt to acknowledge phenomena that begin as 'induced', and recognize space-to-body relations as integral and productive part of their underexplored reciprocities.

Corporeality as the realm of the relation can, then, be concretized, and characterized within spatial detail, involving spatial condition and circumstance as generative aspects with which the relation evolves. An account of spatial circumstance brings the corporeal realm of the relation into tangible presence: it emerges as grained with limits and openings; it is charged with forces, tensions—it exerts diverse and mostly ambiguous influences through which it suggests, and insinuates. It can be explored as the qualified matter out of which and with which the relation actualizes. Potent with manifold possibilities, this material space-field activates and challenges: it triggers the experiential as a modality of becoming, while also proposing terms in which this becoming might come to evolve. The account of its spatial extension, allows thinking the relation in terms of reverberation and exploration that are also inherently qualified—it orients towards a particularization of that which emerges therein.

Examining the relation in terms of the corporeal allows concretizing the potency and vitality of the immediate. It emerges within that phase of experience where the space-to-body seamless and ceaseless intertwining would tend to actualize as an intimate mutuality—'with', and in correspondence. Belonging neither entirely to space, nor to the body, it characterizes both—it pertains to the experience of the relation. This 'feeling with' phase might be fleeting, yet it is never passive. It provides the shifting grounds for that which is more properly conscious: it comes to nurture mental processes of utmost complexity and intensity—feelings, concepts, ideas, and intentions (Langer, 1988). Inquiry into corporeality construed as the fused grounds of space-body-extensions, then, would offer insight into immediate experience as it acquires its impetus, and incentive among divergent circumstances, forces, and impulses, where possibilities actualize as a passing from space to feeling that is at once also a taking form. Exploring the corporeal in such terms allows construing of space as a potential locus of sensibility, forming.

Thinking space at the bodily level where it is construed as integral to and characterizing the experience of the relation, allows pursuing a depiction of aspects of discreet experience through a different trajectory: one that generates from within space—within corporeal diverse 'given' circumstances that are lived with, and intuited inherently to the relation. It renders feeling beyond the sense of the body 'feeling its way around' that characterizes the perpetual explorative state of the body's perceptual systems (Gibson, 1983). Rather it articulates feeling as the bodily way of acknowledging particular conditions—i.e., it marks the possibilities in passing from space to feeling, where features of space configure towards distinctiveness and disparate circumstances become corroborated intensities. It allows construing of the perpetual reconfiguring of phenomenal presences—as these would pass towards becoming apprehended existential conditions. Attending to that spatially generated stratum of micro phenomena at the threshold of consciousness, along with the emotive and mental ingredients emerging therein, presupposes the re-articulation of space as to its unmediated effects and exploring the possibilities arising in the very processes of appreciation and appropriation of space.

Re-constructing material space: perception, experience, and the emergent

This current approach is developed from within the field of architecture, and relies on ways of attending to spatial detail characteristic to this disciplinary field. However, as an alternative approach to built architectural space, in effect it also alters established research techniques, interpretative priorities, and conventional notions, opening up terms like spatial form, spatial effect, or operations of space to re-conceptualization, and analysis. A major factor for this alteration is grounded in the intent to arrive at a conceptualization of physical space that would allow disentangling, analytically, its operations at experiential level from its overall effects as approached in terms of perception. One important methodological shift in this direction is enabled by the systematic re-thinking space in terms of experience, which firmly locates the approach at the level of the corporeal.

Physical space, such as the concrete architectural form actualized in a building or monument, is a permanent and continuous reality which works at multiple levels. Thus, in addition to its presence to perception, space can be construed of, approached and examined in its openness to immediate experience—a modality of the correlation distinct and prior to perception. Spatial phenomena and processes belonging to this generative phase of the continuum experience-perception do not easily come forth—experientially and theoretically. Evolving at a more rudimentary level, less explicit, and less available to consciousness, such phenomena become assimilated into the subsequent phase of correlation—perception, to the interpretation of which they are, consequently, subsumed in theory.

In mainstream research such experiential aspects would tend to remain concealed and relatively less examined both due to established priorities, which keep the focus of study on 'functions' of architectural space, and by the established emphasis on interpretation oriented towards the construction of meanings. This broad and encompassing notion of experience, then, comes to favour the second of the two interlocking phases—experience and perception—i.e., perception comes to be understood as, and stand for the total process. The prioritisation of perception not only confines explication of spatial effects tightly indexed to 'function' and 'meaning', but also maintains 'space' and 'subject' as two distinct entities. Built for a purpose, architectural space is discussed in view of the dominant functions which it houses, facilitates and represents. It is thought of as an object- place that is seen, entered, and used—at once medium, container, and support. Connoting a broader range of correlations and processes, experience in those approaches comes to be understood at a level where involvement is mediated via a predetermined purpose, as well as via the architectural means through which such purpose is expressed. These two entities—space and perceiver/user, then, are in need of re-integration. In architectural theory, this re-integration takes the form of constructing links between spatial features and the experiencing subject facilitated by, and in view of the act of perception—it entails the intent of aesthetic and use-oriented reading of spatial clues which define and represent that function. Experience of space comes to be understood as a correlation to space which is essentially hermeneutic in nature, and is explicated by interpreting the processes through which the perceiver deciphers and constructs meanings. Established in these terms, the correlation with architectural space is readily assumed as a special province of experience, to be accounted for in architectural theory. This reflects on interpretations of socio-cultural import of architectural space, and maintains the unfavourable terms in which that architectural framework is considered to be liable: space comes to be understood as a means to manifest and transmit predetermined content, as well as contain and control—aspects which come forth in critical social theory.

In contrast to such established priorities, this current approach proposes a methodological framework which allows dissociating and re-articulating those occurrences embedded in physical space, which are explicitly direct, non-mediating and experiential. Focusing on the un-mediated, non-contemplative, and corporeally productive, it arrives at a different understanding of certain enduring properties of built architectural space and discloses their operations as a bodily way of attaining meaning and affect. Hence while engaging in most of the same main features that are central to studies on architecture—such as enclosure, configuration, geometrical form, sectional and volumetric properties—this current approach alters the way in which these are rendered and analysed. It shifts research to the empirical level and reconstructs architectural space in its material presence—qualified, affective and open to experience. It locates analysis of space mid-level prior to functional and architectural specifications, and in this way re-orients it towards the operations of space as physical entity and with respect to the situated body. It addresses immediate experience as that which is lived through non-mediated effects and arrives at a rendition of a layer which evolves relatively autonomous both from the assigned foreground functions and from their representational architectural expressions, but is, instead, intrinsically linked with physical space. Based on keen attentiveness to spatial detail this approach particularises, analytically and theoretically, how spatial features configure and build up to experiential distinctiveness— i.e., it attends to the underlying internal mechanisms of the correlation. It discloses physical space in its capacities 'to do'—i.e., it shows how space, by triggering distinct experiential forms, actually engenders alternative, corporeal paths of becoming. By exploring spatial circumstance, it concretises aspects of the empirical reality which underlies the contact, and extends architectural analysis with a conceptualization and speculative inquiry (analogous to approaches in non-representational theory) into the experiential possibilities embedded therein.

By bringing into focus the space-to-body relationships as but one way in which the immediately experiential might evolve, and re-orienting inquiry towards thinking experience in terms of space, this current approach aligns with the shift towards the 'lived' in the larger context of philosophical and sociological thought. Though taking different forms in the various frameworks upholding this shift, inquiry into the 'lived' presents a crucial means of resisting deterministic notions and positions that would presuppose the 'transmission' of predetermined meanings, and a relatively passive 'constituted' subject at the other end. Counter to such positions, the discourse on the lived allows highlighting the active share of agency—constituting and constituted in the course of immediate/lived experience, and establishing a relatively autonomous self at the basis of understanding both agency and the larger ontological and socio-cultural processes.

The engagement of this current study with these key frameworks is two-fold. On the one hand, it allows deriving and involving concerns with self/agency, socio-spatial reciprocity, and processes of constitution and emergence into closer correlation with analysis of architectural space. On the other hand, this engagement is instrumental in formulating the theoretical foundations of this current approach. Hence although no ready framework would emerge from this survey, it is fertile and rich with insights and propositions on which this study relies. In tracing out its rather narrow incision so as to examine how space and experience correlate directly, and establish this as a distinct area of research, this approach does not conflict with the principles of either of these perspectives, but rather confirms the productive nature of that experience while extending on the generative role of space in this towards a particularization of the spatial dimension within corporeal detail.

In spatial theory the resistance to social and spatial determinisms is sought in two fundamental respects: by drawing attention to the very conceptualizations of space and their consequential influence on social, spatial and political practices, and by bringing the context of social practice itself into the explication of the produced nature of space, which is construed as a matter of active appropriation at every level. Foundational to the field of spatial theory, in Lefebvre's (1991) tripartite framework, the conception of 'lived space' presents the theoretical means to counterbalance the effects of 'representational space' (connoting the built environment as architectural monument as bearer of ideologically based pre-conceived ideas on architecture, institution and function), and 'representations of space' (connoting these ideas and ideologies as expressed in distinct conceptual structures). While all of these would be socially produced, expressive of, and reproducing contingent social relations, the potentially liberating instance of these correlations is actualized in the context of lived experience.

The prime concern with architectural space, then, is that it comes to be understood exclusively in terms of its permanent and representational nature. It is in such terms, that the notion of space as 'fixed', 'finished' and 'static' come to be maintained. Hence built space is seen primarily in its liability to lend itself to the uses of power in asserting and conveying dominant ideologies, and enhance the Foucauldian line of criticism in discourse on space. In recent spatial theory, such views are being countered by a different conceptualization of space. Compellingly voiced by thinkers like Massey (2005), this shift towards the lived takes the form of a reading of space as essentially 'open'—'fluid', 'porous' and 'relational'—i.e., constituted and constitutive of agency, where the processes of active appropriation of space are embedded in material practices at multiple levels. Concerned with identifying the socio-political alternatives in re-defining spatiality in the broader context of spatial theory, the shift towards the lived is understood in terms of the attitudes and interventions of active autogenous social subjects. Relying on these insights and extending on the notion of openness, this current study seeks to arrive at a conceptualisation of built space where it, too, can be understood and rendered 'open' to experience and the body, and is confirmed as a vital context in constituting agency and the collective—an experiential field apt to cultivate capacities, engender practices and incite affects enabling social togetherness.

The engagement with the 'process' perspective on experience, as brought forth in the Deleuzeian line of transcendental empiricism, is rather marked. In its very orientation towards the empirical, and the focus on discreet experience, this current approach bears special affinity with that larger philosophical framework, and relies on methodological propositions—such as the focus on the correlation, and conceptual tools—such as the concepts of the emergent and reverberation, at its very foundations. Thinkers in that linage insist on placing the focus decisively on the relation itself and exploring it as a process, because this allows taking inquiry beyond subject-object distinctions. As Dewsbury (2003) explains, this focus on the correlation allows evading two important pitfalls in explicating experience: the linear 'causal' interpretations, as well as the entanglement with issues of origin (of knowledge) unresolved in phenomenological discourse. Instead, it re-locates exploration to the immediate 'pre-discursive' moments of experience, where the relation actualizes—i.e., to the events of encounter construed as inherently 'open' occurrences of 'becoming'. This shift of focus, then, allows theoretical engagement with that which evolves between the lines of representation of meaning and exploring that which is also possible—coloured by chance, inherent diversity and multiplicity, wherein its liberating effects lie. It highlights the 'coming into being' itself as it evolves—the imminent, the 'pre-individual', 'non-contemplative' and thus genuinely singular. Conceptualized in temporal terms—as the moments of interruption of the habitual that allow new possibilities to emerge, discreet experience is posited with emphasis that is not so much on 'what' happens, but on 'that it happens'. The ontological and epistemological import embedded in the relation, then, is disclosed by inquiry into the 'emergent' in encounter, the generative principle of the 'grasping of the thusness' of being, of the 'sensation of place as something more and other than oneself' (Dewsbury 2003). As evidenced in the broader field of non-representational theory, such instances in the context of discreet experience, are, potentially, open to particularization.

In this respect this current approach can be seen as such an attempt for particularization of immediate experience—namely by exploring its generation through the corporeality of its spatial dimension. Deeper down, engagement with the framework of the process philosophers helps verify the appropriateness of the proposed approach as an empirical inquiry into aspects of space, in spite of the fact that in conceptualizing the processes of becoming space is not an explicit issue. The focus on correlations in terms of direct encounter also makes the links with other perspectives on which this study relies, logically consistent—such as the notion of the body as perceptual system, and the conception of the 'sensate' and 'feeling' as essential expression of vitality.

In this current study, a particularization of immediate experience is approached by opening up for inquiry an area that remains invisible in both of these larger theoretical and philosophical frameworks—namely the area of space and the corporeality of space-to-body correlations as aspects which concretise and qualify the zone of contact. In re-constructing the concrete physical presence of space—a corporeal entity as it opens up to the body and experience, it can be validated as a source and dynamic constituent of experience and explored in its generative capacities with respect to the emergent. Extending the relation into its spatial continuation, and examining space at an in-between level, is apt to disclose further essential ways in which this same formed, built, concrete architectural space is 'open'—i.e., productive.

Re-thinking experience in terms of space presents a new area of research which does not conflict with the principles laid out in these above frameworks. Rather it acknowledges a further aspect of the empirical presence of space, and extends analysis and explication of the materiality of correlations with space in keeping with the criteria of sensibility and continuity of sensation. Though rather narrow, this area is worth pursuing. Once opened up for inquiry, it yields a whole stratum of occurrences—discreet processes which offer new insight and extend on aspects of experience as a corporeal issue. It furthers understanding of the emergent with those micro-events that begin as response to material circumstance, disclosing the vital capacities of making contact, and renders the processes of acquisition embedded therein. It in this way inquiry into physical space confirms and complements the principal conditions of experience around which perspectives on the lived converge. These entail the capacities of the self to exceed inwardness, open up to the world, and encounter that which is larger, and internalize possibilities for change that are called forth by that encounter.

By articulating the undercurrent spatial logic of the corporeal situation as a means of characterising the conditions of the contact zone, this perspective brings forth a whole host of vital properties and generative capacities of space, neglected on other accounts. It accesses a cluster of affects and embodied practices as alternative ways of becoming and knowing attained in and through space, which evolve through the sensate and bodily, and which can therefore only be inferred circumstantially. It develops the conceptual tools to derive these as phenomena evolving integral to space, which can only be disclosed by way of minute analysis of the spatial: they emerge in the form of existential conditions open to appropriation in discreet experience. Thus this current approach brings to the foreground a range of aspects pertinent to the processes of socio-spatial reciprocity and mutual co-constitution, that are productive, and evolve in the context of the minute 'material practices' of inhabiting and construction. They concern processes which pertain to and help explicate the reciprocal passage: from space to feeling—to sensibility. It will attempt to particularize how built space at this corporeal level is always a potential, and always open to the body. It will seek to render what this openness might bear with respect to emergent consciousness of the situated agent—accessing aspects and phenomena which are relatively less explored or established in correlation to spatial detail, or addressed elsewhere.

Contextualization: theatre as the case of study
Theatre is a potent and challenging choice as the concrete spatial context to develop, specify, and demonstrate the principles and propositions of this current approach. It is a challenging choice because in approaching theatre space, it ventures into an area of intense research: the problematic of theatre is being explored both within its specificities—in the fields of theatre studies and the corresponding branch of architecture, and in the broader field of the humanities—where it is taken up as a means of understanding issues of the social and public realm. Evolving in terms of multidimensional processes and components, theatre generates and exerts its social and cultural influence in complex ways and at various levels. It presents a compelling foreground function, which is examined as an aesthetic issue through the intricacies of meaning formulation, and whose transformative potential is seen to be embedded both in the practices of production and presentation, and in those of perception. Posited in various terms—performative practice, artistic work, theatrical event, and participatory process, it presents dense and fertile grounds to explore manifold ways in which the theatrical context can support the development of human understanding and consciousness, and even incite altered

states. Taken up as a cultural phenomenon in its ontological and social repercussions, it presents a potent means of research into the broader context of social and cultural practice.

However, similarly to its status in discourse on space, the notion of built physical space retains its elusive status in these various frameworks focusing on theatre as well as these do not address the experiential potential lying with its material presence explicitly and fully. The broader frameworks take up theatre as a cultural phenomenon, and, each in its own terms, focus on forces and factors of a social nature in explicating its ontological and social implications, leaving experiential aspects of space largely unattended. In contrast, for discourse on theatre, space is a central issue. In keeping with Peter Brook's (1968: 11) famous and laconic depiction of the theatrical situation, where space is seen as the primary condition that enables the simultaneous presence of performer and watcher, space is acknowledged as an integral component of the theatrical situation. Yet though enabling the very occurrence of performance, space comes to be associated exclusively with its functions to contain, stage, and frame the performance and, as expressive medium, support the processes of production and perception of theatrical meanings. It is posited as a means in actualising such functions, and interpreted in terms of a particularly theatrical blend of physical and artistic and architectural elements. Highlighting its re-presentational capacities, this notion of physical space renders the nature of correlations with it interpretative, and essentially hermeneutic. The productive potential of theatre as an aesthetic issue is associated and explored primarily via theatrical contents. In keeping with Aristotle's (1985) profound insights, this productive potential is tightly linked to the function of poetry (tragedy), and the utmost point of affect in an individual issuing from the discovery of the unexpected. The rendition of such potential is sought in terms of the theatrical work—the text, the plot, the performance, and their spatial expressions in scenic art as primary vehicles, while the fact that these productive states are also persistently and firmly situated within the shared space of theatre would tend to remain relatively overlooked. The exploration space is indexed to these foreground processes and functions, while the materiality of the setting in its possible experiential bearing, especially with respect to the situated agent, remains a neglected area.

This current approach ventures precisely into this neglected area of direct correlations among the theatre site as physical space, and immediate experience. It builds on a series of previous studies, each of which has focused on particular aspects in the operations of the site as experiential field, and sought to disclose its affective, ontological and social experiential bearing as such (Öztürk 2006, 2007, 2010 a, 2010 b, 2013). Threading a relatively underexplored area, these studies have gradually led to a more explicit incentive: particularising the approach as empirical analytical inquiry into physical space with respect to immediate experience, and clarifying the methodological and conceptual means in theorising the corporeal constructions of experiential effects and conditions.

Hence in approaching the concrete context and case of theatre, this current argument will focus on the role of space holding that this role is not fully addressed and explicated in the established terms and priorities both with respect to the constitution of the authentically theatrical, and as to its ontological and social bearing. It will seek to substantiate that empirical analysis of the case of theatre can help acknowledge the generative potential embedded in the operations of the site as physical space via the sensate and the bodily, and complement on-going research by revealing further aspects pertinent to the understanding of theatre as a concrete context of material cultural practice. It is based on the premise that if theatre experience bears emotive charge and transformative potential in that it opens up alternative paths of being and knowing, the fact that this experience would find us in the shared space of theatre is by far not accidental.

There are several ways in which theatre proves a potent case for this proposed type of inquiry. It presents one of the most formalised spatial entities even when posited at a level prior to artistic and architectural particularization. Built space can be established in its principal morphological features and properties, and examined as an experiential field, addressing a layer of immediate experience which evolves relatively autonomously from the function of performance, yet is integral to its spatial setting. This would allow complementing the inquiry into that which is authentically theatrical by explicating more fully the 'lived' and attending to the shared nature of the event. Instead of the diverging terms in which theatre experience, set in correlation with the processes of production (performer/stage) as distinct from those of perception (participator/auditorium), comes to be interpreted, analysis of the site addresses non-mediating unmediated effects which encompass the entire space, are affective for all participants involved, and offer unifying experiential grounds for the two groups involved in the theatrical situation.

Approached as a social space, theatre emerges as one of the most intensely social spaces, and as one of the most distinct and utterly legible organizations of the collective patterns of activity in the context of performance. Its experiential bearing concerns not only the experience of the theatrical, but entails ontological and social potential partaking in the constitution of agency and the collective. Its analysis thus would offer an insight into the corporeal constructions of some underlying fundamental principles enabling social togetherness.

Construed and re-constructed methodologically as a spatial entity at a potent mid-level, where representational layers are lifted off, yet its major spatial feature and properties are articulate, theatre emerges as one of the most enduring spatial forms. With its capacity to support a range of religious, artistic, and social occasions, this spatial form has been reproduced persistently for diverse appointed functions beyond theatre—intact and in use since its distant origins in ritual practice. As such theatre allows an inquiry into its constitution in and for social practice, offering an insight into space as a means of cultural continuity. It also allows exploring physical space as the shared material context conjoining the ontological and social as an integral part of the theatrical.

These site-specific potentialities offer grounds to shift concerns with physical space, and acknowledge that the impetus and transformative power of theatre is not only a matter of theatrical contents, but is also deeply embedded in the workings of its spatial setting as an experiential field. An analysis of the site can disclose how its properties as qualified material presence would open up further and entirely corporeal ways of affect, discovery and encounter. Focusing on physical space in the proposed terms would offer an opportunity to see how the essential emotive constitution of theatre experience (pity, fear, and pleasure), or the passage into the active modes of discovery, might be supported at the level of corporeal experience.

The analysis of the concrete actual case allows particularising the ways in which space works, in several respects. It enables minute examination of the intricate processes through which spatial circumstances build up to phenomenal presence. It allows identifying how this presence comes to characterise the zone of contact, and hence qualify the events of contact. Probing into the way in which space makes available to awareness the specificities of situatedness, it offers an insight into experiential content embedded therein. By capturing the productive passage from space to sense to sensibility, this analysis attends to the spatial dimensions of the processes through which the situated agent attains a sense of self, of participation, of the nature of the collectivity, along with the pleasures and risks of membership in it. It opens up possibilities to illuminate, through the operations of the spatial, certain special aspects of the socio-cultural role of such sites, and offers insight into the material practices in their construction and inhabitation. It offers a means of explaining the effects of these sites as linked to the capacities of physical space in expressing realities of social togetherness, and enabling the corporeal ways of their appropriation as lived conditions. In a broader perspective this analysis would allow for a glimpse of notions and operations of the social realm through the perspective of immediate experience.

Another important potential of this inquiry concerns the understanding of certain internal mechanisms of the modality of immediate experience itself. It relies on the premise that the site, by conjoining artistic work and collective event, actually tightly embeds the theatrical as a special form of the aesthetic as linked with the ontological. Hence attending to the specificities of the spatial constructions of this experiential layer would allow pursuing a rendition of an underlying homology in the structural principles and conditions among the aesthetic, its theatrical counterpart, and experience, through the shared terms of their most tangible component—space.

By way of a re-articulation of principal features of physical space as affective and productive capacities—circumstances, mechanisms, forces and impulses, this analysis would offer grounds to assert that this spatial entity not only stages and frames the encounter with the theatrical work, but also prepares possibilities for a series of encounters, actualising its experiential possibilities in tempting semblance with the structural instances pertinent to the experiential modality. Theatre space emerges in its capacities as a dynamic framework which sets on the path of bodily becoming and knowing, vitalising the corporeal conditions through which participators exercise socio-cultural capacities and ultimately formulate and re-formulate selfhood.

Theatre as epitome of the social

Theatre presents a fascinating subject for inquiry as a multi-layered social and cultural phenomenon both in that it entails the transformative potential of artistic practices, and as a context of collective social praxis. It takes on a paradigmatic role as source and means for understanding larger socio-cultural issues, projecting way beyond its field, shaping notions, concepts and conceptions at the basis of momentous inquiries in the broader area of sociological, anthropological and philosophical thought.

In Turner's (1982) seminal work, the profound socio-cultural worth of ritual and theatre is traced though the gradual passage from one to the other, traversed within deeper societal processes of individuation, and linked to an explanation of the shift away from 'community' towards the more recent social form—'communitas'. A distinct field of research emerges around the conception of 'performance', which although conceptualised in rather dissimilar terms, helps thinkers as diverse as Schechner (1993) and Butler (1979) focus on explicating social processes: from organized cultural and political proceedings, through festivals, sports and entertainment mass-events, down to everyday attitudes of groups and individuals in terms of 'enactment' or symbolic 'representation' of identity. Theatre's bearing on sociological research at the scale of action and agency finds expression in Goffman's (1959, 1971) dramaturgical approach to social life, which employs the intricacies involved in the theatrical situation itself to analyse strategic forms of interaction as constituents of micro-public order. Along with the notion of the 'social actor' this cross-fertilisation can be traced through concepts like 'incorporation', and 'embodiment' within more recent sociological research, where diverse approaches and perspectives addressing the corporal as part of the active agent are discussed, such as in the work of Shilling (1993), and Williams and Bendelow (1998). Links to what happens in the instance of performing, can be identified in perspectives on the 'lived' also through the concept of 'the performative', employed by thinkers of diverse lineage which seek to relocate the ontological and epistemological within the 'pre-contemplative' processes of self-constitution. While these point to the diverse ways and scales at which theatre is being employed as means for understanding the social realm and the human condition and experience, they also reveal the exclusive emphasis assigned to social factors in explicating its operations. In keeping with the priorities of their respective fields, these frameworks address aspects of such operations in view of societal processes, where the constitution of agency is construed with reference to the complex significations of the context and explicated through the social practices themselves. Space is seen as the field for action, and as but one such background medium of signification. This is so even on the smaller bodily scale, where the spatial—location (front/back stage), distance, or orientation—is implicated as a means manipulated by the social actor so as to implement micro strategies of social ordering. Or, as in approaches on 'the performative', it would be depicted through terms like 'spacing' and 'spatiality' (Gregson 2000: 433-452), or even 'architectures' (Dewsbury 2000: 473-496), which serve to indicate, rather than explicate the spatial dimension.

This current study entails an analysis of theatre space as a concrete material experiential field. Construed as a legible scheme of collective organization which is persistently reproduced in a variety of social sites for performative activities, in the form of theatre space it attains its most legible formalised presence, and can be posited and examined in its tangible corporeal operations. Though this analysis addresses a narrow section of discreet processes—those that evolve as corporeally constructed contact phenomena, these are brought forth with their distinct experiential charge and articulated as phenomena that partake in the constitution of agency and the collective. Unattended on other accounts, these confirm the spatial as a vital dimension in the operation of the site. This analysis, then, would offer grounds to construe the theatre site as an entirely corporeal and spatial model, that bears explanatory potential as to the workings of the social realm from the perspective of immediate experience. With respect to immediate experience, inquiry into the spatial dimension in the proposed terms helps not only particularise the interdependence among spatial circumstance and experiential content, but also render explicit certain internal mechanisms and structuring instances which become available in the course of minute analysis of space.

Theatre and consciousness
One of the central issues in research on theatre is to establish its role in developing human understanding and consciousness. Hence the

context of theatre in correlation with consciousness is taken up both in comprehensive theoretical research, and as an area of active exploration through performative practices. Underlying these inquiries is the recognition that theatre—via experience—bears the potential to open up paths towards transformation and attaining altered, higher states of consciousness. In his seminal study on theatre and consciousness, Meyer-Dinkgräfe (2005) focuses precisely on these potentialities in theatre. He systematizes and discusses the various paths in Western aesthetics in addressing human mind and consciousness, with respect to their reflections in theatre theory and practice, and examines these in conjunction with developments in consciousness studies. This allows exploring essential aspects in theatre aesthetics, experience, practices and techniques as to the ways in which they support the development of human consciousness, which are, furthermore linked with the openings that the principles of atonement in Vedic philosophy would offer in these respects. This complex theoretical context helps identify the multiple possibilities and means in theatre for developing the mental potential and parameters of consciousness. As Meyer-Dinkgräfe asserts, such possibilities are present in ritual, but they also feature in drama (text) and theatre (performance). Accordingly, altered states of consciousness can receive expression through the texts and be depicted in drama. There they can take form in the contents and structure of a work, lead to subtler levels of mind, and enable processes of transformation of consciousness within this aesthetic context.

Yet furthermore they can be attained also in theatre practices. In this, the issue of how radical change in consciousness could be engendered, emerges as perpetual pursuit by way of alternative theatre practices. As Meyer-Dinkgräfe's survey on theatre practices reveals, such pursuits are based on and employ a conception of the activity of performing which exceeds the conventional notion of 'role' playing and representation. Rather, these alternative performative practices would seek to produce shifts in consciousness by emphasizing, within the process of acting, particular techniques and mechanisms embedded in the practices themselves. Revealing of such aspects, some of the most articulate approaches attempt to capture possibilities of activation towards altered states by way of conceptualising such states in correlation with the respective practice: spanning from Mnouchkine's concept of *state*, Grotowski's concept of *translumination,* and Artaud's notion of the actor's *presence.* In Grotowski's laboratory theatre, the implementations of such practices occur in terms of psychoanalytical sessions, where participants would strive to achieve shifts in consciousness by way of developing total concentration on the internal process of self-discovery. Hence the desired process of translumination would be based on states of consciousness and body, where the actor as well as the groups of participants transcend the mind-body-split, achieve totality, and attain 'full presence'. In Artaud's system, this 'magic' potential might be reproduced in specific modes of acting which deviate from traditional performance practices, and are based on a re-articulated mode of physical presence. In this system, language comes to be conceptualized as an entirely physical poetry for the senses—to be attained and matched with the bodily localization of feelings (Meyer-Dinkgräfe 2005: 55-92).

All of these approaches explore the potentialities of theatre practice and experience in bringing forth new forms of knowing and being. Rooted in bodily techniques as much, such potentialities are easier to actualise and explicate within the performative practices on stage. Yet, as Meyer-Dinkgräfe explains, new forms of knowing and being, are also potentially present for the audience. This potential can be located by inquiry into the reception process via three interrelated elements. These entail the spectators—individuals with psychological and social backgrounds and definite positions which influence how spectators would react to the stimuli of the performance. They include the element of the performance itself—which contains the stimuli as dramatic and performative means of guiding the audience. The third element actualises as the merging of these elements in the reception process, which takes place within the spectators and constitutes an interaction of spectators with the performance (Meyer-Dinkgräfe 2005: 127). As an aspect in the reception process, the correlation with spatial components includes the expression of the scene through scenography whose design might support the desired essential rapport, by actualizing a dynamics of space that is in full alignment with the structuring dynamics of the universe. These links among the spatial aspects of the theatrical context and consciousness, then, would point not only to the role of theatre space in developing spatial awareness and spatial cognition, but also reveal how it furthers mental imagery and provides correlations among various levels of conscious perception (Meyer-Dinkgräfe 2005: 127-144).

This current approach relies on these insights which ascertain experience as a legitimate path for inquiry into theatre and consciousness, and disclose the theatrical as an utterly productive process by including alternative performative practices as possibilities of acquisition. Yet it also ventures into a less-charted area of experiential possibilities—those which emerge directly from physical space, retaining an oblique correlation with the theatrical context. Hence, although for analytical purposes it recedes the foreground theatrical function, and lifts off representational layers of space, this analysis nevertheless addresses aspects of theatre, its space, and experience at a more fundamental level. Within the confines of the narrow incision of immediate experience in and through space, it examines the corporeal trajectories of that which is lived and presses towards consciousness, along with the affective and cognitive components it entails, and seeks to open up understanding of the ways in which physical circumstances might condition our passage into the experiential modality. In the specificity of minute analysis of corporeal correlations, it offers an insight into the concrete mechanisms leading to awareness not so much of spatial circumstance, but of the sense of a complex condition—towards a grasp on the nature of the realities of the social situation. It allows probing into the underlying texture of the discreet, space-driven, pre-conscious mental events which activate and mobilise. It attends to experience as it takes form in discovery and the grasp of concrete lived conditions—it links up with the quest for attaining the aesthetic and ontological in conjunction.

Theatre and the controversial status of space
The issue of the role of space in establishing the socio-cultural significance of theatre is central to both theatre studies and the corresponding branch of architecture. Yet although developed through two different paradigmatic notions—the *theatrical work* and *the monument*, both theoretical contexts focus on the processes of production and perception of theatrical contents to which space is tightly indexed. Space is seen in its capacity to reflect the essentially re-presentational nature of theatre as an instance of cultural production, and, correspondingly, its architectural representation in built form. In this way both contexts uphold the priorities of a 'theatrical' trait of theorizing space—it emerges in terms of an inherent ambiguity. At once physical and fictional, actual and artistic, space is always entangled in complex

processes of mediation and representation, and comes to be explained by the help of a set of 'spatial functions'. Thus in the two major disciplinary fields which by definition come forth as the prime disciplines concerned with bodies in space—theatre studies and the corresponding branch of architecture, the workings of physical space with respect to immediate experience and the situated body as such would remain largely unattended.

In theatre studies space is examined with reference to the theatrical work, and construed in view of the complex interplay of imaginative, performative, and material constituents. As a part of this system, space is seen as index, and exclusively tied to the formulation of theatrical meanings. In order to explicate these processes of mediation, then, a whole host of 'spaces' (fictional, scenic, theatrical, architectural, etc.) is instituted and theorized as to their functions. Architectural perspectives focus on the theatre building, which is examined as an artefact that is designed to manifest culturally defined ideas on theatre, on architecture, and on the social institution. Architectural space is to convey cultural values and meanings. On the functional level, too, theatre is studied as a building type, connoting a particular spatial organization and configuration, which houses the diverse functions involved in the production and presentation of performances. In this regard architectural space, though acquiring overall ambience, is also meant to act as backdrop for a variety of theatrical expressions. Both of these frameworks of theatre uphold an essentially representational conception of space, the correlation with which is essentially hermeneutic and interpretative in nature.

Furthermore, the theorisation of theatre in view of two distinct processes: that of production/presentation and that of perception, underlies the explicitly divergent terms in which theatre experience, the lived nature of the event, and the correlations with space are being accounted for in view of the two groups involved in the theatrical situation. In the practice of the performer, experience takes the form of live explorations of the performing body, which is productive both in terms of its animating craft within the space of the stage, and in terms of incorporation and embodiment, perhaps even to the extent of attaining those altered states of consciousness. Yet the experience of the static emplaced audience, on the other hand, is interpreted in terms of mediation and perception, and firmly attached to the social, political, or cultural mission of the theatrical work. This indicates that for the participator experience would be linked to represented realities, and would rely on re-cognition and volitional imaginative modes.

While the social and collective nature lying at the core of theatre is acknowledged both in regard of the work as text and in view of the event-nature of the performance, this aspect, too, is indexed exclusively to the distinct foreground function—theatre. Hence research on that social nature of theatre focuses on the ideas represented in fiction, and on the essentially communicative practices of the specifically 'theatrical mode of community' brought about in the very 'nature of performance' (Barr, 1998). In this way the intensely social character of the site is tightly indexed to and blended with the unique form of artistic production. It comes to be explicated in terms of the experimentation with and the collective questioning of these (represented) ideas and emotions—i.e., as linked to the theatrical work. The absence of research on the site in its entirety itself as the corporeal setting in which the encounter with the theatrical unfolds, allows tracing out a distinct area for a more rigorous inquiry into the generative capacities of physical space at the level of immediate experience.

Spatial form as site of emergence
Oriented towards the immediate bodily experience evolving in and through space, this current approach institutes an alternative notion— *the theatre mode of spatial organization* as grounds for analysis. It employs the term *mode* in its twofold capacities: it denotes space at a potent mid-level—prior to artistic and architectural particularization, while at the same time suggesting the ways or manner in which space works. Hence by way of temporarily suspending concerns with the mediation of the theatrical work, and its representation in architectural space, this concept captures spatial form in its resilient morphological features. It allows the rendition of architectural space in its principal spatial form and inherent properties—a distinct spatial entity which is open to an exploration of unmediated non-mediating effects. This, then, allows complementing on-going studies on functions of space, with an analysis of its operations and effects conducted at an empirical level. Construing theatre space in terms of *mode* bears analytical and explanatory potential in several respects. It facilitates a re-articulation of architectural space its affective potential. Physical space can be acknowledged in its palpable qualified presence and examined as it opens up to the bodily and experiential. It can be analysed, identifying

experiential possibilities that emerge within concrete spatial circumstances, mechanisms, and relations. It can be understood in its capacities to 'do'—as it would assist those subtle ways of feeling and knowing that are acquired and actualized in pre-contemplative practice.

In particularizing the operations and experiential effects of the spatial form, this approach introduces three analytical concepts— 'isolation', 'exposure', and 'collective containment'. These are construed as inherent, recurring, and generic conditions to this spatial form, and employed as analytical tools. As such they are established in their threefold function: as concepts—denoting ways of occupying space, as spatial terms—identifying physical constitution of effects, and as existential conditions. These concepts enable a conceptual and analytical reconsideration of immediate experience by tracing the passage from space through sense to sensibility, depicting experience—forming. As spatial terms impressed upon theatre space, they allow conducting an analysis of spatial effects at multiple levels, and conjoining these so as to explicate the overall operations of the spatial formation with respect to the performance, as well as their minute effects with respect to the situated body. As spatial terms they economically re-describe the architectural elements and components characteristic of the site in keeping with its fundamental functions to define and protect, to facilitate presentation and perception of an act, and to accommodate and organize. As conditions, they identify distinct ways of being in space, articulating links between spatial circumstance and experiential content—they allow inferring forms of experience towards which the corporeal correlations might tend to condense.

On a larger scale, the spatial form can be understood in its tight correspondence to the primary function it embeds: it is structured by and coheres with the performance as a structured event entailing the processes of production, presentation and encounter with the theatrical work. Hence the overall constitution of the spatial entity is characterized by, and reproduces this principal structure, through which it simultaneously enables these functions, establishes the performance as a distinct occurrence, and configures the collective. It also suggests reciprocal reliance of the performance on specified spatial effects, disclosing one further fundamental way in which space and performance correlate in physical space.

Each of the concepts attends to the experiential potential of the overall operations of the site, yet also specifies such potential through and within each, in this way disclosing the shifting nature of spatial effects, the diverse experiential charge of concrete physical circumstances, and their specific internal mechanisms. These concepts prove potent analytical tools. They help understand the workings of space as coextensive with the correlation—they offer insight into the specificities of the zone of contact. They allow detailed analysis of the spatial constitution of unmediated non-mediating effects, while evading any suggestion of definitive outcome. These conditions come forth as possibilities in engendering experience, while they themselves generate: they compose towards phenomenal distinctiveness, to be grasped in the form of a condition—they present both the actual and the possible. They are not purely phenomenological either: they work at the level of potential presence—they are not contemplated, but attained by way of a bodily encounter with a way of being in space. They take experiential form only once sensed and acknowledged as an existential condition. While embedded in the materiality of space they emerge to phenomenal presence—i.e., these conditions extend to qualify the discreet processes of experiencing the relation. This way a possibility emerges to conceptualize the operations of the site as spatial construct in terms of mental occurrences, feelings and states (suspense, activation and absorption/concentration), as these build up towards certain more dynamic processes structuring experience—i.e., analysis in terms of the proposed concepts allow construing how spatial circumstances instantiate the phase of stabilization and accumulation, as well as that of destabilization and outward move, which enable the sensate and bodily paths of acquisition.

Linking up of experiential effects at various levels renders this spatial form not only experientially consequential, but also experientially diverse. It opens up the opportunity to approach physical space as a shared corporeal framework—an experiential field that can be examined at the level of the corporeal in its possible unmediated effects. It can be rendered tangible in view of possibilities emerging within concrete spatial circumstances and relations, and in this way help access the productive processes embedded in the corporeality of space-body relationships—a stratum of phenomena that evolve in immediate 'lived' experience. In contrast to established perspectives on theatre, where the focus on production/presentation and mediation/reception as distinct processes leads to the interpretation of the experience of the two groups involved in the theatrical situation in radically different terms, the proposed approach posits theatre space as a concrete material framework that is shared, affective, and productive for all participants involved—i.e., it allows establishing the corporeal as a unifying experiential platform for all participants involved.

However, this approach also extends the particularly architectural analysis with a (speculative) inquiry into the discrete experiential possibilities embedded therein. Thus it comes to addresses experiential ingredients which cannot be observed directly or evidenced, but can be only re-constructed circumstantially, arriving at a range of discreet processes and practices that actualize at the pre-contemplative level. Equipped with the specificity of spatial circumstance, analysis begins to disclose space-to-body reciprocities as these evolve. Approached at the empirical level, then, architectural space is established as dynamic constituent: neither deterministic (seen as prime cause) nor elusive (fused in representation and perception, or neglected for being self-evident) it presents a qualified physical framework, particularized in terms of experiential possibilities and open to appropriation.

Examining this spatial form in the case of theatre is especially revealing, because it is as theatre that it can be understood as an original prototype and a model which precedes design. Re-traced within its historical emergence in social and ritual practice, theatre space can be linked to its constitution for and through a distinct pattern of collective activity, and acknowledged as an artefact proper—a product of material culture. It comes forth as an enduring model, which has been handed down and incorporated throughout its historical evolution and diverse modifications. As such it comes to highlight resemblances, links and continuities among varying actualizations—and in this way offers grounds to construe the possibility that a few, but fundamental principles governing this kind of social organization, might have come to be solidified and expressed in its distinct spatial conditions. It might be that precisely in this way this modality becomes affective —it supports, engenders and cultivates sensibilities, enabling social togetherness. While such capacities can be taken to account for the persistent re-production of this spatial form, it is in the case of theatre, where the possible presence of these conditions would emerge in their most articulate and formalized actualization. Hence the analysis of theatre-as-lived-space would help re-construct a stratum of phenomena that pertain to the spatial practices of inhabiting—offering insight into the discreet processes through which such fundamental principles might be internalized. This approach, thus, allows addressing and concretizing less-charted aspects of socio-spatial reciprocities both in terms of space-activity correspondences at the level of the site, and at the minute scale of space-to-body relationships—in the practices of inhabiting built space.

Yet furthermore, this analysis offers an opportunity to depict the corporeal ways in which spatial conditions structure the experience at performance. It issues in the form of instances of affect—activation, suspense, absorption—which resonate with the structuring instances emerging in various frameworks centralizing on experience. This allows approaching discreet experience through its corporeal construction, and explicating events of emergence in terms of deeper internal mechanisms—in and through space. Physical space emerges in its capacities to materialize the possibilities of being drawn into a unique, authentic and irretrievable modality—reverberation. It confirms the corporeal as a vital dimension of space, and as a source and site of alternative bodily paths of emergence and becoming.

Method, structure and organization of the book
This inquiry ventures into an unexplored area, namely that which entails the direct relations and correspondences among space and experience. In this it aims to re-construct a relatively autonomous layer of experience through the immediate corporeality of space-to-body correlations, and disclose the generative potential lying with space, through the possibilities it opens up to further insight into the discreet processes linked with emergence. Therefore the argument in this book evolves at two levels and entails two major aspects. One concerns the reasoning and validation of the proposed shift in re-thinking space as integral to experience, establishing the legitimacy of the proposed area of research this engenders. The other concerns the institution and development of the alternative methodological and conceptual tools apt to render and address built architectural space in its generative capacities.

Though oriented keenly towards this narrow incision linking up space and experience directly, the study is located at the intersection of discourse on architecture with diverse perspectives converging around the key issues of space, self, experience, and consciousness, and hence contains many strands and links with on-going discourse on these. I have tried to organize the argument as legibly and logically consistently as possible into two parts—theoretical formulation and concretization upon the specific case, and structured the course of its development into six subsequent chapters.

Part one—*Rethinking corporeality: physical space between theoretical obscurity and experiential potential*—entails two sections, chapters one and two, following this introduction. It engages on a systematic discussion of the larger discourse on body/agency, space and experience focused on the specifics and issues which are immediately relevant to the argument. It builds up towards establishing the theoretical foundations, and the principal methodology of the approach. In reconstructing built physical space in its material presence with respect to experience, it draws concerns with agency/self and the possibilities, instances and mechanisms of formation, transformation and acquisition, into the discussion of architectural space. Hence the choice and juxtaposition of diverse frameworks is intended from the perspective of the current argument—seeking out notions, insights and propositions of pertinence, bringing unlikely frameworks into proximity and building up on the underlying connections among these. This allows grounding, theoretically, the necessity, possibility, and explanatory potential of this approach, and arriving at the outline and formulation of the methodology of the approach as a conceptual reconsideration of both built space and experience from within the confines of this proposed perspective.

Chapter 1. *The 'lived': from 'body' to the body with space*—engages on notions of the lived body in social theory and the wider area of the humanities, tracing the diversity of aspects characterizing the resurge of concerns with lived experience around the concepts of embodiment and incorporation. It brings forth and discusses some prime reasons for the tacit status of space in this context, and seeks out other complementary frameworks, such as those of the performative, as well as those on the physicality of the body's perceptual systems to bridge the passage to space. In conjunction, these allow deriving theoretical grounds for a more experience-oriented perspective on the body, arriving at a rendition of correlations in their immediacy: depicting the body as emplaced within space and in its active explorative modality at the basis of re-considering the potential of inquiry at this corporeal level.

Chapter 2. *From 'lived space' and experience to the materiality of experience*—covers two theoretical contexts engaging with aspects lived experience. Hence the principal conception of experience is traced out as discussed in spatial theory, and as approached in philosophical frameworks. The meta-theoretical perspective on 'lived space' brings forth the notion of lived experience in the context of the complex processes of mutual co-constitution. It highlights the area of material practices in understanding the productive aspects in the experience of socio-spatial reciprocities and correlations. The philosophical frameworks engaging with experience bring into focus the conditions and possibilities of establishing a shared world. They help identify some more particular mechanisms enabling contact, pointing to that contact as a prime location bearing potential for change and transformation. Hence the concepts of the emergent and becoming come forth as linked with movement, outwards and towards an encounter. Building on these insights, the argument proceeds by a re-consideration, extending these conceptions as 'reverberations' at a more rudimentary, corporeal level. This theoretical re-consideration relies on a framework of feeling, which restitutes the concept of feeling as a process, recovers the productive status of the sensate and establishes it as mark and mechanism of the mind. This chapter concludes with the specification of methodological propositions and the conceptual tools of the approach, arriving at a particular rendition of architectural space, open to the body and experience—and to the analysis of these.

Part two—*Corporeal constructions: theatre as a context and case of inquiry* develops and specifies the approach at the concrete empirical level of physical space based on the case of theatre space. It discusses the challenges and potentials of locating and implementing the approach within this particular spatial form/mode of organization—theatre.

Chapter 3. *Theatre space—artistic functions and productive capacities* elaborates the theoretically established potential by focusing on the particular case of theatre space as a context for inquiry into lived experience. It pursues rendition and understanding of the operations of the spatial dimension along two veins, both special to the context of theatre. One explores the space-experience correlation—socio-spatial reciprocities in terms of the continuity of this spatial form since its origins and into its manifold reproductions—depicting its constitution for and through social practice, and its appropriation in experience. In the collective context of performance activity, it traces out links between the material practices of formulation and those of inhabitation as valid constituents of the experiential. The other special line of inquiry concerns the potential of theatre as space and site which conjoins theatrical experience as form of the aesthetic and lived experience, and thus opens up understanding of operations of space in its ontological and social-cultural aspects, as linked with the aesthetic. This allows construing and pursuing the rendition of essential homologies in the structure of experience—in its actualization in the performance event, and through its most tangible rendition—space.

Chapter 4. *The generative potential of the corporeal: Physical space as dynamic locus of the actual and the possible* entails the detailed rendition and analysis of theatre space as lived. The spatial form/mode is disclosed in terms of the logic of operations, the physical construction of distinct conditions, linking up spatial detail with experiential content. The analysis arrives at an explication of the intensity of the site as experiential field and the possibilities this intensity presents in triggering and nurturing the experiential—the productive modality of becoming. This is taken as grounds to extend, speculatively into the distinct forms of experience towards which spatial conditions might come to actualize.

Chapter 5. *Discussion*

This chapter recuperates the various strands discussed above, towards confirming the relevance of this approach and highlighting its findings with respect to the socio-cultural role of theatre, with respect to the understanding of the spatial dimension in the workings of the social/public realm, and with respect to the conceptual reconsideration of built space, and immediate experience.

The ***Conclusion*** is brief and focused on the openings towards future research, embedded in this approach.

PART ONE

RE-THINKING CORPOREALITY:
SPACE BETWEEN THEORETICAL OBSCURITY AND
GENERATIVE POTENTIAL

Chapter One

The 'lived': from 'body' to the body with space

Space and space-body relations in terms of the body

The polemic surrounding the notion of space is partially rooted in the dominant physical presence of built architectural space. It concerns the prevailing conceptualization of correlations with space, which are conventionally being resolved as exclusively bound to the framework of perception. Yet, although deriving from the explicit distinction between perception and experience, which the shift towards the 'lived' augments, this polemic also reflects some more subtle issues pertaining to the material presence of space. These would be understood better by calling to mind the ambiguous ways of depicting the nature of physical space and the theoretical difficulties it poses. Space figures not only as an object-reality (an enclosing wall, floor or ceiling, a column or pediment), but also in terms of the less tangible void that is both materially formulated, and permeable. It is also invisible. Capturing and explicating both is a challenging task- a challenge which results in the diverging theorizations of space. These and related issues would point to some of the reasons why, in the larger context of thought on self/agency, experience and consciousness, space attains the controversial status of a dimension that is somehow ever-present yet also notoriously elusive, theoretically. As physical presence, built architectural space appears to be too disturbingly materially manifest, immutable, solid, firm and defined—and therefore also possibly definitive or even 'causal'—to be perceived as genuinely productive. In the close-up of immediate experience, space is too self-evident to be pursued as a source in its own right, or explicated. Hence the inquiry into physical space is characterized by a gap between positing space in its evident distinctive presence as an entity to be perceived, and rendering its materiality transparent in immediate experience.

In its own terms this current argument attempts to address some aspects of this narrow intermediate area awaiting theoretical work. It relies on the premise that the experiential and social potential of space is not fully explicated by way of interpreting its expressive representational powers, or through its practical affordances. Space in its physical presence is a continuous matter, at work at multiple levels, and especially with respect to the situated body and in the modality prior to perception, it actualizes a rather different range of capacities. These are immediate and affective, bear potential to influence and engender experience, and, in this, offer possibilities for grasping realities of being within the social and material world. Hence this study sets out to rearticulate space at a level where its physicality can be construed as an integral experiential dimension. It probes into the possibilities of re-constituting the generative capacities of space with respect to the emergent embedded in the corporeality of space-to-body relationships, and further understanding of physical space as it opens up to the body. At that level, by exploring its tangible palpable presence, space could be affirmed as a subtle, yet qualified and affective physical framework appropriated in the sensate ways of bodily experience, and as a source and site through which we exercise cognitive, creative and emotive abilities—and ultimately re-think and embody selfhood. A step could be made towards attaining a fuller account of the potentialities lying with built architectural space.

However, the mainstream conceptualization of architectural space which prioritises representation and perception, is a powerful one, and has come to stand for the totality of effects of physical space, screening off other possibilities. Built architectural space is visible, firm and expressive—a framework that is evident, image-based, and shared (objective). This notion of space would be supported in field research as well, because the subtler effects of space would not readily come forth in the terms in which they arise, such as pre-contemplative sense or feeling, but would rather immerse in more recognizable mental phenomena, such as perceptual ones. That which is immediately felt and experienced in and through space would pertain to an area of discreet processes that can be derived only circumstantially and reconstructed speculatively. Instead, space would tend to be registered and reported only through the more properly conscious processes of perception, where it figures as a rather immutable permanent part of the phenomenal world. In this way space comes to be understood exclusively through its visible features and effects—it is linked to image and representation, as well as to foreground purposes and functions. Together, these are taken to offer the prime grounds for meaning formulation. Hence perception appears as the appropriate explanatory framework, within which the theorization of the correlation to built physical space has come to be conventionally accepted.

This 'space of form', then, is to be dissociated decisively from the 'lived', immediate, and the experiential. Permanent and fixed and hence possibly also determining, architectural space would need to be excluded from concerns with the autonomy of the subject/body, and even more so from the possible paths of attaining liberation. This exclusion reflects especially on discourse on the 'body'—the form which the shift towards recovering the relative autonomy of the subject takes in social theory and the humanities in general. There it amounts to an almost total absence of an account of space in correlation to and in the vicinity of the body.

In its representational apparently immutable form, built architectural space appears to be of a different category from other sociocultural entities, such as the systems of practice, attitude, intention, or values which, though expressive, become so in an immediate and constituted way. Hence by contrast, the whole area of correlations with space can come to be denoted as a special kind of correlations—namely those of seeing, reading, using, and meaning formulation (of space), and taken to form a separate province of experience altogether. Discussion of this separate realm, then, can be omitted from discourse on the lived and the bodily, because architectural space appears to be sufficiently accounted for in the image-based re-presentational referential framework of perception. In the absence of alternative 'experiential' conceptualizations of built space that might offer paths to its integration into the explanatory framework of the immediately experiential, this omission becomes even compulsory: in establishing the autonomous subject, lived experience takes the form of liberation from the effects of formulated space.

This omission is also justified, because in foregrounding its appearance, built space comes to be seen as a framework that manifests, and conveys and in its own ways defines the formulation of meaning. Its physicality at use level facilitates utility and purpose, emplacing the order of systems, equipment, framing circulation patterns and relations among social subjects. Seen in these terms, architectural space—the 'space of form'—becomes suspect in the sense that both as a medium and as means it is liable to the misuse of power. 'Fixed' 'finished', and 'static', it can be posited as a close correlate to other frameworks of social determinism. As brought forth in Foucault's critical perspective, it appears as but one of the expressions of governmental regimes, and is readily associated with the 'disciplinary' frameworks of institutional systems for social control. Space can be seen to purport control both over the ways in which the respective range of practicalities will be conducted—to the extent of eliciting 'behaviour', and over the processes of meaning formulation—through which dominant ideologies are encoded, conveyed and 'received', in perception. Hence built architectural space has come to signify determinist positions, which presuppose not only notions of space based on its capacity to 'frame' functions—practical as well as referential and symbolic and in this way facilitate the 'transmission' of predetermined knowledge, but also the notion of a relatively passive 'constituted' 'discursive' subject at the receiving end. Hence the disappearance of an account of the spatial from theorisations of the 'lived' and bodily can be understood as the dual effort to evade the space of control and representation, and as a shift away from the static notions of the social subject. Consequently this shift towards the 'lived' is being discussed by thinkers in mainstream social and spatial theory as tightly bound to the body itself and the autogenous processes through which it appropriates data and makes sense. The 'lived' is being understood in terms of the capacities of agency to resist such possible channels of determination whereby the reciprocal correlation of agency to space comes to highlight mainly the active modes of intervention and intentionality.

While in the vicinity of the social body built space in its physical appearance along with the possible determining aspects of this presence can be allotted to a separate realm of correlations, concerns with space cannot be entirely evaded in view of immediate experience. In the nexus of immediate experience space is integrally present, and however subtle that presence would be, this presence may not be entirely neglected. Yet in theorizing that experience the place of analysis of the spatial dimension as a possible factor in its formulation is being occupied by spatial terms that indicate, rather than explicate its role with respect to lived experience as an ontological and epistemological issue. Hence terms like 'spacing', 'spatiality', 'architectures', by denoting space as omnipresent, actually preclude further inquiry. Brought to mind in terms of distance and dimension in positioning—such as 'with respect to' or 'among' objects (floor, wall and chair), or properties ('redness', 'stability'), space is rendered 'experientially' transparent. It is effectively excluded as an explanatory tool through which aspects immediate experience and the body might be understood. In relation to 'the lived' and bodily, then, space recedes to a void or field where its material presence is replaced by way of evoking the social situation and relations, by accounting for physicality in terms of movement—act, becoming and event, or in terms of the actuality of time—instance, moment, duration.

In mainstream research on the body, then, such ambiguities surrounding the notion of built space are being evaded. Explicating 'lived' experience takes the more 'social' route—i.e., through depicting the aspects of the socio-cultural realm, which entail the account of the foreground activities, practices and relations of a social nature. Hence the 'lived' body, as source and locus of ontological and epistemological acquisition, comes to be examined and explicated in terms of the import of the processes pertinent to the respective practice, activity, or relational context—i.e., processes that are autogenous (as distinct from those that are induced), and occur closer to conscious awareness and are therefore not only more readily recognized as subjective, but also help posit the body-subject in an undeniably active mode of existence.

In turning to the body, the survey and discussion in this chapter is twofold. On the one hand it seeks to trace out insights and findings relevant to the aims of this current study—i.e., propositions that would support approaching physical space with a focus on the generative possibilities embedded in the corporeality of space-body relationships. On the other, it seeks to identify some of the reasons which impede the account of space, so that it recedes into theoretical obscurity especially as immediate physical presence. This would help address some the more persistent problems of established notions of space in detail, and trace out some of the areas of theoretical work in opening up physical space to analysis with respect to the body. Ultimately this should lead to establishing and exploring space as integral dimension of experience, furthering understanding on its generative capacities, and ascertaining these as a legitimate part of the social and cultural potential of space.

The selection of perspectives in this discussion is guided by the aim to prepare the grounds for retrieving the experiential potential of space by exploring its corporeal properties with respect to the situated body. In this regard, the seemingly disparate perspectives which are brought together here, offer depictions of the body in its correlations with material surrounds in an increasing particularisation of the physical aspects of these correlations. In this way they also help build up and concretise the notion of the corporeal theoretically, so as to arrive at asserting space as the material context encompassing the correlation. This prepares the grounds to posit physical space in the vicinity of the body, and understand the correlation as a productive and open-ended process.

The first two sections of this chapter engage with discourse on the body in the larger field of social and cultural theory focused around the concepts of embodiment and incorporation. The main sources referred to are seen to be ground-breaking and foundational in that they deal with the restitution of the body to theoretical thought. They identify the major approaches to and trace the prime directions for research on the body as an active foundation in the constitution of the self/subject. Along with concise discussion of these issues, they offer an anthological overview of the diversity of concerns and aspects involved in exploring the lived in terms of the body. In this respect the concept of embodiment emerges as a major theoretical tool in over-coming the body-mind dichotomy, and establishing the notion of the self within the dialectic correlation between body and mind, lived experience and perception of social realities.

Incorporation is taken up in discourse as a larger framework of thought on the body-subject, which helps exceed the binary models in conceptualizing the correlations between the living organism and its social and material surrounds. At the same time it also brings into account the fundamental condition of change which characterizes the contemporary human condition in terms of the larger evolutionary processes. On the body scale incorporation highlights the capacities of the social subject to assimilate the challenges of the 'life-world' by capturing and the adapting to the specific patterns and effects generated by social and technological development. Both of these conceptions further understanding of the social subject in terms of the dialectic correlation between formative and formulating processes. In establishing the relative autonomy of the 'lived' body and the productive import of the experiential, in both frameworks the prime concern is with the active share of agency.

In turning more specifically to immediate bodily experience, certain theoretical and philosophical perspectives will be taken up, that highlight the body in two experiential modalities: the performative, and the distracted, both of which do indicate links with space at this immediate bodily level. Though of diverse lineage, these perspectives focus on immediate experience in ways that allow glimpsing the body in its explorative correlations with the surrounding world in general, and allow deriving implications as to the correlations with space in particular. The productive and emergent in these perspectives comes forth as embedded within the discreet occurrences—doings, events and processes, in which the body is involved, and is emphasised as a shared capacity and tendency in human experience.

The last of the approaches to the body discussed in this chapter posits the body in its most corporal—an organism as it works though its perceptual systems. Yet it does consolidate certain essential propositions of these above theoretical frameworks, and extends the account of the body in terms of the physicality of its correlations. In this way it also helps confirm the presence of corporeal space in the immediate vicinity of the body as productive, and eases the passage towards a re-articulation of built physical space as a possible generative dimension in immediate experience.

'Body' and 'embodiment'

One of the major forms in which the larger turn towards the lived in social and philosophical thought takes, is expressed in the resurge of interest in the body. The broader field of body research is formulated by a vast variety of cross-disciplinary approaches spanning from neuroscience, medicine, and sports, through to ethnicity, religion, ethics and aesthetics. It revolves around the diverse issues and forms in which the body emerges as a vital source in evolving our capacities as human beings. This shift reasserts the body as a locus and expression of the socio-cultural realm. It entails the exploration of the complex processes of identity and self-creation in the context of assimilation and transformation of the surrounding material, social and cultural world at various levels. In social and cultural theory, diverse perspectives engage with theorising the lived and bodily as a foundation of the re-constitution of corporeal existence, and its crucial import in understanding the formation of the active agent. As pointed out by Shilling (1993 2007: 1-18), these perspectives do offer fresh approaches towards 'embodiment', although they would frequently be taking their points of departure from former frameworks, which might even be linked with the 'disciplinary project' of the 'founding fathers' in modern sociology (Durkheim, Weber, Simmel, Mannheim). The major aim in theorising corporeal existence around the concept of embodiment is to exceed the dichotomies between body and mind by positing the constitution of the body-subject on unifying grounds. This involves re-instating the body as an active foundation in understanding the formation of the subject, and offers means of conjoining concerns with lived experience in the explanation of core issues such as social power and cultural production.

As Shilling (2007: 1-18) asserts, arriving at a 'fundamentally embodied sociology', would offer a long overdue alternative to social deterministic positions, which are based on frameworks concerned with control over change. He explains the emergence of the 'disciplinary project' at the historical turning point of transition from traditional societies to industrialized capitalist societies, which had been characterized by the acute problems of secularization, and had required placing the priority of sociological research on establishing the conditions for democracy and citizenship also in correlation with capabilities for human agency—order. These capabilities, then, came to be equated with rationality, consciousness, and the controlling capacities of the mind. The special attention given to abstract cognitive capacities and conceptual thought in these frameworks allowed upholding notions of the subject as 'discursive' and constituted—largely by and through pre-conceived social forces and factors, and promoted developing theories and notions of the subject as controlled. The body came to be assigned the status of a 'pre-social' 'natural' phenomenon to be understood in terms of mere sensations—i.e., it was employed to offset the notion of the agent as the rational and conscious member of social order and shared knowledge.

Hence by recovering the body from this degraded status, and by establishing the role of bodily experience and corporeal existence as a formative basis in the accumulation of knowledge, theoretical discourse on the body can be perceived as a major means in countering both the deterministic approaches, and the explanatory frameworks of production of knowledge, which the disciplinary project had come to bear (Shilling 1993: 20-25). Furthermore, as Williams and Bendelow (1998: 208-213) argue, bringing diverse approaches together, allows attaining a grasp over the diversity of processes of embodiment and the corporeal awareness, the practical modes of mastery and hermeneutic 'techne' these involve. The concept of 'embodiment' is proposed as central to a sociology which 'puts minds back into bodies, bodies back into society and society back into the body', a position that challenges the dualist legacies of the past, and enables addressing the deeper ontological questions concerning the nature and status of the body and its relations to the larger socio-cultural processes.

In this theoretical context, 'embodiment' emerges as a conceptual resource to advance a variety of subjects, where it is established as a multi-dimensional factor in the creation, reproduction and transformation of social phenomena. In spite of the diverging views on the nature of the human body, and its employment in different frameworks, this concept is taken to discuss some of the prime issues of sociological research—the issues of bodily conformity and the associated problems of corporeal transgressions in relation to the prevailing socio-cultural historical order. In this regard, alongside of the 'discursive body' and the technologies of power of social constructionist positions (Foucault, in Williams and Bendelow 1998: 1-48), other alternative explanations help assert agency within less predictable and more active processes. Hence the notions of the 'symbolic body' and the role of ritualistic beliefs in its formation (Douglas, in Williams and Bendelow 1998: 1-48), and especially the notion of the 'civilized body' coming about through the long historical civilizing process (Elias, in Williams and Bendelow 1998: 1-48), span through a range of alternative features. They offer analyses of the body in terms of the dynamic interplay of biological and social factors influencing the constitution of the self, and allow perceiving more embodied beginnings for sociological research (Williams and Bendelow, Williams and Bendelow 1998: 5-6). That the body need to be understood as a 'cultural and historical category' is consolidated in manifold ways: conjoined with the insights on desire, transgressing practices, liminality in collective festivals, and the symbolic reinforcement of morality through ritual (Bataille, Bakhtin, Durkheim, in Williams and Bendelow 1998: 1-48).

The body-subject as social phenomenon
The crucial importance of the concept of embodiment is that it allows theorization of the body as a 'sensory and sensual, as well as sensible being' (Williams and Bendelow 1998: 48), which marks a decisive shift away from the passive and towards an active model of agency. Inquiries into the lived body and embodiment as the vehicle for cultivation of particular types of lived experience, allow not only sustaining a balanced relationship among intention, self-instigation and the given external—i.e., social factors. Such inquiries also affirm the 'preconceptual and non-propositional structures of experience' as productive in building up the understanding of the world, and allow positing the body as a legitimate locus in the acquisition of practical knowledge. This experientially grounded view on human embodiment as the existential basis of being in the world, therefore, helps establish a broader understanding of the relationship between body and self, culture and society.

'Embodiment' as a theoretical concept, then, is seen to require building up sensitivity to the capacities of embodied subjects to be shaped by their social environment, as well as recognizing the social consequentiality of the body's materiality. It emphasizes the need of exploring the interplay between order and control, experience and representation in their dialectical relationships, through which bodily 'interiority' becomes 'externalized', and social 'exteriority'— 'interiorized' (Williams and Bendelow 1998: 208-213). Hence for instance in the context of consumerist culture, the body as a 'surface phenomenon' presents a framework showing how it works as a marker of identity and status, pointing to both its increasingly reflexive nature, and as its expressivity in projecting identity. In this, the body image is developed and constructed not as isolated self-enclosed activity, but rather in and through social relations—it is always accompanied by the image of others (Williams and Bendelow 1998: 97).

This expressive nature of the body, then, comes to underlie approaches in the field of cultural studies as well. In more specialized studies—such as those that would focus on the awareness of physicality in everyday experience, the concept of 'embodiment' is developed in terms of issues like 'body-image', as well as in terms of expression of emotional states, where such awareness is approached by employing a phenomenological framework (Nettleton and Watson, 1998). Or the body comes to be analysed as a 'contestable' signifier in the articulation of identities, which emerges within cultural practice, a line of inquiry which offers lucid accounts on the historical construction of the notion of embodiment (Atkinson, 2005).

Explanation of the context within which the body is posited is focused on an account of the social features and characteristics of that context. Space is denoted insofar as it becomes organized in keeping with fundamental bodily coordinates and in this way can provide reference and orientation for body activities: vertical/horizontal, left/right, backwards/forwards. Hence whether approached through the larger framework of phenomenological analysis of the body-subject (Merleau-Ponty), through the investigation of cultural and cultivating potential of its body techniques (Mauss), the study of micro-politics in the encounters and interchanges of social actors in everyday life (Goffman), the notion of the corporeal is delimited to the body itself. Embodiment as a conceptual tool is understood in terms of its capacity to address the complexity of the processes conjoining the physical and the mental. In this, the issues of connections between bodily drives and social motives, practical and imaginative capacities, interaction and self-identity, technical skills and performative capacities—are ultimately and exclusively set within and explicated in terms of the context of the (social) activity itself.

This observation is confirmed in theorizations of 'embodiment' as a research tool itself, such that proposed by Crossley (2007: 80-94). This theorisation brings forth the multivalent links among various sociological issues embedded in the concept. Examined in relation with Mauss's study on body techniques, the concept of embodiment allows arriving at a rich range of aspects involved. It can be studied as to its social and cultural aspect, revealing how the body comes to be a product of social labour, external and learned, and thus allows identifying the ways of assimilating the normative basis for culturally appropriate bodily action and coordination—aspects which account for variability among socio-cultural settings. It can be examined as to its mindful aspect—revealing the capacity of the self to embody knowledge and understanding, as well as the ability to employ these in improvised play, through which embodied techniques issue as forms of practical reason. Furthermore, for being learned and practiced in social contexts, body techniques allow linking up with the inter-corporeal context in which these are used—allowing engagement with embodied subjectivity and agency. As such, Crossley concludes, the concept of embodiment can attend to issues of meaning, understanding and normativity in action. It also allows linking the subjective life of the body with its objective sociological situation.

It can be perceived that while all of these diverse approaches help assert the body as exhibiting active and passive sensations, subject and object relations—a body that is the locus of exchange between inside and outside (Williams and Bendelow 1998: 95), the explication of this exchange is also clearly delimited to the body-subject. In keeping with this, the possibility and nature of social feelings are posited and sought primarily in terms of conjoining intellect with embodied emotion.

The expressive body in social practice and interaction
More specific research into issues of social interaction, too, would be based on examining the dialectic correlations between the mental and the physical aspects of the performing social subject (Frank, in Williams and Bendelow 1998: 55-66). These are illuminated by examining the body-use in action around four central dimensions. These entail the dimension of social control—which addresses the question of how predictable its performance will be, the 'desire' dimension—related to whether it is producing or lacking, the manner in which a relation with others is taken up—monadic/closed, or dyadic/open, and the issue of self-relatedness—whether body consciousness associates or dissociates itself with its own being. These form a matrix of four principal types: the disciplined body, the mirroring body, the dominating body, the communicative body. Each type is discussed through a set of predominant communicative means/patterns, and a preferred site as a socio-spatial model: such as the monastic order, the department store, or warfare. However, in the depiction of these models, features of social and spatial are merged, to the effect that the spatial features appear to serve as a metaphoric associative reference of the

social context in correlation with the character of relations it presupposes. Hence for instance the type of the 'communicative body' is set within the context of dance, community rituals, shared narratives and caring for others. The model as explanatory tool relies on denoting the social character of the site, to which the type's operational medium—'mutual recognition'—already belongs. Mutually enhancive and explanatory of each other, these appear to suffice as explanatory factors and preclude the necessity of accounting for spatial properties of the model.

As Williams and Bendelow (1998) assert, the concept of embodiment proposes and enables re-thinking the social subject in terms of the corporeality of the body. It helps evade the separation of dualistic models of thinking, supersedes 'static notions' of the self in terms of 'essence', as well as supports the shift away from thinking in terms of passive 'states' and towards thinking the self in terms of dynamic/dialectic processes. Seen to be located within the 'webs of power and resistance', research on the body is developed in terms which allow highlighting the subject as relatively autonomous—in its capacities to resist imposed systems and frameworks. However, in the theoretical context of discourse on the body the corporeal would tend to be defined in the terms of, and confined to the social context. Rarely explicitly mentioned, space is employed referentially, such as in the associative models of Frank's typologies of the body in action noted above (Frank, in Williams and Bendelow 1998: 55-66), where the 'model' refers to certain generalized tendencies of dispositions, attitudes and behaviours promoted by the respective social setting. Or, as brought forth in Goffman's (1982) analysis, space assumes the role of a means in resolving the micro-politics of a social situation, where the social actor utilizes the spatial in the positioning and negotiation of social relations and roles. Research on the body through the concept of embodiment highlights concerns with the capacities of the social subject to appropriate the social context, disclosing the dialectic nature of body-mind correlations, and locates the productive and emergent properties within their mutual dependencies and co-definitions.

Spatial contexts of identity and the social
Beyond the referential and representational role of the image of space and identity, the powerful correlation between identity and the spatial context at a more bodily level is also increasingly being acknowl-

edged, suggesting that there could be more to be disclosed about the self, by way of rigorous study of experiential properties of space. Hence for instance the notion of 'situational personality' comes to reflect the observation that behaviour of an individual would vary more under different conditions than the behaviour of different individuals under the same conditions. Situational personality It in this way comes forth as a notion through which psychologists seek to denote the possibilities of precedence of the temporarily acquired over the pre-dispositional in human attitudes and actions. It also suggests the correlation with a temporary situation as an active process of acquisition and formation. Deviating from the representational priorities of mainstream research on architecture, certain perspectives explore the role of architectural space with respect to identity at a deeper level. Hence for instance Pallasmaa (1995) theorises the correlations of the dweller with space in the context of 'house/home, drawing on philosophical and phenomenological perspectives. Based on the manifold intimate mechanisms of identification revealed in the thought of Bachellard, he explores the correlation phenomena as authentic acts of direct encounter with space, asserting space in its potential to symbolise and hence support human presence and existence. In this perspective the mental significance of images is approached though an introspective phenomenological survey of recollection and imagination attached to space, where identification emerges from the emotional components borne in such acts of direct encounter (Pallasmaa 1995: 131-147).

More specifically oriented towards the social realm, there are also studies that address the active share of architectural space in the constitution of social properties of collective sites. Hence for instance the relevance of detailed account of architectural space to the very nature of the social, is revealed with special lucidity in Kracauer's essay 'The hotel lobby' (1995: 173-188). Here, a critical discussion of the human condition in modernity is based on contrasting two collective social spaces—the church and the hotel lobby. Although the focus of discussion is on the changing notion of the aesthetic—which in modernity shifts away from evoking the sublime and towards self-referentiality, these two sites are analysed with a meticulous sense for the integral linkages between spatial and social. Hence this analysis allows construing a diversity of ways in which the social realm, and the architectural space that formulates it, intertwine with aspects of the human condition.

The social and ontological consequentiality of these two sites is established not only in view of the different nature of the experience as defined by their functions. The key role of space comes about through the particularly spatial means and features which materialize, or fail to do so, some deeper purposes—such as those of formulating a 'congregation' where the effort for unification is based on connecting with an elevated realm and outgrowing the imperfection of communal life. Hence effects of space may partake actively in the constitution of the social beyond a random aggregate, and augment the prospect of togetherness and bonding. Or, as in the case of the lobby—it might come to actively obstruct such a possibility. In this respect, the two models effect the sense of equality and its social correlates in rather diverging ways. While in the spatial context of the church this sense is seen to be supported not only by architectural detail and expressivity of space that would point beyond the social and towards an elevated sublime, but also by the physicality of in positioning, and orientation, through which space proposes particular correlations of bodies. Thus it would support the event as collective and shared both in that it points, aesthetically, beyond itself to give the event voice and expression, and in that it integrates, physically. The lobby in contrast presents a social site where the quest for the aesthetic is confined to the aesthetic appearance of the space as such. At the level of the body it operates by way of dispersing random individuals, actualizes an 'evacuation' of—invalidation of togetherness—coming to reflect 'the inessential at the basis of rational socialization' (Kracauer 1995: 173-188).

In this account certain means of particularly spatial nature are disclosed as partaking in the constitution of and support of social bonding and communication. Beyond its influence over dispositions, the role of space comes to involve the affective and ethical that can be grasped experientially. Though aspects of representation are depicted along with dimensions that derive from direct bodily situatedness, space is nevertheless rendered experientially consequential—as it generates feelings and phenomena of a social nature. Such a perspective allows construing of the legitimacy and potential of inquiry into architectural space in conjunction with other social aspects. Analysis of space also offers an opportunity to address a special range of as`pects of the formulation of the social/collective realm through a spatial and experiential perspective, and further understanding of its operations.

'Incorporation'
The body within the systems of the material world
Incorporation presents a more complex and inclusive conception of the correlations of the body, which allows substantially extending the notion of the corporeal into the context of material conditions. As Crary and Kwinter (1992: 12-16) assert, this conception offers potent unifying grounds for a diversity of contexts and approaches which seek to identify challenges and potentialities characterizing the human condition in modernity. In this way it presents a position towards the human condition for the series of essays, each in its own terms offering a theoretical basis to supersede (established) separations and oppositions between 'soul and matter', 'essence and body', body and milieu, and, at the macro-scale—between 'superstructure and infrastructural relations of production' (1992: 12-15). The conception of corporeality also formulates the deeper underlying project to exceed models based on binary ways of conceptualizing the material conditions and the living organism itself, and chart the forces—aesthetic, technical and political—with which things combine to form novel aggregates and patterns, diversifying the challenges with which our being, life and subjectivity are confronted.

While addressing the body, self and subjectivity at diverse levels spanning from philosophy through to neuroscience, from the aesthetic through to the technological, these perspectives nevertheless share a mode of viewing subjectivity. They converge in their understanding of the social subject as emerging within the correlation between organism and its living conditions—i.e., in terms of the 'dynamic, correlated, multipart system'. Hence in spite of their apparent diversity, these perspectives share a focus on the processes of formation and co-formation themselves.

Resistance and assimilation as transformative forces
Crary and Kwinter (1992: 14) identify two directions of research into the correlations of subject and system. One direction engages on tracing the lines of development and transformation of 'biological and technological arrangements'. These types of inquiry help ascertain

that such developments need to be construed as embedded within the continuity of the fundamental historical process of evolution, and not as the result or sign of some recent shift in cultural paradigms. Essays within this group seek to identify the status of the subject in view of the driving forces for the increasingly accelerated change in the organization of social and material circumstances. Hence Guattari's (1992: 16-36) larger systematic overview of the processes accompanying industrialization and urbanization and their effects on ideas about social organization, offers critical insight into the new 'managerial' and disciplinary techniques developing within and through the 'great state bureaucracies' and 'industrial assemblages' (Guattari 1992: 16-36). He identifies a historical turning point, beyond which a marked and systematic transfer of the 'human will to mastery away from the non-human world of nature' and towards the knowledge, management and control of a human nature as well, takes precedence. Beyond that turning point, the status of subjectivity is seen to be gradually formulated through a 'series of 'reductions' and 'deprivations'—enforced by the rationalizing imperatives of the capitalist 'mega-machine'. Life thus becomes increasingly reduced to 'finite quantities of force and sensation', and hence can be efficiently subsumed to institutions—i.e., to organization and control which issue through the diverse forms of 'regimes of power production' as in the 'collective apparatuses' of 'subjectification' (Guattari 1992: 16-36).

Employed on the larger scale, the concept of 'incorporation' comes to highlight the processes of integration of human life forces into larger-than-human systems of social and technical organization. Yet it also allows exploring how the continuous transformation of the 'life-world' evolving in an on-going process of modernization, becomes linked to the production of 'ambient milieus', and construe these as 'sites of invention and transformation' (Crary and Kwinter 1992: 15). This is so, because on the smaller bodily scale, the concept of incorporation entails and highlights the human capacities to cope with material circumstance—i.e., it the capacities of the subject to 'capture' and 'adapt' to change. Hence the concept of 'embodiment' rethought in view of this broader context is taken to indicate the finer-grained strategies of the subject to combine with and assimilate the 'minute, shifting, often invisible patterns and rhythms of the concrete historical milieus within which it unfolds' (Varela 1992: 320-338). The notion of milieu serves to depict the possibilities for incorporation and invention: it is seen as to emerge, and evolve by way of reciprocal and mutual incorporation with other emerging structures. Regardless of the variety of approaches spanning concerns with the explicitly bodily (Mauss), through to the construction of perception/mind (Finkel), the issues of intentionality (Sartre), or the principles of individuation (Gilbert Simondon), subjectivity is seen in close interdependence with the volatile forces and resourcefulness which are mobilized in that correlation with ambient milieu. Hence, as Varela (1992: 330) argues, the body-subject can be construed as always involved in the immediacy of the given situation—a micro world which is both already constituted and under transition, and where the repertoire of behavioural patterns is composed. While having the readiness for action proper to every specific lived situation, it is the 'micro-breakdowns'—i.e., the stream of recurrent micro world transitions—that would tend to generate new modes of behaving. The subject's practical relation to its milieu, then, emerges as a dynamic system of local, interdependent, self-updating movements, perceptions and gestures (Crary 1992: 13).

In the broader context within which they are explored, both incorporation and embodiment as concepts allow positing the issue of subjectivity in terms of the capacities of the subject to capture and adapt to its milieu while at the same time also resisting definition. Subjectivity therefore would need to be understood in terms of 'unknown and unforeseeable' capacities for cognitive and cultural transformation lying with the subject. Furthermore, especially the concept of incorporation highlights the interrelatedness and mutual influences of the individual with its surrounds, ascertaining that neither human subjects, nor the material objects or entities among which they live could be meaningfully studied as separate from the 'dynamic, correlated multipart systems within which they arise'(Crary and Kwinter 1992: 15). However, while the notions of 'system' and 'milieu' support a unifying view on correlations, and the body-subject is posited 'with' a given site or surrounding, the focus is on the capacities of subjects in acknowledging, adapting, and incorporating. On the part of the subject this involves the engagement with specific socially and technically generated patterns and effects, such as new industrial speeds and rhythms as well as new fluid models of human movement. The reality of circumstances and conditions appears in the generalized terms of their bearing and effects—speed, fragmentation, mechanization, sensual reduction and intensification of complexity, rather than in terms of material constitution. Hence even in the broader frameworks addressing the complex processes of incorporation, space as part of the correlation either remains a tacit notion—somehow merged with patterns of activity or implicated in milieu, or it is posited as a separate, and in a way self-contained subject.

'Space as event' versus 'static' space
Architectural space presents the distinct subject of inquiry in Eisenman's essay 'Unfolding events' (1992: 422-427). It brings forth significant propositions for a long over-due alternative theorization of space, although its primary concern is with the capacities of new design to alter the urban environment. The argument is oriented towards replacing the notion of architectural space in traditional theory, because it maintains the space as object within two static conditions: figure (solid building) and ground (voids between them). Instead, this essay discusses the potentials of a different notion—the 'space as event'—as a foundation for design. Employing the Deleuzean conceptions of 'displacement' and 'fold', a new way of construing and constructing space is asserted, where, based on the principle of 'event,' space would present itself as a third type of object—one that is neither old nor new, neither figure nor ground, but rather containing aspects of both. New structures could be designed so as to assume the role of 'unfolding events', incorporate existing static components of the urban environment, and alter it to reveal latent conditions as possibilities for new readings. It is such new structures, then, that would attain capacity to restructure and reformulate the system of other, outdated, physical components of the urban system, allowing that system to emerge as a site potentially open to new interpretations.

Oriented towards design in new ways that bring forth space in its potential to alternate and shift and hence destabilize existing systems of built space, this perspective suggests the possibility of a theorization which evades fixities and definitiveness associated with built architectural space in mainstream theory. It asserts the notion that physical space could be construed as productive in that it can be made to cohere with the structure of an 'unfolding event'—i.e., as a physical structure that would work in terms of a process. Although such capacities would appear to be the special and exclusive province of these new structures—i.e., of a new design through which space might come to actualize such special capacities, this perspective nevertheless allows associating events of change with physical space. It insists on construing space through a third alternative figure, which opens up established notions of architectural space, so as to accommodate thinking and theorizing space in terms of the potency of the 'both-and'. Hence the productive potential of space is affirmed in its capacities to accommodate or even instate an event, while also reconstituting its environs—firmly grounded in its corporeality. However, the concept of incorporation in this reading appears in exclusively spatial terms: it comes to denote the correlations among physical structures in the urban context.

These ideas on capacities of space, and the means of envisioning it could be brought to bear on a theorization of space that would involve not only the events of change at the large scale produced by radically innovative design. It would also capture the subtle ones—those that pass almost unnoticed in the vicinity of sensing bodies, and allow reinstating the processes of incorporation within the corporeal correlations of bodies with space. Furthermore, such a theorization would also address capacities of built space in general—linked with existing space of form, and could be reoriented towards explicating how, alternatively, space might trigger events of embodied affect, or 'knowing' within the very experiential modality of existence which it underlies and enables.

The concept of incorporation allows addressing the body, subject and subjectivity in the integrative terms of system-self correlations: it posits the body within the dynamic correlations with an extended field, and these correlations as base of understanding the complexities in the formation of experience and the subject. It is important to note that these subject-system or subject-milieu correlations are brought forth not only in view of the active interventions of the body but also involve the capturing, adaptation, and assimilation of factors and forces imposed by the larger system as equally active aspects of the correlation. It is there—in these ceaseless interactions, where the 'lived'—hence emergent—is seen to be embedded. Bringing to the fore the capacities of the subject to grasp and productively integrate with that which is larger, incorporation comes to highlight the transformation in the very techniques of knowledge generation and acquisition. It, then, comes to be suggested as 'the new primary logic of creation and innovation in the late modern world' (Crary 1992: 15).

The theorization of 'incorporation' as a dynamic and active process in all of its facets confirms the necessity of thinking the constitution of the subject within its correlations. It also proposes construing these correlations in terms of the continuity of self-with-system. These propositions could be taken as grounds for a further extension in thinking the concrete corporeality of these correlations, as one that would also accommodate an account of space as an integral dimension through which the body's correlations evolve.

Immediate experience and the body
'The performative'—generation of space

More explicit involvement with concerns of a spatial nature come forth in approaches exploring immediate experience by way of a close up on the body-in-activity. These seek to establish the relative autonomy of the body-subject and the processes of productivity and emergence within the context of activity by focusing on these processes themselves. While the framework of 'the performative' examines the body in its active mode of operation within the world, the conception of 'distraction' allows probing into a less intentional modality of mutual and reciprocal correlations in terms of some more subtle processes.

The concept of the 'performative' presents a theoretical tool to address those aspects of subjectivity, inter-subjectivity, and identity and generation and the emergent that become constituted through and with the activities in which the body is involved. As different approaches develop their inquiry at different levels, the performative would come to denote different sets of issues pertinent to the immediately lived and bodily. In the context of practices, the performative is taken to highlight distinctions among static and dynamic, and explicate the productive role of the latter in the formulation of performing selves. When explored in terms of the concepts of event and encounter, it comes to disclose the very processes of becoming. In a different line of thought, a special 'distracted' modality of immediate experience in the urban context would be denoted, suggesting how the body—environment correlations might be also less intentional or intervening yet still autonomous and active. In each case it is the links to possibilities of emergence and generation which render the 'lived' immediate experience liberating.

Gregson and Rose (2000: 433-452) theorize the performative in terms of practices spanning from those that are every day and corporeal, through to the academic engagements at the level of discourse. The conception of the performative itself is developed by juxtaposing Butler's critical thought on the practices which produce and subvert discourse and knowledge in correlation with performance, and Goffmann's 'theatrical' notion which focuses on interaction and engagement among conscious, active, and acting subjects. The element of signification implicated in the concept, is productively exceeded by giving further emphasis on the active 'doing' which 'enacting' entails. It is this 'doing', then, which would be seen to bring space into being, where each particular performative instance would be bound to articulate its own spatiality (Gregson and Rose 2000: 446). In this, both the performed practice and the processes of emergence are seen as something dynamic, and would therefore depend not on established form—i.e., pre-existing built space, but on participatory learning by doing. The productive, then is firmly bound to the performed practice and entails the construction of that alternative space, which is being performatively generated.

This perspective vocalizes the alternative way of attending to spatial issues which underlies thought on the lived and the bodily in frameworks seeking to oppose determinations associated with formulated space. It renders explicit the essential split in the notion of space itself, which appears to correspond to the experience—perception distinction. Hence the 'space of established form' is construed as static, assigned a special status, and is decisively dissociated from the possibility of generating dynamic and productive processes, both physically and metaphorically. The other aspect of this distinction pertains to the type of activity. In Gregson and Rose's (2000: 433-452) perspective the productive nature of 'performing' is rendered legible by contrast with 'just being located in space', that is somehow taken to implicate inertness and passivity, and also in a way subjection.

The performative, the body, and space appear conjoined in Dewsbury's (2000: 473-497) work, focusing on the philosophical conception of 'eventness', flux and perpetual re-constitution in the thought of Deleuze and Guattari. Working from within this nexus, Dewsbury discusses this approach to immediate experience by identifying the principal properties of 'performativity' in a threefold way:

indeterminacy, irretrievability and excess. These properties, he argues, come forth in the temporality of the event—as it happens. Linked to the present moment and construed as an act of immediacy and spontaneity, the performative allows acknowledging the centrality of the visceral body and the 'non-contemplative mode'—the think-feel state characteristic of it. Hence the performative involves the settings through which events take place as situations entailing both risk and chance. Indeterminacy lies in that the event is not entirely under control of the body but also belongs to the situation. Its excessiveness derives from its openness to multiple possible outcomes. Its affective nature is based on excitation as the contact phenomenon with the world. In this way the performative event can be understood as located at the very centre of emergence, and its theorization can be traced within the principal reciprocities among the becoming subject and the objective world. These circumstances are 'intelligibly felt', as they organize possibilities of instrumental action and offer points of contact for the body to become situated. In this way an 'increased potential' towards some of the possible encounters would be constituted 'out of and through' the 'architecture and situation of the event'. However, in this theoretical framework the role of space is indicated insofar as to show that it would provide possibilities for the performative 'actualizations'—acts which are seen to entail both 'sensual embodiment' and 'etching out space' (Dewsbury 2000: 473-496).

Emergence and generation, though linked to circumstance, are embedded in the potential of the performative event itself for re-enactment. Simultaneously emergent, core and subjective, re-enactment entails the active intervening 'doing' of the body, which is continuously mobilized in everyday becoming. Suggesting the links among the emergent, immediate experience and space, this and related perspectives centralising on the processes of becoming provide an essential part in the theoretical foundation for this current study, which seeks to particularise the generative potentialities lying with concrete spatial circumstance at the level of empirical experience.

The 'distracted' as productive mode

A different perspective on the subtle processes through which the body maintains its perpetual contact with its surrounds is brought forth in Latham's (1999: 451-473) exploration of the notions of 'distraction' and 'habit' in Benjamin's thought on the urban experience under modernity. He argues that in contrast to prevailing ideas that in dealing with the complexity of urban existence the individual disconnects and screens off increasing flux of information in acts of self-protection, analysis through the notions of 'distraction' and 'habit' provides an alternative and rather different understanding of the urban experience. These concepts allow bringing forth a very subtle and special modality of being, based on and maintaining correlation at the level of the habitual and practical, non-intentional and non-directional, yet also continuous perception. It operates through two poles: one of these poles employs the distracted mode to deflect stimuli from entering conscious perception, while the other entails adopting an 'emphatic stance' which, in a way, attains closeness 'mimetically'. In this way this modality ensures that one remains connected without actually contemplating the connection. Hence the urban experience is to be construed also in terms of those bodily modes of on-going perception which are grounded in tactility and habit, and through which the body-subject maintains an uninterrupted, though also un-focused contact with its urban surrounds.

This 'distracted' form of perception is embedded in the workings of the body and its negotiations with the immediate context. It highlights the body employing its sensorium, and therefore needs to be understood as founded on bodily encounter. It can be understood as a modality central to the everyday experience of social space in that it discloses other ways of getting hold of the urban, and allows accounting for the active learning involved in these processes. 'Distraction' depicts a state where the tactile maintains its links in the form of on-going perception, while having attention on something else in the foreground. Quite distinct from contemplation, it depicts a way of 'feeling' one's way around the place, noticing and knowing of external objects, in passing. It denotes a kind of perception that both disrupts the smooth flow of the habitual, and at the same time builds up to becoming itself a practical and habitual way of encountering the urban. By far not devoid of affect and arousal, this mode of inhabiting social space is, then, productive of a kind of knowledge which is embodied, and lies as much in the objects and spaces of observation, as in the body and mind of the observer—it can be seen as a mimetic way of connecting. As Hallam (1999) explains, in Benjamin's thought this more immediate but disconnected experiential mode ('Erlebnis') would not quite amount to the full genuine affective experience

('Erfahrung'), yet it is nevertheless established in its productive potential. This modality, characterized by distraction and the habitual, offers a valid path of examining the capacity of self for 'meeting the world within structures of mutuality'—it is founded on encounter. Addressing aspects of the ethics of encounter, it can be revalorized as a powerful experiential way of relating to the world, and explored as to its social potential.

The productivity of this modality of being, as Latham asserts (1999: 456), concerns not only embodied learning, but is also suggested as a potential in generating attitudes that are of social and ethical import. It allows construing embodiment in terms of a perceptual modality that is profoundly urban, pointing to the subtle interplay between distance and closeness, empathy and boredom. In its positive reading 'distraction' presents a more individualistic, yet no less intense way of meeting the energies of the urban which are both inspiring and destructive. It presents a modality of correlating which keeps the multitude of the urban flux as well as the co-presence of others in a subdued background position, so as to evade the rules of direct engagement and interaction. Yet it nevertheless also contains the affirmation of contact between strangers. This affirmation takes the form of distance negotiation, where the encountering and confronting does not come to mean a dissolution or transgression of the other. It is also about a gesture of recognition and awareness of mutual humanity as shared condition of subjectivity, and about acknowledgement of the self with the other. As an emphatic yet pre-conscious correlation, this distracted modality also defeats the authority of the material surrounds. It stands in contrast to the use-oriented practical intent, and therefore serves to draw a limit to the omnipotence of the self, while also at the same time drawing the self into the world (Latham 1999).

This perspective offers insight into aspects of immediacy in the context of everydayness, practice, and the habitual by highlighting a different kind of bodily engagement with surrounds, which builds up to other aspects of 'embodiment'. It also brings forth the correlation in terms of its corporeality, and confirms the human sensorium at the basis of capacities for genuine experience. It, then, could be taken to complement those notions of the lived and the body which rely exclusively on the active share of doing and intent, with the human capacity for a kind of sensing and operating within the world that is less intervening and less or oriented—as a mode that is both 'distracted' and productive. This would allow extending the physical presence of space, which can be confirmed as affective in bodily terms, and hence included in the framework of what that which is experienced immediately.

The explorative modality of sensation: the body as a perceptual system

The theorization of the body in its active and transformative correlations with its immediate surrounds denoted through the conception of 'incorporation', is extended towards the open-endedness of bodily encounters in the context of the performative, and complemented with the conception of the distracted modality through which the body maintains a ceaseless subtle mimetic connection with its surrounds. For the purposes of this current study, however, it is crucial to acknowledge that these theoretical propositions on embodied capacities are supported at the empirical level as well. Hence concrete research on the body in terms of its sense relations to its medium, posits these processes of correlating at their most corporeal, and, by extension, would offer grounds for probing into the very materiality of these correlations in terms of space. Based on extensive scientific research, Gibson (1983) proposes a holistic approach to understanding the physicality of the body by way of examining and explicating the operations of its sensory apparatus. He establishes a model for thinking the body and the bodily activity of explorative correlation with its surrounds, which offers a productive empirical extension of the above theoretical approaches. This perspective on the body, then, both confirms certain propositions with scientifically established findings, and complements the understanding of bodily experience, and its possible conscious correlates, with fresh insights into the physicality of the processes of their constitution.

Senses, Gibson insists, need to be regarded not as producers of visual, auditory, or tactile sensations, but as active seeking mechanisms for looking, hearing and touching—as systems for immediate perception. In this, distinguishing between sense impression and sense perception is of crucial importance. This distinction helps explain how we are able to have the constant perception that is needed for effective action, and understand this as an active modality of the body, entailing both the processes involved in discovering new stimulus invariants, and those in extending the repertory of responses that can be applied.

The body operates through five such perceptual systems which are not only active, but also intrinsically interrelated. They overlap in focusing on the same information, and hence are not mutually exclusive but mutually supportive—they are complementary and coordinated. Viewed from this perspective, the perceptual systems can be established as out-reaching mechanisms that search out and detect required perceptual information about the world in which the body as organism exists.

External senses have a double role—to make us feel, and to make us perceive. Sensations, then, while being primarily engaged in detecting the world, conjoin with the conception of the existence of the external object, in that they also detect the corresponding impression made on the perceiver. Sensation and perception correspond also in that they are produced at the same time, yet they have different attributes. The fact that senses may obtain information without the intervention of intellectual processes, and that not all input may arouse sense impression, help understand how perceptions may form without having to enter consciousness in the form of sensation.

As Gibson (1983) explains, there are two levels of sensitivity that can be distinguished in keeping with the fact that the sense organs are of two different sorts: the passive receptors which respond to forms of energy that surpasses their (measurable) thresholds, and the perceptual organs which depend on receptors but work as active systems, searching out information from the stimulus energy. While the body responds to both permanent and changing properties of the environment, in its operations it relies on constant perception—i.e., on its ability to detect invariants. This condition of 'paying attention' reveals that organ-systems are not anatomical, but exploratory: they orient and investigate for relevant information. Hence the body is construed in its perpetual involvement and active exploration of immediate surrounds—its correlation being one of resonance. The body resonates both in view of the perceptual systems always seeking and extracting information, and when seen as a whole system whose input and output resonates to external information. This relation of resonance is performatory, and entails perceptual learning through which the individual can take account of and cope with objective facts.

This aspect of the body as a source of practical knowledge is confirmed also in studies on cognition, where even the most primary (sensory-motor) experience is shown as it works as an 'embodied' learning mechanism integral to the cognitive unconscious, such as in Lakoff's seminal work on bodily experience as formative of the mind (1999).

Among the perceptual systems, the most relevant to furthering understanding of the corporeal nature of space-body relations is the haptic system, dealing with the sense of touch (Gibson 1983: 97-135). This system requires special attention and highlight, because although the haptic always accompanies and underlies visual sensitivity, for humans visual attention takes precedence over the haptic and visual input dominates haptic awareness. Hence while the two systems work together and produce facts that are registered in two different ways, the haptic would tend to go unnoticed. The haptic is a special system in several respects. It denotes the sensibility of the individual to the world adjacent to the body obtained by the use of the body. However, the information it yields concerns not only the environment, but also the body itself, as well as each as relative to the other. The haptic— involves two separate senses: skin pressure and kinesthesis. Hence unlike the other perceptual systems, the haptic sensory system in- volves the whole body with its members, and its entire surface—the skin with all its appendages.

The other exquisite capacity of this system is that the explorato- ry sense organs are also the performatory motor organs—i.e., the equipment for 'feeling' is anatomically the same as the equipment for 'doing'. With the exception of the mouth, this combination is not found for the other systems. However, as motor activity is more de- manding, the whole system would be taken rather in its motor capaci- ty, while the exploratory haptic perception might not be registered.

Yet, as Gibson (1983: 97-135) explains, the haptic system yields a surprising amount of information, although we would become conscious of haptic awareness only in the dark, when vision fails. This derives from the capabilities of the haptic-somatic system to address both the environment and the body itself in their correlations. It can yield information and perform its relationships both with respect to the frame of the body and to the framework of space. In the system of touch, the layout of the environmental surfaces that come in contact with the body, and the disposition of the body go together. The haptic system registers velocity, motion and acceleration, force and pressure. Via gravitation, it can attend to the vertical and the horizontal, and identify plane inclination. The haptic perception of relations to an object identifies linear direction, informs of alignment, dimensions and distance. The exploratory touch, which may palpate, prod, press or rub, does permit both the grasping of an object and a grasp of its meaning through the object's tangible properties. Hence such meanings would be grounded also in geometrical variables (shapes, dimensions, proportions, edges, slopes, or protuberances), surface variables (texture, smoothness or roughness), or material variables (mass, heaviness, rigidity, or plasticity). While some of these are consolidated visually, there are those which come forth only in haptic perception. The notion of haptic space, then, builds on the sense of the touching surface, which can be either empty or solid. The haptic system is special also in the sense that it presents the same stimulating event in terms of two possible poles of experience: objective and subjective. By touching a solid object one may attend either to the external resistant thing—the edge of the table, or to the impression on the skin of the hand. Consequently, as Gibson discloses, an account of objective reality in this mode of perception may follow both poles (1983: 97-135).

These insights of this scientific research on the body in its sense relations offer grounds for a conceptual reconsideration of physical space as an immediate experiential field. Such reconsideration allows understanding the reasons why the notion of movement so readily replaces the notion of space. It is embedded in exploratory perception through the haptic-somatic system, the awareness of which conjoins the sense of movement with the sense of space. Hence attending to the specificities of the experience in terms of space, would require special attention to the properties of physical circumstance, and yield a different body of experiential contents acquired in the course of exploratory perception. Furthermore, positing space in the vicinity and in terms of the sensing body obliterates the persistent solid-void dichotomy and allows construing, rendering and exploring space as qualified material presence that encompasses features of both solid surface, and void. This opens up the opportunity to approach and reconstruct the sense of space by way of analysis of concrete physical features and properties—of space.

Corporeal reverberations: the body with space

This survey has offered a glimpse on the diversity of aspects characterizing the nature of embodied experience in discourse on the lived body. It has also helped highlight a number of issues to be addressed in grounding the validity of thinking built architectural space in correlation with the body and the immediately experiential. The prime impediment for acknowledging the generative potential of built space appears to be linked precisely to the powerful permanent material presence of the built space of form, and the theorization of space as the fixed and image-based visual realm of representation which has come to dominate mainstream approaches to space. It is a conception of space which posits the correlation firmly within the framework of perception—i.e., it presupposes the correlation as distinct, and separate from the flow of lived experience. With alternative frameworks not as readily available, this type of mediated and mediating correlation has no place in the quest for establishing the relative autonomy of the body-subject. Space effectively disappears from discourse on experience, receding to cautious indications in terms like 'material world', 'spatiality', 'system' or 'milieu'.

However, the survey of discourse on the body around the concepts of embodiment and incorporation, the performative, as well as in terms of the body's perceptual systems, also allows tracing out possibilities of re-constructing physical space in the vicinity of the body. It articulates several theoretical shifts in understanding of and accounting for the materiality of human existence. In the shift away from the body-mind split and the notions of the passive subject, embodiment highlights the active share of bodily existence in the formation of the subject. This notion of embodiment places the emergent within the dialectics between social factors and the capacities of embodied subjects to be shaped, while also recognizing the social consequentiality of the body's materiality. The conception of 'incorporation' furthers understanding of the 'lived' by asserting an alternative to established subject-object distinctions, proposing integrative frameworks through which to explore the human subject within and as part of the larger social and material systems. Hence 'milieu' is a site of formation and transformation—where subject and site are seen in perpetual mutual emergence. The concept of the performative places the productive potential decisively within the intentional active interventions and capacities of the self. It focuses especially on those doings, modalities or states that render the immediate and bodily essentially open—i.e., it points to 'events' of becoming as the locus of the unpredictable, non-discursive and pre-conscious processes though which the emergent emerges.

Few of these approaches engage in explaining the reciprocal correlation with space. Rather, they theorize the body in terms of a variety of modalities, all active, all live, and all denoting the productive import of the very actualisation of its contact with the world. The corporeal existence of the body is being established as integral to the processes of constitution of the social subject. Through the notions of 'system' and 'milieu', the account of correlations extends to incorporate social and material structures, through which the presence of the world becomes increasingly physical, hence also, possibly, spatial. More explicit links to spatial aspects come forth in the context of 'the performative', where the productive and the emergent are seen as embedded in immediate experience, and therefore also in space. Yet space is denoted rather as that which comes to be generated in the processes of becoming.

In another vein, certain depictions of the bodily ways of being render correlations with immediate surrounds of a different kind—distractedly. Non-intentional, non-intervening, yet also not confined to an act or activity but continuous, this mode of correlating nevertheless does bear emotive cognitive and social import. This allows construing the body and its corporeal existence at a more discreet physical level—as founded in the perpetual activity of pre-conscious sensual exploration. This perspective is confirmed by empirical research on the operation of the body through its perceptual systems, which evidence the body in its perpetual explorative, performative, and resonating correlations with the material world. This allows positing these corporeal correlations as vital aspects of immediate experience, which actualise also at this empirical level, and as founded on bodily encounters with material surrounds. Formulating the most tangible component of that materiality, space can be included in an account of the generation and emergence—it allows inquiry into another layer of discreet corporeal ways through which sensibilities are attained, and capacities constituted.

Physical space is not only a special separate province of perception. Its relevance is not confined to the visible representational reality with which it has come to be associated in mainstream perspectives. This same space of built form has a presence which is also non-mediating: in the vicinity of the body it continues its existence. Here its materiality is neither determining, nor limited to practical affordance. It surrounds, immerses, and affects—it is a shared matter for both the performing, and the situated body. Though their engagements with space occur in different terms, and perhaps result in different productive formulations, both the performing and the situated body are involved, and actively so.

The 'lived' as the bodily relations with built space is not confined to 'resistance' to pre-determination, where space triggers a kind of negative productivity in that it would stimulate the formulation of tactics of opposition, transgression, or the formulation of alternative spatialities.

The relation of being simply situated, too, is not one of passive reception, but an active form of reverberation. Bringing about physical circumstances, properties and mechanisms, space takes shape as a qualified matter which is being continuously explored—itself. Construed in these terms, space emerges as a vital and vitalizing inextricable dimension of experience, one that mobilises and bears affective, cognitive and social potential. It can be linked to events of becoming and the emergent. It can be construed in terms of the relation it nourishes, as this relation evolves—continuously and corporeally, though also somewhat distractedly. With space, the body's corporeal existence is founded on the perpetual processes of exploration, confirming the relation as one of reciprocity, and resonance. Though it might not be readily registered, such resonance is a form of active exploration. It is open-ended, too. The relations of resonance and reverberation entail a fair share of indeterminacy—they do not foretell experience as an outcome. While perhaps not producing space, the engagement of the situated body with built space can be understood nevertheless as equally productive—it generates experiential forms, it actualizes. Positing physical space in the vicinity of the body articulates a different, still more minute level at which the modality of becoming evolves.

Thinking corporeal space in the vicinity and in terms of the body allows understanding space as it situates—it allows, or forbids the body to find its points of contact. It proposes relations and hence possibilities for affect or action. It envelops and thus entails sensory engagement. Based in substance—physical components and spatial form—its effects are cumulative. They may build up to intensities that work dynamically—to be felt as forces, blending in with and magnifying other, human, impulses. All of these bear potential to trigger the immediately experiential and its discreet exploratory outwards extension—the sensing body which is inextricably and perpetually engaged in survey without distance, from within. Whether construed as the 'distracted' mode of experiencing (Latham/Benjamin), as the embodied form of 'sensory becoming' (Deleuze, 1994), or simply as an expression of vital processes (Gibson), this correlation is a kind of direct emphatic involvement. Hence employing a rather full sensory apparatus—the tactile and kinetic along with the visual, the body resonates, registers and acknowledges. The tactile feels its way around, tracing physical presences, voids, limits and openings. The kinetic detects forces as alterations and intensities, both outer and bodily, in correlation. Corporeal space affects and mobilizes—it addresses the whole body as the zone of contact. The body partakes in this correlation in various ways, all intense, and all relying on sense, investing as well as attaining practical knowledge. Whether constructing its relations and performances, or appropriating distractedly and non-intentionally, it explores and reverberates, it is involved in a productive exchange. These two corporeal entities, then, not only coalesce and correspond, but also intensify and augment that process of correspondence. Space is intelligibly felt and apprehended, while excitation (the contact phenomena) entails the visceral, intuitive, affective processes of sensing and grasping realities of the social and material world.

The conceptualization of built physical space can be extended to the realm of the body; it can be rendered tangible in experiential ways—as it comes to be sensed. It can be explored as it opens up on immediate experience, allowing the body to live with and grasp meanings from within corporeal presences—both space and the body itself—attending to palpable properties, exploring possibilities, and engaging with the discreet events of contact phenomena. Discourse on the lived in terms of the corporeal existence of the body does not require evading and excluding concerns with built space entirely. Understanding corporeal experience within its spatial dimension only calls for special analytical attention. It requires thinking of space in different terms, and its re-articulation in view of the passage from space to sense to sensibility.

Chapter Two

From 'lived space' and experience to the materiality of experience

From space to the body—the problematic of built form
Thinking experience within its spatial dimension grounds it, immediately, within the 'here' (space) and the 'now' (time). Yet it is space that bears a special potential: it brings forth the realities of existence as shared in a physical concreteness, which the temporal dimension does not provide. Space is the most tangible framework with which experience evolves. However, in establishing its socio-cultural, onto-logical, and epistemological import, an account of space in its material presence, as integral correlate to experience, and especially with re-spect to a body-subject who is situated, appears to be problematic, and such potentialities of space remain relatively unexamined. The prob-lems impeding such an account are two-fold. On the one hand, there is the fact that immediate experience is construed of as already immedi-ately spatial and temporal, which renders both of these dimensions somehow self-evident. On the other hand, there are certain issues as-sociated with the possible effects of that which is physical and exter-nal, which renders this narrow area of effects in and through space controversial, or simply negligible.

Construing space and time as already immediately belonging to, and present in experience, leads to their status of being left theoretical-ly relatively unattended. In theorising experience, it frequently would suffice to denote a 'space-time' as conjoined coordinate system and context in which experience can be construed of as immediately set. In this way the notions of experience and time become almost inter-changeable in representing the process itself, such as in the case when terms like 'instance', 'moment', or 'interruption' are taken to depict immediate experience *per se*. Yet each of these dimensions—time and space—correlates with the processes and events involved in the experiential flow in rather different ways. In contrast to time, which pertains in equal terms to each of the totality of processes and phenomena that are lived, the logic in which space relates to each of these is far from straightforward or univocal. This would require the differentiation of the terms of the account of space in accordance with the respective distinct process in focus.

Space embeds, and opens up to processes of different nature, magnitude and scale, evolving at different levels, and in varying dependence on its physical presence. There are those foreground activities and processes, for the purposes of which space would have been constructed. These would tend to be more readily recognized as they formulate the context of functions and actions. There are those experiential processes which are construed as relatively less bound to space, because they involve and appear to be governed by factors of a different nature (social, cultural and ideological). Processes of this category would, more frequently than not, tend to point beyond space and towards themselves as prime sources in explicating experience, a trait which came forth in the context of the 'lived body'. There are also those practices, activities and events, which, together with but also beyond the functional affordance, entail direct engagement with space—appropriation, formulation and re-formulation, which evolve as essential aspects of social correlations. This is the vast and complex category of processes which are brought forth through the analytical conception of 'lived space'—i.e., these come forth by thinking experience in spatial terms. Attending to these entails establishing potentialities of space in terms of the reciprocal correlations, which are taken up from the perspective of a relatively autonomous agent—it is oriented towards understanding how space is open to intervention. Then, there are those concrete activities which develop directly with and through space—such as motion, or movement, in relation to which space can be explained in the simple terms of distance, measure and affordance.

All of these components of life are immediate, and hence also integrally spatial. However, though contained and supported by space, these appear not to require extensive analysis of concrete physical properties of built space. In the stream of lived experience, they formulate a complex context of occurrences, practices and processes, which in effect screen off other, more subtle ways of being and becoming with space—such as those that evolve through the cluster of phenomena embedded in the materiality of space-body correlations.

This cluster of phenomena is intertwined within the rich and complex texture of space-supported life, evolves at the level of sensate bodily involvement with its physical reality, and belongs to experience itself intimately and integrally. Yet although they would partake and characterise each of the experiential layers noted above, these phenomena cannot be observed, but only inferred, circumstantially. They can be rendered accessible by thinking experience in terms of space—i.e., they present a narrow section of the lived, and require keen attentiveness to the palpable qualifying specificity of built space in its capacities to articulate the concrete existential conditions that are shared, in experience.

Bringing these subtle ways of becoming with space to the foreground and making them available to the on-going discussion of space, the lived and experience in general, is the principal aim of this study. It relies on the premise that this aim can be pursued by way of empirical analysis of material space. Such analysis, by virtue of capturing the relation with space in its intimacy, where no direction is yet proposed, would be both disclosing the generative capacities of space, and tracing out the forms of experience, which its unmediated effects might trigger.

Instituting this layer of experience as a distinct area of inquiry is necessary because the study of space in its physical presence has come to be posited primarily within the framework of perception. Perception as a modality distinct from experience presents a subsequent, more properly conscious phase in the process, includes the occurrences of an immediate nature, and therefore has come to stand for the wholesome process. Furthermore, for being primarily visual, closer to conscious awareness, and entailing intellectual capacities (cognition, aesthetic judgement, memory, imagination) perception formulates the outcome of the process, and as a 'final' phase lends itself to rational explication. Therefore, in mainstream research on built architectural space, it is in terms of this modality—perception, through which interpretation of the complexities of spatial effects is being sought. This would mean that there is a gap in understanding space in that whatever has been experienced in and through space becomes assimilated, and dominated, by explication of the purely perceptual properties of physical space.

Theoretically, these two modalities—experience and perception—would presuppose different types of inquiry into physical space that complement each other and in this way would fulfil the principle of continuity of experience. However, discourse on built space has come to be located exclusively within the framework of perception, assimilating the experiential, and standing for the whole process. This evidently simplifies the terms of depiction of architectural space and research in that it helps reduce effects to their visibility and legibility, where they can be described and interpreted. It maintains the 'object' nature of space, and facilitates its association with capacities to express preconceived forms of meaning. It also enhances the tendencies in conceptualizing physical space in terms of spatial stability, through which it would attain the powers for a problem-less referential transmission of identity—aspects of space that present the focus for intense criticism in discourse on built architectural space. However, in order to overcome such pre-conceptions, and re-construct physical space as a productive experiential field, it is crucial to recognise this confluence of modalities of correlating with space, understand the actual ways in which the experiential becomes submerged. This, then, would allow formulating the methodological means in disentangling and bringing to the foreground that which is particularly experiential. A more particular discussion of this conceptual commingling underlying the theoretical ambiguity of architectural space will be attempted in the concrete case of theatre, as it allows tracing out the status of space within two different disciplinary contexts—theatre studies, and the corresponding branch of theatre architecture.

The other important obstruction to a particularly experiential account of physical space can be intuited as related to the 'induced' nature of its effects at that level. Though embedded in tangible materiality—solid, empirically present spatial phenomena, such effects may not come to be recognised fully consciously. Awareness of these is too subtle in that it begins as sense perception and evolves from the periphery inwards and hence lies deeper in the pre-conscious. The 'sense' of such un-mediated effects, would therefore tend to remain un-registered, for being too fleeting and transitory in its tendency to pass into other more complex processes of a properly 'subjective' autogenous nature, perhaps becoming involved in the motivation and intents called forth by the dominant activity context. In this way, though utterly integral to experience, space would not directly come forth in its generative potential: such potential needs to be re-constructed, circumstantially, from within the very form of its actualization in experience. Acknowledging and validating the spatial in its qualifying influences at the level of immediate experience requires not only special attention to a cluster of discreet processes that can only be derived. It also entails the institution of the conceptual and methodological framework that would be apt to re-articulate physical space as an empirical entity, open it up for analysis, and explain its operations in the terms of the corporeal.

Thinking experience in terms of space appears to offer a potent path in attaining a rendition of these experiential phenomena characterising the zone of contact. It allows capturing that which is generated by living with and through the materiality of built form, attending to the unmediated effects and the existential conditions towards which these might intensify, and arrive at the affective, ethical and cognitive inherent in it. It addresses a narrow area awaiting theoretical attention and particularization in research. This area is significant because it presents possibilities of recovering an account of physical space in its continuity as shared framework with respect to experience as well, in keeping with the condition of the continuity of sensation and sensibility, and offers an insight into space and experience from this perspective.

In turning to the larger frameworks of space and experience, the aim is to survey certain key perspectives in philosophical and sociological thought, through which thinkers of diverse lineage and orientation approach the re-constitution of the 'lived'. This would help trace out possibilities in which these perspectives might inform an analysis of architectural space within the intended direction. It would allow locating the study, support the built up of the theoretical base of the approach, and help establish whether and how built space could be recovered and explored as a generative dimension, at the corporeal level of immediate experience.

Discourse on the 'lived', marks the decisive shift within the broader field of the humanities towards obtaining a deeper grasp on the complexity of processes involved in the constitution of agency, and counterbalance deterministic positions. Lived experience is posited as an essentially liberating component and an active foundation in ascertaining the relative autonomy of the subject, and as a crucial means in furthering understanding of the larger socio-cultural processes. In spatial theory, this discussion forms around the conception of 'lived space'—a vital principle in the formulation of agency and an essential aspect in the social production of space. This conception enables the articulation of experience as it is thought of in spatial terms, and is instrumental in bringing forth that which is suppressed and excluded from the setup of rational space and representation into the explication of experience.

The discourse on the 'lived', and space develops at the meta-theoretical level, where prime emphasis is given to the very conceptualization of space. Lefebvre's (1991) framework provides the foundational theoretical structure of analytical concepts, which allows distinguishing the various levels and operative modalities of notions of space, and shows the dialectical correlations of these notions as embedded in the larger social processes of the production of space. The 'lived' is theorized in terms of 'appropriation' which entails both the experiential correlation with existing concrete space, and its gradual 'secretion' through the various processes involved in 'spatial practice'. The framework as a whole seeks to address the problems of various conceptual confusions in discussing space, and the consequences of such confusions for theory and research.

Another issue impeding the development of research and knowledge of space is brought forth in Gibson-Graham's (1997) analysis of discourse itself. It entails the problems arising with the 'spatialization' of discourse, which takes up the place of engagement with spatial issues, and obstructs the definition and understanding of the material and social realities of space. This tendency is revealed in its effects of supporting two types of theory, both of which rely on the correlation of spatial form and identity. In contrast, focus on these realities would offer an opportunity to take account of a range of alternative practices outside these frameworks, at the basis for a 'fluid' ontology. Still another set of issues are articulated in the work of Massey (2005), who engages in the conceptions of experience and the self which are expressive of ideas on space in philosophy and theoretical discourse, holding that the way in which space is posited bears implications as to how it will be intended, designed and explicated. Her rigorous analysis with respect to features and properties through which space is understood, discloses various persistent conflations of space with time, of mental and material. These, then, maintain the entrapment of space within dualities and oppositions at different levels: global/local, space/place, concrete/abstract and mind/body. In overcoming the notions of space based on a predetermined 'essence', a different reading of space is asserted, one where space is essentially 'open', 'porous' and 'relational'—i.e., embedded in material practices, enhancing the emphasis on the 'lived' as a shift towards a more liberated social subject at the basis of (radical) social and political theory.

In spatial theory, establishing the 'lived' as a liberating context relies on bringing to the foreground the manifold practices through which the possible determinisms associated with formed physical space are resisted and productively surpassed. This is achieved by shifting the focus away from 'the space of form' and towards the 'material practices' performed in, through and upon that space, which are seen to be expressive of the active share of agency. In evading a predetermined definition, correlations with space are denoted in terms of the practices of intervening, forming and reforming spatial realities, and it would be primarily those practices to be brought forth as the sites of co-constitution, and where the productive and emergent is seen to lie. In spite of the fact that these perspectives shift away from 'the space of form', there are insights, notions and propositions that could be re-examined and taken up, and allow grounding this current research as an alternative complementary approach to built architectural space. The proposed analysis is theoretically and methodologically intended as essentially coherent with the principal notions of these above frameworks. Re-conceptualising architectural space at the empirical level with respect to the situated agent opens up possibilities to seek an account of built space in its experiential potential and to recover its socio-cultural import in ways that would not conflict, but rather particularise and confirm its productive capacities. Once re-articulated built space could be analysed, disclosing its generative capacities in the form of a narrow yet also productive stratum of correlations that belong to lived experience. These are embedded in its material presence, work in terms of unmediated effects, evolve through the body, and bear relevance to the understanding of how our sensibilities and capacities for social togetherness might be engendered, and actualized in particular (collective) socio-spatial configurations and through qualified spatial form.

The larger philosophical frameworks focusing on lived experience offer insight into the ways in which thinkers of various lineages approach the fundamental principles and conditions of establishing a shared world, and explicate the crucial potential of the experiential modality in correlating and attaining that world. This entails an inquiry into the processes through which the immediately experiential engenders change—i.e., an inquiry that seeks to explain the fundamentally different ways of being and becoming, along with the alternative ways of knowing inherent in them. Though diverging as to the ways in which the subject, experience, and even 'sharing' are understood, as well as in their methods of inquiry, the primary concern of these frameworks lies with the very possibilities of 'correlating' to that which is larger and other than the self. This entails explication of the capacities of self/subject to connect meaningfully with the given physical, social and cultural realities, and the capacities to incorporate what this contact or 'sharing' is apt to produce—i.e., the capacities to undergo change. The survey of these frameworks also allows tracing out propositions and insights as threads that might support positing lived experience within the concreteness of given spatial circumstance.

Approaches in the broader phenomenological tradition give explicit precedence to the possibilities of contact with the phenomenal presence of the world at the basis of experience. While the notion of self would vary in depiction, taking shape in conceptualizing the 'interpreting mind' (Gadamer), or the 'sentient body-subject' (Merleau-Ponty), these frameworks maintain a distinctly polarized relation with the world, which is bound to the intent of the active subject-pole. However, genuine experience always potentially entails a generative moment of 'breaking out' and extending towards the world, through which the world can be perceived and internalized.

Thinkers in the lineage of transcendental empiricism seek to overcome that polarity by focusing on the very processes of correlating themselves. These processes are conceptualized in the immediacy of their very occurrence as lived events founded in encounter. Hence the correlations of the self with that which exceeds the self can be construed not in terms of domination—either way—but rather in terms of open-ended and productive exchange. This allows seeking an account of multiplicity and un-predictability inherent in such events—placing 'the emergent' as the foundation of a reconfigured ontology of 'becoming'. Addressing the lived in the area of formation before and beyond identity and subjectivity, these frameworks posit and explore experience and self as sites of manifold possibilities and unexpected linkages—i.e., the lived is brought forth in terms of the discreet processes of emergence. However, in spite of the concreteness of the micro-events in which experience is analysed, this conceptual system is in a way also less tangible and material, because of the emphasis on establishing the very possibilities of these events, rather than on 'what' happens. Nevertheless the processes are construed in terms of the empirical corporeality of the correlation, and articulate the body in its fundamental vitality and active modality of correlating expressed in the conception of 'reverberation'. While this larger framework is taken up at various levels (such as non-representational theory) emphasis would tend to remain on concretizing the nature of the processes of emergence in terms of 'movements' or 'moments'. Space would tend to remain a tacit notion, latently present insofar as immediate experience is always already spatial.

The persistent reluctance to engage on the issue of experience in terms of space reveals that built space is a suspect subject not only when viewed as the 'ordering' and 'representational' presence at the perceptual level. The neglect of spatial circumstance in explication of processes and phenomena that belong to the 'lived' and experiential, would suggest that these aspects remain underexplored not only because these might be somehow 'attached' to the frame of perception, or be disregarded for being too minute or minor, but also because these are associated with an aura of controversy.

Such controversy concerns especially effects of that which is external to the body and presents itself as objective material reality: direct effects of this kind appear to be determining and hence passive in nature. Therefore spatial features of this category are seen to pertain to the lived insofar as they offer the context for action (allowance), or as frames to be transformed or transgressed (negative productivity). Unmediated effects generated in built space, especially with respect to a body which is firmly emplaced, would clearly tend to fall into this category because as such they would have to be considered as 'given'—i.e., only 'sensed'. The absence of the aspects of intent, intervention or alteration, would render these difficult to construe in the liberating terms of the 'lived'. This, on the one hand, would stem from certain remnants of thinking relations with physical aspects of the world in terms of causality. On the other hand, it would reflect the still persisting divide in understanding the workings of the mind, experience and consciousness along the lines of the 'subjective' (autogenous) as distinct from 'objective' (induced) processes.

Foundation to exceed such obstructions come forth in Langer's (1988) profound philosophical essay on the human mind, based on an altered conception of 'feeling' and its reconstruction as a process. By establishing that which is 'induced'—i.e., that which is felt as sensory stimulus on equal grounds with 'autogenous' processes, this framework allows ascertaining aspects of sensibility, awareness, excitement or suffering as belonging to those events (rather than as products of the event), and construing the operations of the mind in unified terms. In this way the full range of mental processes come to be explicated as vital activities that chart the entire domain bounded by the human body. Thereupon, processes beginning as 'induced'—such as through unmediated effects of space, can be ascertained as valid and potent constituents of experience, as these would differ from autogenous ones only as to their origin, but not as to their active and generative nature. The processes of 'sensing' external physical properties and circumstances, therefore, would need to be understood in their dialectical transient relationships with mental processes that are 'subjective'. This allows extending the notion of the corporeal and corporeality beyond the bounds of the body and encompass the relation with space as active and open, explore that relation in terms of immediate bodily encounter and seek explication of experience as it opens up to spatial circumstance.

Having attained the principal theoretical foundations, the current approach, thereupon, is defined in terms of a series of methodological propositions and a conceptual framework. These are discussed in their capacity to enable re-constructing the spatial dimension as integral to experience at this discreet level of the relation, and conducting inquiry into the immediacy and involvement with concrete material space as a relatively un-treaded territory of lived experience.

'Lived space'

The social production of space: experience versus perception

One of the prime concerns of social and spatial theorists is the very conceptualization of space, which bears far-reaching consequences in that it renders space open to ideological manipulation. This theoretical context is characterized by rigorous engagement with and close scrutiny of prevailing conceptualizations. It seeks to reveal, oppose and supersede tendencies of conflating aspects and notions of space, through which issues pertinent to the abstract/mental level begin to blend with those belonging to material/physical space. Lefebvre's (1991) seminal work on the social production of space presents the turning point in laying out these distinctions. 'Lived space', the key conception in this framework is posited in its essential potential in theorizing lived experience, and brought forth as the means of countering and evading deterministic interpretations of built 'representational' space, along with its instrumentality of bearing ideological underpinnings via 'representations of space'. Hence the conception of 'lived space' allows addressing how socially produced space is being appropriated and transformed into 'lived experience', by bringing in the active share of the experiencing subject. While that which is 'lived' allows and suggests taking the physical, sensory and phenomenal of the given realities into account, it nevertheless brings into focus the active and hence open-ended processes of appropriation and intervention of these realities highlighting the correlation in terms of the relative autonomy of agency.

Coined by Lefebvre, the conception of 'lived space' is integral to his tripartite analytical framework. Entailing 'representations' of space and the 'representational space' of their realization along with the 'lived', this framework explicates space as set within the broader system of production and reproduction of social relations. Hence these concepts address the diverse processes of production of space at all levels of the operations of a society, and set it firmly within the forces and mechanisms of the social structure as defined in a particular mode of production in its historical place and time. Although this framework directs inquiry from space itself towards the analysis of the processes of production of space, these two—processes and product (space), are to be construed as two inseparable aspects, and not as two separable ideas.

Lefebvre insists on recognising both the integral links, and the crucial distinctions between the notions of conceptual space ('representations' of space), built space as it is perceived or 'read' (representational space), and 'lived space'. This latter concept denotes not only the context of spatial practices of appropriation, but also implicates that there is a direct experiential involvement with concrete built space—i.e., it is experienced. It sets these immediate interrelations within the historically specific conditions of social production—i.e., in correlation with economic, ideological and political processes. The 'representation' of space, denoting space as 'conceived', is tied to relations of production and especially to the order which these relations impose—i.e., to the knowledge, ideas and conceptualizations of space. Concerning the terms in which space is imagined, as well as the conceptual and visual representation of ideas regarding space along with the signs and codes these implicate, it underlies, but is also distinct from their possible realization in actual built space.

As but one of the more overt means of mediation between this idea level and its realization in concrete constructions, design is seen to involve, and frequently also augment established dominant ideologies. 'Representational' space is where representation of these ideas attains material realization in the form of buildings, monuments and works of art, and hence comes to embody the complex symbolisms expressive of and representing the relations of production. The powerful visual appearance of this physical presence, then, is revealed as it would tend to take precedence over the merely experiential, come to govern intellectual and visual (image) perception, and promote the primacy of the 'gaze' and the logic of visualization. It is in countering these tendencies, where the 'lived' attains its special formative and liberating import. In this the conception of 'spatial practices', highlights the realm and productive functions through which space is socially 'secreted', 'mastered' and 'appropriated' in lived experience. There, in the context of spatial practice, space is always directly lived before it is perceived and conceptualized—captured and internalized as knowledge.

Hence the 'lived' attains the status of a theoretical tool to reconceptualize space in ways which allow confronting the speculative primacy assigned to the conceived/perceived—a primacy which in conventional research causes the disappearance of the whole realm of practice, along with life itself, from discourse on space. Instead, reasserting the context of practice allows for a broader account of correlations with space which highlights the pre-conscious level of lived experience *per se* (Lefebvre 1991: 34-39). It is there, at the level of lived experience, where perception of 'representational' space (indicating a more passive 'reading' mode) is complemented by active processes of direct involvement. This entails 'affect' and 'imagination' on the part of agency, along with the whole range of practices pertinent to the situation and through which space is appropriated. The 'lived' is also distinctly bodily—involving all the complexities and peculiarities of bodily lived experience, and in this way also drawing into account the range of cultural factors formative of the body (40-41). The crucial issue, Lefebvre insists, is that the 'lived', like the two other concepts of this triad—'perceived' and 'conceived', is not meant to serve as an abstract model, but attains its relevance in grasping and explicating reality when applied to 'concrete' built material space.

Space, then, is to be construed as a 'material substrate' which both embodies and conceals social relations. This is so because social relations for being concrete abstractions, would not have any real existence outside space, but come about in and through space. Consequently, space is to be understood not only in terms of the 'representational' it materializes, but also as it embeds, physically, an active and affective kernel—i.e., as it 'embraces' loci of passion, of action and lived situations. While this kernel may be characterized in different terms, such as 'directional', 'situational', or 'correlational', in each case it would come forth not only as fluid and dynamic but also as essentially qualitative. Hence in Lefebvre's perspective, 'lived' space is to be understood not only as rooted in the context of the lived practices it supports—the spatial practices of appropriation (417). For a full account of these practices, space would have to be construed also in terms of its material presence, which, prior to being perceived or read, is experienced, first.

By bringing into account the context of life/practice, and rendering 'experience' as a correlation with space that is prior to and radically different from perception, Lefebvre's framework allows for and proposes an analysis of the productive appropriation of concrete built space—as founded in the dialectical relationships between the perceived, the conceived and the lived (42). These constructs, then, offer powerful analytical tools, which allow superseding the thesis of 'mirror-consciousness'—i.e., the possibilities that perception is about reflecting pre-existing structures and pre-conceived meanings in a process of transmission, and grounding the social subject in its active role with respect to 'lived space'. While 'lived space' would come forth as a realm that is also produced in practice, it is also suggested in terms of 'concrete' space which is first experienced, then 'read'—a physical presence whose articulation at this level would be meaningful to pursue, as it would help concretize further aspects of the lived.

The 'porous' and 'relational' space of material practices
In recent spatial theory the persistent problems underlying the conceptualization of space are addressed in Massey's intense work *'for space'* (2005). Taking up a broad historical perspective, this work engages on and examines the intricacies in the evolution of notions and discourse on space in the thought of key philosophers and theorists of diverse lineage, seeking to reveal and exceed the shortcomings which impede the full acknowledgement of its potential in constituting agency. This examination reveals the various tendencies in theorising experience of giving precedence of an account of time over space, of conflating different aspects of space that blur distinction between abstract and concrete and experiential and perceptual, as well as those which entirely replace space with other notions, such as 'place'. These are brought forth as major and momentous factors that obstruct acknowledgement of, and hence research into, the manifold spatial realities which the materiality, sociality and produced nature of space actually bear.

Building up on the distinction among 'perception' and 'experience' already embedded in Lefebvre's analytical concepts, Massey lays out a more precise definition of the material practices in the context of which space is experienced as 'lived', placing special emphasis on its 'produced' nature. This entails the shift in the very notion of space: away from the 'fixed', 'finished' and 'static' entity of perception that frames it within 'representation'. As Foucault's critical analyses demonstrates, this notion of space maintains it in terms of aspects of space, through which it becomes a liable tool of power—instrumental in constructing and conveying certain 'regulating', 'normalizing' and even 'disciplining' effects. In opposing such liabilities, the project of 'the lived' is oriented towards asserting a different reading: one where space is essentially 'open', 'porous' and 'relational'—i.e., embedded in material practices, and thus co-constituted and co-constitutive of agency. This helps supersede the 'object' notions of space, and put into question positivist views and explanations of correlations with space in terms of causal chains of thinking. It allows seeking understanding of the processes of correlation in rather more liberating terms. In Massey's analysis the 'lived' is discussed from the perspective of radical social and political theory, pointing to potentialities of space in that it remains open and can accommodate the active share of agency—i.e., it allows acknowledging and augmenting the processes of re-formulation triggered in the active engagement and contribution of agency. Instead of conceptualizations of space which frame it to some pre-determined essence or meaning that is perceived, space is to be re-thought in terms which allow exceeding the formed and formulated, and allow emphasizing its potential through other characteristics. Hence in this reading space is seen as 'fluid', 'relational' and 'porous'—i.e., open to contestation and re-formation. This notion of space would allow an account of the practices of coexistence which entail the complexities of co-formation and conflict. These, then, would ground a politics of negotiating the configurations which our 'throwntogetherness' demands and presupposes.

This reading of space, Massey argues, allows shifting away from the closure and inevitability of 'bounded place' which at any level—enclosure, home, or nation—is seen in terms of fixed meaning and hence can be posited as loci of identity and loyalty. It also evades the theorization in terms of free flows that would maintain the condition of instability of ambivalence or of difference. As both of these directions might be open to prior conceptual determination and maintain relations of dominance through 'stabilities' of meaning, or 'instabilities' of meaning, an alternative conceptualization of space would need to go beyond 'openness' or 'closure'. Hence space would need to be construed as always under construction, as a place which is always productive of the new and where material practices of negotiation are at the same time construed as invention—i.e., space is to be seen as it marks the emergence of the conflictual new, which 'throws up the necessity of the political' (Massey 2005: 162). Space is specified as the sphere of relations, of contemporaneous multiplicity of trajectories, of multiple histories—i.e., as the sphere that entails the negotiations within and about place (147-8). This perspective highlights space not as an abstract category, but as the space of the reality of throwntogetherness, as the event of place, and the concreteness of co-existence with which one has to engage, on a daily basis. In Massey's perspective, the 'fixedness' and 'finiteness' of build architectural presence and of perception, are overcome by locating experience firmly within practices through which space is both appropriated and generated. It allows seeing the materiality of place in that it embeds the unexpected and multiplicity, as a concrete combination of risk and chance. It proposes a theorization of space which seeks to address the manner of being there—the manner in which we relate to ourselves and others, and which would allow understanding this manner of being as a possibility to depart from something determined towards something other, which evades certainty. As Massey (2005: 161-189) argues, at the level of the event, place/space can be seen as collective achievement, formed through practices of contestation and negotiation of intersecting trajectories, while the practice of place is to be understood as practice through which the constituent identities are moulded continuously, too.

Fluid ontology and alternative practices
The critical position of Gibson-Graham (1997: 306-323) addresses another essential reason for the problematic status of space at the meta-theoretical level: the excessive and imprecise use of spatial terms and metaphors in theoretical discourse. This survey reveals the 'spatialization' of discourse itself as a recent trait, characterized by an abundance of spatial terms and their metaphoric employment by thinkers of diverse orientation, such as philosophy and social and cultural theory. Hence 'discursive space' is 'occupied', speaking positions are 'located', disciplinary boundaries are transgressed, territory is de-territorialized, theory flows outside and inside a conceptual landscape that is mapped, producing 'cartographies of desire' and 'spaces of enunciation' (306-7). This tendency in the language of contemporary feminist, postmodernist and post-structuralist theory, Gibson-Graham argues, is problematic. It bears political effects in that spatial terms are used to describe the theoretical context, instead of performing their primary functions—to facilitate and enable understanding of the spatial realities themselves.

This 'spatialization' of theoretical discourse is seen to owe thinkers as diverse as Foucault, Deleuze and Guattari, as well as pre-poststructuralists like Althusser, and other thinkers in the Marxian tradition. It would tend to evolve in two types of theory, both of which represent space as constituted by, or in relation to identity. Thus while in Marxian theory the focus is on the performance space of one type of form—the mode of production of capitalism, in post-structuralist theory this representation is concerned with the performance space of multiple and non-specific identities. The theoretical status of space is still further conflated with the tendency to promote a 'philosophic-epistemological notion of space', such as in the work of Foucault,

Derrida, Kriseva and Lacan, which leads to the effect that the mental realm comes to envelope the social and the physical ones.

Replacing the 'stable' spatial ontology which relies on 'the presence of form to give meaning to space', Gibson-Graham's altered reading insists on positing and examining space an 'open' field of indeterminacy and excess, and as a domain of 'practices that are alternative to the performing of a function' (306-23). However the project of acknowledging the reciprocity between space and agency in these terms is necessarily based on re-establishing the active role of agency. Such a line of inquiry, then, comes to rely primarily, and even solely, on the acts of intervention in explaining the correlations of active appropriation.

Productive materiality
Thinkers from the broader context of social and political theory converge in their concern with the very notions and conceptualizations of space, as these conceptualizations form the base of the complex socio-cultural processes involved in its production. Hence in critically examining these conceptions, the aim is to re-cover, bring forth, discern and acknowledge lived space in its formation, which presents the active basis of rendering the relative autonomy of the social subject/agency. Thinking lived experience in spatial terms brings forth the import of a whole constellation of material practices pertaining to the reciprocity among agency and space which highlight the re-constitution of space as it partakes in the co-constitution of agency. In these, the conceptual layer underlying spatial representation is disclosed as a necessarily ideological construct (Lefebvre), the space-place dichotomy and proliferation of associative usage of spatial terms is pointed out as a critical condition in that it has buried important distinctions between different meanings of space in current theoretical thought (Massey), and the recent trait of the 'spatialization' of discourse itself is shown as problematic in that it renders space open to ideological manipulation in still new ways (Gibson-Graham).

What is at stake at this meta-theoretical scale is the issue of conceptual confusions, through which conceptual representations of space—i.e., the abstract notions addressing space in mental, metaphorical, philosophical and epistemological terms, have come to envelope and screen off the variety of meanings of space in its social and material realities. As a major consequence of this conflation, spatial form has come to be put forth as a source and bearer of pre-conceived and transmitted meaning, through which it is rendered open to manipulation. While it would be this conception of built space as a representational medium, which is being resisted, this resistance has led to an explicit shift away from 'the space of form' altogether. Instead, the account of space is sought in terms that involve, along with the conceptual and the mental import of that which is perceived, also the social and physical realms—a proposition which allows construing the 'lived' as that which is produced as much 'discursively' as 'materially' (Massey). However, in re-establishing the 'lived' in its liberating ontological and socio-cultural potentials, it (the lived) comes to be construed exclusively in terms of the active share of agency in material practice, and less and less in correlation with the material realities of space. However, underlying Lefebvre's conception of 'lived space', there would be still traces of built space in its concreteness that is experienced before it is read. These implicate the possibility of distinguishing, analytically, this aspect of the experience due to space from the amalgam with the life and the spatial practices it embeds. Yet in subsequent accounts, the lived would come forth exclusively as the realm of 'material practices' of co-constitution—i.e., in terms of that which occurs within, through and upon space (Massey), rather than 'due' to it.

Accounts of the spatial as the domain of alternative practices that are not subsumed to determination and form the basis of a 'fluid ontology', presuppose a still further disengagement from existing built spatial forms. In this way the possibilities of the emergent, of 'indeterminacy and excess' are posited and explored as the realm of the productive interventions (both material and discursive) of social subjects, rather than in terms of analysis of the materiality of built space as to its generative potential with respect to experience. Socio-spatial reciprocity comes to be understood as the 'co-constitution' actualized in the resistance, intervention and re-formulation of the 'given'. Concrete built space, in this way, is left over to the reductionist approaches prioritizing its 'representational' features. Its liberating potential is sought by construing space as foothold, situation, field for engagement—a site for the 'lived' in terms of its negative productivity—it is seen to trigger practices of resistance, evasion, re-formulation. Space as material and phenomenal presence recedes to a backdrop and effectively disappears from the vicinity of experience as a positively generative source. Thus the possible import of space as physical framework with which we correlate experientially remains unexamined. The productive and emergent of ontological and socio-cultural significance comes to be seen exclusively with the material practices of co-constitution—i.e., within capacities of agency to oppose, transgress, and intervene into and re-formulate pre-existing space as well as with the generation of alternative 'spatialities'—highlight capacities of resisting determination associated with the space of form.

Yet, as this current argument sets out to establish, this 'space of form' might be not only about the functioning of physical space as a finite or fixed framework that is shared in the phase of perception, where space is interpreted as index and means of transmission and reception of pre-conceived meanings, however modified this reception may become by what the agent introduces into the relation in perception. Recovering its liberating potential at the level of experience by receding its object presence and rendering it open—porous, relational and fluid with respect to the context of lived practices and appropriation, might not exhaustively explicate its generative capacities.

Built space does not dissolve in the phase of experience, but continues its presence as a tangible framework with phenomenal properties. It retains its materiality, but it works in different terms, which can be disclosed by lifting off representational layers, and re-conceptualising its presence as affective qualifying immediate extension of direct correlations. It is this particular cluster of phenomena embedded in the materiality of space-to-body correlations that remains less examined, for appearing to bear on causality and definitiveness with which 'outside-in' effects, however subtle, would tend to be associated. This study will attempt to substantiate that physical space can be accounted for in terms of effects that are un-mediated and non-mediating, open-ended and generative. It holds that an account of such features and properties of space with respect to the situated agent does not impede but rather augments the productive in the modality of lived experience, articulating still other aspects of the alternative ways of becoming and knowing.

Experience

The broader frameworks of the 'lived' at the philosophical level, seek to establish experience as a generative modality of being and becoming, while grounding the very principles and conditions of change and transformation within possibilities of sharing. Thinkers of both the phenomenological tradition and the process philosophers of the empirical lineage aim to supersede dualist body/mind conceptions, and shift away from the deterministic positions purporting the 'constituted' subject and confinement of the knowledge construction to the modes of rationality and instigation. This is enabled by establishing the centrality of experience in engendering acquisition and change on its own terms.

Establishing a shared world
Thinkers in the phenomenological tradition (Gadamer, Merleau-Ponty, Husserl and Sartre), insist on the importance of acknowledging the phenomenal presence of the world as a shared foundation of experience, and on placing the subject in a condition of 'openness' towards it. In Gadamer's (1996) perspective the correlation is based on the essential condition for all experience—namely the simultaneous presence of mind and world. In this way experience becomes linked to the necessity of a contact and engagement with something other than the self. Though based on the linguistic model of dialogue, and explored in terms of a subject with an interpreting mind (rather than an embodied one), it nevertheless ascertains 'interpretation' as active engagement with phenomenal realities. In the phenomenological tradition, as Strohmayer (1997) argues, interpretation is to be understood not as an 'additional procedure of knowing'; rather, it is to be construed as constituting the 'original structure of being in the world', through which 'understanding' necessarily entails transformation. This insistence on the recognition and an account of the aspects of reality with which contact is made allows not only construing experience as a form of acquisition, but also acknowledging the aspects of reality as grounds for the very possibilities of communication and sharing.

Phenomenological polarities: the sensing self reaching out
The power of Merleau-Ponty's (1992) phenomenological approach is in that it includes the sensing self within the phenomenal reality. Experience in this way is firmly located within a 'historical situation', through which the possibilities of sharing and inter-subjectivity are established. Building on Husserl's recognition of the fundamental importance of space as the prevailing material condition of existence, it offers a framework that seeks to place phenomenal properties back

into the objective world. The sentient subject, then, can be re-integrated into the flow of life and with the materiality of the world, while at the same time evading empiricist/physicalist notions of direct causal connections between the intelligible and the sensible can be superseded. This analysis of the sentient body-subject aims at an explanation as to how precisely the mind engages with the body in the act of perception. The quest for meaning is seen as a 'reaching out' and 'discovery'—i.e., it is construed as a productive process pointing outwards and towards a common world of 'learned practical skills' and 'existential understandings'.

However, while this framework places the sentient subject back into the physical world and depicts the correlation as a mutual 'possessing' of two corporeal entities, it is also inherently directional and remains polarized. This polarization is implicated in the particular notion of the embodied subject, whose corporeal presence within, and 'carnal' correlation with the world are expressed and enabled by intent and deliberation. In this way, the act of perception, as immediate it may be in the 'silence of primary consciousness', nevertheless comes to involve aspects of contemplation along with the purely experiential. This directionality and polarization also come to influence the account of space. While instated as the primary feature bringing forth 'facticity of being' with the world, and the foundation where the relation entails the direct 'primordial contact' with the thing 'as is' allowing for 'direct access to truth', which precedes knowledge, space emerges primarily in terms of that intent and directionality, beginning with the subject. Space in this account comes to be depicted as the field within which things become correlated. It embeds the qualities of these things, and can be posited in terms of distance and measure—i.e., it is explored (by the gaze) and understood in its major property—its affordance as the field and potential for movement (Merleau-Ponty 1992: 243-298). While asserting the primacy in accounting for the phenomenality of the world in understanding experience, and experience as an alternative and essential form of knowledge, this framework does not readily entail the tools for analysis of the reverse condition—from corporeal space to the sentient body-subject. It retains the role of space with regard to immediate experience in a problematic status, in that it involves conflicting propositions in the explication of the correlation.

The process of the correlation: encounter, reverberation and the emergent

The 'process' philosophers in the lineage of Bergson (duration), Deleuze (event, becoming), Agamben (encounter), or Dewsbury (event/performativity) trace out a different approach of explicating experience, which shifts away from causality, as well as from the uncertainties of seeking origins of knowledge (phenomenology). In this framework, the liberating power of lived experience is theorized in terms of processes even further removed from intent and into the non-contemplative impersonal zone beyond the subject/object dichotomies: it is explored by venturing into the discreet area of the correlation itself. Based on the analysis of experience through a 'pre-discursive moment'—the event-encounter, which enables exploration of experience as to that which may be also possible, thinkers of this lineage arrive at a radically reconfigured ontology centred on the concept of emergence. In this approach the focus of inquiry is placed onto the subject-object relations themselves, holding that while still pertinent to both, these relations as such do remain external to their terms—neither subject nor object. This principle, then, grounds a different kind of empiricism: it proposes thinking not in terms of things or people, but rather in terms of the in-between—in terms of their relations as events. This shift allows highlighting the ontological and epistemological importance of the 'coming into being' itself, as a way of construing the event in its very unpredictability. As Dewsbury (2003) explains, this kind of inquiry allows moving away from meaning centred on the consciousness of the individual subject, towards a 'pre-individual' and 'impersonal' zone, the issue being not 'what' happens, but 'that' it happens.

Therefore diversity and uncertainty, the 'indefinite' which the event entails, is not to be seen as a mark of empirical indetermination, but rather as a 'determination of immanence' and the possibility for the emergence of the singular. As Dewsbury (2003) puts forth in discussing Deleuze's import for 'non-representational' theory, that which is not represented, is so because it is too common. Hence, the focus of this type of approach is seen in the orientation towards that minute significant something which is within everything, but is not fully actualized or captured in any one representation: the grasping of the 'thusness' of being, the 'sensation of place, that something more and other than ourselves' (Dewsbury 2003: 1913) come forth as occurrences that might have little tangible presence in that they are singular and therefore not immediately shared. However, what is shared is the tendency of having that experience, and the task of bringing these to the fore so as to be shared grounds the project of non-representational theory. Construed in these terms, the 'event' is seen to be perpetually present as a possibility, a moment that can be posited as that which is perhaps the most truly personal, embedding therefore the conditions for 'difference' and 'multiplicity', the experience of which would be imperceptible and irrevocably lost unless it is investigated, and re-presented so as to be communicated (Dewsbury 2003).

It can be observed that the conceptualization of the event in these approaches evolves in primarily temporal terms. The generation of the experience in question is seen within the moments of interruption—i.e. these approaches would tend to highlight the temporal as triggering mechanism. While the spatial is acknowledged as a principal ever-present dimension, it is not taken up as an explicit aspect for inquiry and remains a tacit notion.

More tangible links and implications with respect to the possible influences of corporeal circumstances on the event of encounter can be sought in view of another key conception in Deleuze's thought: reverberation. It is a foundational conception, which allows approaching all forms and levels of 'becoming'—'affect', 'percept', and 'concept' in terms of the vitality of the correlation. Theorizing each of these in terms of reverberation allows transcending the problem of establishing the origins of knowledge (Deleuze and Guattari 1994: 163-201). Reverberation is put forth as a dynamic, creative and intrinsic constituent of life. While 'becoming' entails and expresses the constructive force of encounter, 'reverberation' intrinsically pertains to that process and characterizes the essential aspects of the correlation. It is important to recognize, these thinkers insist, that once understood in these terms, reverberation exceeds imitation, identification, resemblance or sympathy, and comes to denote an exchange, a passing from one to the other as between two equal entities (Deleuze and Guattari 1994). This understanding would allow pursuing the rendition also of processes embedded in the reciprocal passage- from space to the body as belonging to the event of encounter.

Movement

While this larger framework of experience provides profound insights into the discreet processes and mechanisms of emergence, and asserts the empirical reality of the correlations as the site of such emergence, it also maintains discourse on these at a level that is rather detached from actual material presences. In this respect, a significant extension of this framework into the reality of the body and movement is proposed by Manning (2009). She employs and concretizes this conceptual framework in a convincing argument on movement, re-establishing the discreet experience of becoming by exploring the trajectory from bodily movement to thought, and asserting the concept of movement as a generative principle. This particularization allows rendering these processes of emergence more inclusive, and establishes how movement, while evolving as subjective exploration, marks this emergence immediately within its social and ethical-political dimensions. Placing emphasis on embodied cognition, Manning's inquiry aims to shed light onto the generation of thought and action by foregrounding a range of discreet occurrences and events that would otherwise pass unnoticed, and depicting and explicating these in empirical detail. This is taken up in a conceptualization of the processes involved in terms of the fundamental encounter underlying the modes of embodied experience and thought. In this way, on-going experience can be understood in terms of the 'cross-genesis of action and perception' that 'open onto thought' (Manning 2005: 2).

In contrast to notions of movement as 'displacement', which rely on measure and position and do not account for the inherent continuity of the experiential flow, movement is re-conceptualized in ways that allow spanning and interlocking the physical and the mental in their continuous mutual fertilization around the integrative nexus between action, perception and conception. Construing these in terms of 'incipient movement' and 'pre-acceleration' allows accentuating the productive potential as a pulsation towards directionality—i.e., as an event in the making that does not foretell a definitive outcome in terms of location, position or form. The Bergsonian conception of 'duration', rather than in temporal terms, is construed as the process of a becoming aware, where the sensing of duration presents the first instance of drawing events into awareness or perception. This amounts to an articulation of immediate experiential 'space-time' marking the plane of experience where occurrences begin to be registered. This instance is analyzed in further specificity through the system of concepts in Whitehead's philosophy: 'actual occasion', 'causal efficacy' and 'symbolic reference', which are employed as explanatory and/or mediating tools. Examining movement in terms of the micro events at this level, then, leads to an altered understanding of both movement and consciousness. Shifting the focus towards movement allows understanding the 'taking form' itself, and demonstrating how thinking is more than the final form it takes in language. Rather, it is embedded in the auto-genetic potential of ideas as they become 'articulations' while movement takes form (Manning 2005: 29-113).

This exploration of the sensing body in movement helps ground the notion of 'becoming body', where the 'self' resists pre-definition in terms of subjectivity or identity, but is rather involved in reciprocal exploration of thought that is not strictly of the mind, but of the bodily becoming. Brought to bear on immediate experience, this perspective offers insight and explication of the ways in which the body reverberates with its 'constructed environment'. Yet the notion of reverberation appears to be associated primarily with the acts of construction themselves, and hence would give priority to the potentialities of the environment as affordance, rather than as qualifying or conditioning circumstance.

Corporeal contact—a source of emergence
This survey reveals that the emphasis on the active and constitutive share of agency prevailing in the conceptualization of experience in the context of 'lived space', is also maintained at the philosophical level. Both the phenomenological approach, such as in Merleau-Ponty's work, and in process based inquiries, such as Manning's, the properties of the immediate environment—that which is 'given to perception' as a sense of space, be it void, object (chair), or property (redness), is denoted—i.e., such properties are pursued insofar as the autonomous self in action might come to perceive them. The notion of movement comes to serve as the medium for and the means of experience and perception at the micro level, both when construed in terms of bodily 'distance', 'displacement' and/or the mental 'reaching' outwards (Merleau-Ponty), and when explored as a 'generative principle' in its opening up to thought (Manning).

Construed as central to experience, movement fulfils an important function: it allows thinking the act of relating to an outside milieu in terms of undeniably autonomous—i.e., autogenic processes. Movement, as well as its correlate—rest, is visible and describable. It comprises a shared capacity and way of being, which would tend to be immediately registered as a mode of presence within a shared world. It is undeniably active, and invokes the notions of advance and change—it is explicitly productive.

Movement, along with the discreet autogenic processes it renders, thus has come to occupy 'lived' experience, in full. Be it in terms of physical intervention and its spatial correlates—field, distance, measure, or with focus on the very happening and its time dimensions—duration, instance, interruption, the liberated autonomous subject emerges primarily in terms of capacities of generation of space and auto-genesis. The role of the spatial dimension comes to be understood within its affordances. In this context, then, it would suffice to depict spatial circumstance in as much as it offers the potential for possible acts, physical or mental, or denote its negative productivity—evasion, transgression, alternative space formulation. This would tend to foreclose more detailed inquiry into the possible import of existing material circumstance, quality or condition, and leave a small but significant area pertaining to experience unattended, through which other forms of correlations are overlooked as irrelevant to the understanding of the autonomous subject.

Some of the roots of this omission lie with the character of the processes that pertain to this area. That which might be generated in the corporeal correlations among space and body, by virtue of being sense-based, would tend to be too subtle and fleeting. It would be less likely to result in explicit expressions and hence also difficult to observe and evidence. Yet reluctance to engage with and seek an account of the spatial as a corporeal dimension in the context of immediate experience, lies also with the fact that by virtue of coming from without, these processes of correlation appear to be of a different nature. In this respect it also concerns the diverging terms in which the correlations of the self with its surrounds are being conceptualized, and indicates that for coming from without, spatial effects would tend to be assigned a radically different status, being suspect of bearing also deterministic underpinnings.

However narrow, this underexplored area is worth pursuing. Once opened up for inquiry, it would yield a whole stratum of occurrences and processes that can further understanding of the emergent. It would offer novel aspects of the immediately experiential within those mental events that begin as 'response' to physical circumstance, and disclose other dimensions of the vital capacities of making contact, corporeally and productively, with the physical, social and spatial realities, along with the alternative ways of knowing and acquisition which are embedded therein.

Such inquiry would not conflict, but confirm and complement the principal condition for experience around which perspectives on the lived converge. This principal condition entails the capacity of the subject to exceed inwardness, break out and open up towards the world—i.e., encounter that which exceeds the self, and internalize the possibilities for change which this encounter inevitably calls forth. Attempting the class of phenomena generated in the corporeality space-to-body relations, prepares grounds to involve that layer of experience which evolves in terms of space into the 'lived'. It allows taking up and extending on conceptions like resonance and reverberation in their most direct connotations: as the living through and with a qualified condition, and, in this way, attaining a direct grasp on what the surrounding spatial reality has to offer. In this respect, an account of experience in terms of spatial circumstance, would offer further detail and extend the empirical basis in understanding how conditions for exceeding inwardness might actually be supported spatially — triggered and recuperated.

The 'induced': 'feeling' as constructive mental process

Attaining the sense and feeling of a tangible physical presence, such as space, can be thought of in different terms—as an active 'doing'. This possibility is established in Langer's (1988) profound cross-disciplinary essay on the human mind, where she reconstructs the concept of feeling as a process, and asserts it as the primary methodological tool in explicating human mentality. Feeling can be taken in its broadest possible sense—as whatever is felt in any way such as sensory stimulus, or inward tension, and re-thought as a process. As such it emerges as the mark of mentality: it issues from the very vitality of the living organism, and entails activities of great complexity and high intensity, which chart the entire domain bounded by the human body. As Langer explicates (1988: i-xv, 1-60), this conception of feeling allows ascertaining that aspects of sensibility, awareness, excitement, or suffering need to be construed as belonging to those activities or events, rather than as adjuncts or products and hence of a different category. It roots elaborate phenomena (ideas, images, fantasies) in the fabric of preconscious processes. It allows substantiating that the entire field of human conception, responsible action, rationality, and knowledge, can be understood as a vast and branching development of 'feeling'.

One of the crucial problems that can be resolved in this conceptualization of feeling at the basis of mentality is the physical-psychic paradox, which, once dismantled, allows founding the understanding the operations of the mind on unified grounds. This, Langer asserts, entails showing that the processes which begin through a sensory stimulus, are in fact not radically different from those that begin as inward tension. Hence the distinction of the two modes of feeling—that which originates from without, is felt as impact, and perceived as induced, and that which is felt as generating from within and more readily perceived as autogenic action ('subjective'), does not concern their nature, but rests only on the terms of how these are attained. The conceptualization of feeling as phase in a physiological process allows construing both of these modes as embedded in the nature of vitality itself. Therefore, the mental events pertinent to either of these two modalities would need to be seen and understood in their continuously shifting transient relationship. They both are part of, and constitute the tightly interwoven fabric of pre-conscious processes, pressing the threshold of conscious perception towards the phase of 'being felt', then falling back into their latent pre-conscious phase. It is, then, important to acknowledge that a 'phase' is not an added factor, but rather a mode of appearance (Langer 1988: 1-46).

A major difficulty that these propositions allow confronting, is the legacy of causal thinking rooted in the Lockean empiricist tradition, that would take effects that are induced from outside sources as 'imprints' or 'entities' contained by the mind. This view leads to a model of the mind based on the principle that it is moulded on the material world, and hence attempts to relate causally two orders of basic elements. Such an attempt would be problematic in that immediate experience is set up on a double standard—sensation as distinct from emotion, and maintains a basic misconception in assuming feelings as ingredients or products of any kind. Instead of hypothesizing acts as entities, a fundamentally different understanding can be attained by taking feeling as the verbal noun it is: it allows construing feeling as the 'doing' of something, and highlights the process nature of mental activity (Langer 1988: 7). This reconstruction of the conception of feeling as process, then, has far-reaching import: it proposes rather inversed terms in which to rethink the very notions on how we relate to our bodies. Exceeding the notions of being 'in' our bodies, or even those where body and mind are seen to almost form a single entity, Langer asserts a radically integrated notion—asserting that we are never not embodied, feeling is our essence as human beings, and rational thought is but one of its more perspicuous modes (Langer 1988: v).

Feeling thus includes both emotion, and sensation. Sensation takes up a major role in establishing the contact with an outside: it entails the felt responses of our sense organs to the environment, those of our proprioceptive mechanisms to internal changes, and those of the organism as a whole to its situation as a whole. These two modalities involve millions of processes, which are normally not felt, but might come to acquire distinctiveness and enter the phase of 'being felt'. Hence a deeply engendered process might gradually pass to the physical phase as a vague awareness or a fleeting emotive moment, a feeling tone from which more acute tensions built up to specific experiences, such as a pain response, or the feeling of shock and terror. As Langer explicates, this 'transiency and general lability of the psychical phase', then, would account for the importance of preconscious processes in the construction of such elaborate phenomena as ideas, intentions, images and fantasies', making obvious that these are rooted in the fabric of totally unfelt activities, which in Freud's thinking would be denoted with the substantive term 'the unconscious' (Langer 1988: 9).

The autogenous class of mental events springs from the constant functioning of the central nervous system itself. An act that is engendered from within—i.e., without the attack of a sensory impact of external stimulation, is felt to arise differently: its mental phase begins as a gradual rising from a general body feeling and a texture of emotive tensions. The 'mental state' which these gradually compose includes the body feeling as a constant somatic factor. In this way these mental events are rendered usually nearer to the psychical phase. Against this background, more specifically articulated acts are felt as envisagements, cogitations, insights, intentions, decisions, etc. These mental acts proceed from within and towards their termination in expression, which may be muscular motion, or the formation of an image. They evolve not as acts of coping with impinging forces. Their structure is organic and developmental. In contrast, sensations are a class of felt activities which typically stem from peripheral sources. They are processed by sense organs that work as protective peripheral outposts, and always carry some indication of an impingement to be dealt with. These build up in terms of essentially centripetal action, and, together with those sensations that come from within the body constitute a major department of feeling—sensibility. The felt activities of this class are reactive and improvisational in nature (Langer 1988: 11).

Within the fundamental relation of the living system with its surrounds, both of these two modes express, and rest on the nature of vitality itself: the organism is the centre of activity, always under the influence of the world around, and always affecting its immediate neighbourhood. Though the trait of this interaction is asymmetrical— the (inanimate) world—what is given—having the gross control, while the fine control—what is taken—lies with the organism, this interaction is nevertheless to be understood as a relation of exchange.

This above reconstruction of the concept of feeling allows understanding processes that are 'induced'—entailing sense and sensibility as active mental processes, akin to those of autogenous origin, and confirms the workings of the mind on unified grounds. For this current study, it offers theoretical grounds to ascertain space as the corporeal realm co-extensive with and qualifying the correlation, and examine space-to-body correlations as productive processes of reverberation. Hence these correlations can be construed as processes that are founded in the intricate links with sense realities, expressive of the explorative involvement which such links entail, and marking the passage from space to sense and sensibility. Construed within a space-body-mind continuum, immediate experience can be particularised both in terms of its corporeal constructions, and as to the possible experiential content that these engender.

Built physical space: a shared experiential framework
Theoretical foundations

The physical presence of space—such as the concrete architectural form actualized in a building or monument, is a continuous matter, which is at work at multiple levels. This continuity is clearly implicated in Lefebvre's conceptual system. While asserting the primacy of lived experience as a modality distinct from perception, Lefebvre, nevertheless, does establish these as two consequent and interlocking phases within the total process of correlating with concrete existing socio-spatial realities. Hence, prior to the more conscious acts of perception, through which symbolic and referential features of representational space would be 'read' and come to support the formulation of mediated meanings, there is also an experiential phase, where physical space is suggested as an 'affective' presence. The fact that in the broader context of the 'lived,' the presence of built architectural space would tend to remain a suggested, rather than examined aspect of lived experience, is rooted in the priority assigned to the second more conscious perceptual phase in mainstream discourse. In this way built space has come to be understood in perceptual terms, and perception has come to encompass the experiential aspects of the correlations with it.

The project of the 'lived' entails re-constituting the phase of immediate experience into an account of the correlations with actual 'spatial' realities. It entails re-thinking experience in spatial terms, and brings forth, potentially, the whole realm of the 'lived' at the basis of understanding the relative autonomy of agency. In spatial theory the import of lived experience is rendered most express, by focusing on the reciprocal agency-to-space correlations, where this relative autonomy is explicated in terms of mutual co-constitution, and highlights the active share of the social subject. The role of built space is construed in terms of its negative productivity, based on the issues of how it is being evaded, transgressed, or re-formulated.

For this current inquiry, which ventures into exploring precisely this neglected area of intimate and intricate experiential involvement with concrete features of built architectural space, one methodological proposition is to allow this full flow of the 'lived' to recede. Instead it brings into focus a narrow and specific section—the stratum of discreet phenomena evolving 'due' to space itself. This opens up an opportunity to bring into account features of space that are already there in empirical presence in a way that would disclose their un-mediated non-mediating effects and access another layer of subtle processes of correlating which in their own terms are productive, open ended and generative of meaning.

Thinking experience in-the-terms-of-space actually entails only a slight shift in the perspective on space, which is proposed for analytical purposes. Yet it requires the explicit rendition of the-terms-of-space—i.e., it is a means to re-construct built architectural space in its material presence, for experience. Different from the more integrative perspectives that would fuse experience and perception, this current approach seeks to disentangle and bring to the foreground aspects of space that are explicitly experiential.

Thinking space in terms of experience entails the recognition that built space does not materialize suddenly so as to appear into view and formulate the framework of pre-conceived and received meanings—the shared context of perception. Neither does it work solely through its representational powers as rational space. As dominant and evident its object-presence and architectural orders may be, accounts and criticisms that are based primarily on the visual regimes of space and their reception in perception do not exhaust, or explicate the materiality of space in full.

Space is there in its physical presence, all along—a corporeal entity which is open to experience. Thinking experience in terms of space necessitates acknowledging the consequentiality of this presence, for experience, and with respect to the situated agent, as well. At this empirical level space emerges in entirely corporeal properties and affective capacities—a continuous material presence which envelopes, and emerges into and out of phenomenal distinctiveness, a qualified matter with which the body is perpetually in contact, exploring and reverberating. Inquiry into these intricate correlations, then, entails bringing built space forth in tangible physical detail. It entails its conceptualization so as to render its workings with respect to the sensing situated agent. Approaching space with respect to the experiential possibilities it generates, entails keen attentiveness to the shifting configurations of spatial features, to the undercurrent logic of the corporeal situations these might engender, to the minute subtle ways in which concrete circumstance qualifies the correlation, to the fleeting affects pressing towards awareness. It offers a path of inquiry that is apt to access the co-responding forms of feeling and knowing triggered when existential realities attain material-spatial presence—i.e., when they actualise as possibilities by being grasped as such.

The proposed research method, that would inform this type of analysis into built architectural space, and take inquiry beyond the descriptive, interpretative or purely phenomenological, is, therefore, necessarily hybrid. In this, the exploration of the corporeality of space-body correlations would rely on analysis of spatial phenomena, yet would also need to exceed the implications of intent and contemplation that tend to accompany inquiry into the means of perceptual attainment of a particular spatial feature. For the subtlety and the 'distracted' and peripheral way in which un-mediated correlations with space would tend to evolve, the empirical framework of the 'process' philosophers offers potent conceptual tools in understanding the nature and mechanisms at work at the micro-level of encounter. Focused on the correlation itself, this framework locates explication within the pre-discursive, pre-individual area of direct encounter, and hence exchange. In this way the 'lived' and experiential are construed in their embeddedness in 'reverberation' with empirical realities in presence, and reverberation can be understood as the active modality of bodily becoming. In the context of reverberation, the event of encounter presents itself as site of emergence, entailing chance and multiplicity. However, with its focus strictly on the instance of 'becoming' as an instance of actualising but one of multiple possibilities, this framework maintains 'that which is beyond the self', and is being encountered as an omnipresent, albeit tacit notion.

Yet, in analogy with other methods of particularisation, such as those around movement (Manning), this current approach proposes to concretise aspects of the encountered spatial reality, holding that this would offer an opportunity to understand aspects of the processes occurring at the 'plane of composition' in further detail. Particularising experiential content would show how sensation actually goes beyond excitation and reaction, and come to involve that which it 'extracts' from a given condition. Or it could disclose how spatial circumstance might come to characterise the process of encountering, reproducing in corporeal terms its principal mechanism. Open to the explorative reverberation of the situated body, the existential reality, which space brings into phenomenal presence, can be posited as concrete and shared site of emergence. This would not only confirm that the tendency of having that experience is shared, a tendency which, as Dewsbury (2003) argues, helps construe that experience as both singular, and common. It would, furthermore, also concretize it, perhaps shedding light on how actualizations of multiple possibilities take particular direction. Yet more importantly still, it would allow positing this instance of encounter is as open to other possibilities of sharing. This is so, because space, while designating the facts of contact, as concrete material framework also embeds the potential of the acts of communication and sharing. Therefore inquiry into the spatial extensions of the correlation would not conflict with the principles laid out in these larger frameworks, but rather, by foregrounding processes that begin and evolve in corporeal terms, would meet the empirical criteria of sensibility, as well as those of sensation continuity, and extend on aspects of immediate experience.

In ascertaining the experiential potential of material space with respect to the situated body, the re-construction of feeling as a unifying foundation in understanding human mentality bears special importance. Such a reconstruction allows evading misconceptions and remnants of causal thinking which would tend to overshadow that feeling which originates from external sources. It allows re-thinking physical space as the corporeal context and extension of the correlation and explore its generative capacities. Hence even when considered solely as a concrete sensory source and stimulation, a spatial feature or property can be understood as inherently productive in that it is potentially present—it acquires distinctiveness, and, by passing fleetingly into the phase of phenomenal awareness, assists the generation of a particular feeling. The fact that 'response' is both re-active—i.e., linked up with sensory stimulus, and improvisational, helps recovering the 'induced' and sensate that is experienced through the body, as a legitimate and active 'phase' in a total phenomenon or process, and allows addressing physical space as basis of sensibility.

This opens up the opportunity to establish space as an area of research in such way that that it does not contradict, but rather enhances and extends on notions of productivity embedded in lived experience, such as depicted in the concepts of event, the performative, becoming, and the emergent. As much of what could happen in the bodily encounter with phenomena of a spatial nature, can only be reconstructed, circumstantially, arriving at a depiction of experience in-the-terms-of-space could be approached by way of analysis—of space.

Conceptual tools for an analytical approach
As but one way of arriving at a re-construction of built architectural space in its concrete material presence with respect to experience, this approach institutes the conception of *mode of spatial organisation.*

This conception is developed as a methodological tool, which addresses space at a potent mid-level, prior to architectural particularization, and allows exploring the logic through which it works. Hence while casting off the representational layers of space, it captures spatial features in their physical presence, examines their effects at an empirical level as properties and conditions that generate in its materiality—i.e., it allows attending, analytically, to the intricate and intimate direct correlations between physical circumstance and the situated agent.

Different from integrative perspectives on architectural space, that would conjoin the expressive (symbolic, presentational, signifying) with the experiential and interpret effects in a holistic as well as perceptually based amalgam, this approach seeks to establish and address built space as a distinct area of inquiry into immediate experience. In positing space with respect to experience as a phase distinct from and prior to perception, it foregrounds the less-charted realm of corporeal constructions concerning both the very formulation of spatial conditions and effects, and the cluster of experiential phenomena potentially embedded therein.

The shift away from the representational features of space is important, because it helps evading those effects through which space would come to be associated primarily in its regulative capacities, both as affordance and as appearance. In terms of representation and perception built space is brought forth exclusively in its designed and desired effects as 'rational space'. Representation, along with the corresponding prioritization of visual strategies of knowledge acquisition, marks built space as an area quite distinct from the principles and potentials of 'lived' space, and immediate experience. In contrast, the proposed conceptualisation allows construing of built physical space as a generative source with respect to the emergent, and of space-to-body correlations as a layer of vital processes integral to the lived.

Methodologically, this proposed re-construction of physical space in terms of mode of spatial organisation requires rethinking and re-conceptualising the conventional terms and notions, such as that of architectural form, through which architectural space is being understood. Hence in mainstream discourse on architecture, 'form' is seen as the expression of time-and-place-specific ideas on space, manifesting the respective sets of rules and standards of order in the architectural ensemble, and is closely associated with the varying stylistic motifs in structural elements, surfaces, and decorative detail.

Instead, approaching physical space at the level of the *mode of spatial organization*, allows construing and conceptualizing *spatial form* in rather different terms. Though its constitution is rendered through the elements conventionally addressed in research of architecture—enclosure, configuration, shape and volume, these, and the principal properties of spatial form are attended to at a more rudimentary yet also entirely empirical level. Spatial form is construed as the relatively stable and distinct expression of the logic of operation of the mode, actualising its principles and properties as a monolithic entity. This allows thinking built space beyond the solid-void distinction. Rather it emerges in terms of its material presence which generates its dynamic mechanisms and effects by merging features of both.

In order to approximate understanding of the manner in which physical space brings into concrete presence the specificities of situatedness, this analysis proceeds from *spatial form* through to *forms of experience*. With respect to the experiential bearing that issues within this zone of direct contact, this allows pursuing the passage from space through sense to sensibility. With respect to insight into the very nature and structure of immediate experience, it allows acknowledging the intricacies of the bodily processes through which this situatedness comes to be felt. Hence one further methodological proposition concerns the conceptualisation of the mode in terms of its principal properties, which are construed not in terms of single spatial features, but as complex effects—as experiential conditions. This methodological principle helps evading both deterministic and purely phenomenological interpretations. Instead it ensures that analysis into spatial effects attends to features of physical space at multiple levels and conjoins these to establish their un-mediated experiential charge—i.e., analysis probes into potential configurations.

Construed in these terms, built space emerges in its dynamic constitution. The operational logic of a spatial modality can be understood in the perpetual re-configuration of its spatial features and elements into different effects—i.e., experiential circumstances come forth as potentialities composing and re-composing into and out of distinctiveness. It is in this configuring of spatial features through which ever diverse but marked and intense *conditions* would be brought to phenomenal presence—a potential which renders material space utterly 'open'. Built space can be understood in its capacity to present both the actual concrete and material reality, and the potential—the corporeal correlations with spatial circumstance come forth as a matter of emergence. As these conditions are at once spatial and existential, *forms of experience* would issue as the actualizations of the experiential possibilities generated therein.

This conceptualization of built physical space discloses its openness and inherent ambiguity. Re-constructed in the specificity and intricacy of its workings with respect to the situated agent, material space can be linked with the Deleuzean notion of 'emergent form', although originally this notion is reserved for that which remains unexpressed in physical form and is associated with possibilities of future construction. Hence for instance in Ballantyne's insightful analysis of Deleuze's thought, emergent form along with the correlated conceptual system, is brought to bear on design thinking and interpreted as a framework for architectural practice. 'Emergent form' is brought forth as denoting those implicit forms at the 'plane of immanence' which may or not come to be actualized, but would, nevertheless, still hold an influence on the design process and its outcome—in the concrete design solution. Viewed from that perspective, emergent form along with the constellation of related concepts are being highlighted in their relevance to experimental design, which might seek to actualize that which is excluded from norm and contractual conditions. By giving such implicit features articulation, design could achieve their unexpected presence—a quality, which sometimes would come to characterize the novel and unconventional (Ballantyne 2008: 30-36, 90-98).

Yet, approaching existing built space in terms of 'mode', does offer grounds to extend the relevance of the notion of emergent form, and assert that emergence might be a quality which is not reserved to exceptional design thinking. Rather, emergence can be construed as inherent in all spatial form, and as an essential quality becomes apparent when formalized space is construed in terms of immediate experience and the body. Explicated in terms of the concrete experiential encounter with spatial circumstance, ambiguity, openness and generative potentiality come forth as foundational properties of built form. They are integral to understanding the workings of material space.

Analysis at the level of spatial mode helps disclose that built architectural space might not be the permanent environment it is considered to be, and which would preclude experience by proposing clear and stable conditions that elicit straightforward response. Rather it emerges as just the reverse: what is permanent about space at this empirical level is its capacity to implicate a diverse range of experiential possibilities, and trigger the experiential as a distinct modality of becoming along with the alternative paths to acquisition and forms of knowing these would open up.

The mobilizing potential and possibilities of emergence lying with space, do come forth not only in view of sensual experience, which as an active modality of exploration and improvisation is inherently open-ended. Such potential derives also from the very nature of material space itself. As subtle as its effects may be, as distracted and un-attentive the situated agent might be to this discreet correlation, space is always affective. It is charged with forces, triggers impulses and is, hence, engaging. Its effects are never quite clearly defined, but fluid and controversial—they are always in a state of configuring. Therefore its capacities to 'do'—relate, incite, and mobilize, are always potentially productive. With respect to experience built physical space—i.e., form, property, circumstance, mechanism and condition, emerges as always under construction—a texture of multivalent possibilities. It is fluid in the sense that the same principal spatial features enter into shifting correlations and come to intensify different qualities. Built space can be understood in terms of its spatial logic—it works through both the immanent, and the imminent, and in this way renders the existential conditions that are being brought into phenomenal presence ambivalent.

It is precisely this transient nature of generated effects qualifying its operations even where space would be quite formalized, which make the system of built space interesting for inquiry at this level. Much of what is potentially embedded in its corporeality exceeds or defies the planned affordances or intended expressions of an original design. While coming about through the concrete features of built space, these operational capacities attain generative power in terms of the logic inherent in the spatial modality—magnifying, conflicting, restructuring and altering the overt orders of 'rational space'. Regardless of the degree of distinctiveness, or their fleeting nature, these properties of material space would still tend to characterize the bodily encounter as challenge. Material space would summon latent capacities, be it by way of the hesitancy over ambiguous impulses, the tension among strict emplacement and dynamic impetus, the vague insinuation of apprehension, or simply by way of the necessity to probe and attend to the perpetual re-combinations of spatial mechanisms and circumstances.

Living through and with material space affectively undermines the certainty of grasping the self in unequivocal terms—its vagueness, incompleteness and controversial suggestiveness do render the situated body open. The inquiry into experiential possibilities in terms of material space discloses an utterly productive texture of spatial and bodily phenomena—a texture of complex and shifting, yet also definable corporeal circumstance with which immediate experience would come to evolve. Space, in its tangible palpable presence, can be construed as a dynamic constituent of experience, and examined in its capacity of an entirely corporeal, and shared framework through which we exercise creative, emotive and cognitive abilities—and ultimately re-think and embody selfhood.

Chapter Three

Contextualizing corporeality: theatre space between mediation and generation of experience

Theatre as setting and physical space: embedding the theatrical, the aesthetic, the social and the immediate

So far the argument was focused on establishing physical space, theoretically, and methodologically, as a distinct area of inquiry into immediate experience, asserting the relevance of such inquiry to the understanding of its generative potential. Conceptualising corporeality as the shared realm of space-body correlations has prepared methodological grounds to locate this inquiry on the empirical level, where it would facilitate analysis of concrete material circumstances and processes. The proposition to conceptualise physical space as the extension of the correlation which qualifies the events in the zone of contact, has allowed confirming the cluster of events and processes evolving therein as an experiential layer inherent to immediate experience. Analysis into built architectural space in these terms, thus, has come forth in its potential to further insight into discreet processes linked with emergence. In establishing the validity of such inquiry, a range of perspectives and notions of space were discussed in view of possibilities and propositions that might lead to re-constructing space in its materiality with respect to experience, and the situated agent. This survey has brought forth the necessity of taking physical space out from its latent self-evident state in current perspectives on experience, and into account at this level as well, an account that would not contradict, but ensure the principles of continuity of sensibility and experience. It has also helped depict the explanatory potential in rendering built space in its material presence and open to the experiential phase of correlation, distinct from and preceding perception. Furthermore, an alternative complementary way of conceptualizing built architectural space was proposed, arriving at the outline of an analytical approach, and tracing out the principal methodological propositions and conceptual tools to enable a re-construction of built architectural space at this level. By instituting the concept of *spatial modality*, inquiry has been located at mid-level, lifting off representational layers of space. In this rendition physical space is neither elusive and fused in perception, nor deterministic and seen as a prime cause. It is not construed in purely phenomenological terms either, but rather brought forth as an empirical entity, which can be understood as an entirely corporeal experiential field and approached analytically in terms of its possible un-mediated effects—it can be examined as to its generative capacities with respect to the emergent.

This part of the study entails the particularization of these propositions, by way of implementing and adjusting the approach to the concrete context of built space, focusing on the case of theatre space. This particularization involves and builds on a series of former studies on the experiential potentialities embedded in theatre space as issues that are relevant to the understanding of the ontological and socio-cultural role of space in theatre. The reasons for choosing theatre space for this type of inquiry are threefold:

> As one of the most formalized and articulate realizations in built form, theatre space offers a potent field to explore the workings of space in terms of forces and mechanisms, circumstances and impulses of a spatial nature, and establish space as a dynamic constituent of experience—i.e., reconstruct, circumstantially, aspects of the immediate experience in, through, and with space, along with its affective, cognitive and ethical import.

> As a distinct actualization of a social site—namely that particular kind of collective organization which is formulated in the context of artistic performative activities, it allows linking up such experiential potential with aspects of the constitution of agency and the collective—i.e., it helps disclose immediate experience as an already social and cultural issue, and the spatial as a vital dimension in cultivating sensibilities which enable social togetherness.

As the space within which a unique art form evolves as a participatory live event, it embeds the theatrical as a form of aesthetic experience— i.e., it bears potential in construing the experience of the performance event also from the perspective of and in terms of the immediately experiential. This, it will be held, opens up possibilities to capture an entirely different way in which space might be pertinent to the theatre experience and, by extension, the aesthetic. By locating inquiry into experience of performance at the level prior to the modes of representation, it comes to access that experience in its foundational formative phase. This offers insight into the inherent dependence of experience on space for its constitution, while also construing its essential links with the work, meaning and context. This type of inquiry would allow recognizing the coherence of physical space with the logic of that experience, and help render its role in reproducing, in rudimentary corporeal form, instances inherent in the structure of experience within the spatial economy of theatre. Ultimately, it would complement established notions of theatre experience and functions of space based on interpretative methods, with a rendition of that experience derived though analytical inquiry into the operations of space at the corporeal level. This would further understanding of the properties of the site and setting as physical context, within which the theatre experience as an aesthetic issue has been, all along, also firmly situated.

Implementing and developing the proposed approach based on the case of theatre is also challenging in several respects. Discourse on theatre—unique artistic form, context of complex processes of aesthetic and cultural production, and participatory event, is a well-established research area, and forms the firm basis of establishing the socio-cultural significance of theatre. Theatre experience as an aesthetic issue, and the role of space in its mediation, are prime subjects extensively examined in theatre studies, as well as the corresponding branch of architecture. Oriented towards understanding the complexities of the diverse processes of production, presentation and perception of the performance, theorization of theatre experience takes an inclusive and complex form. The role of space in this is construed as the primary means in the formulation of meanings, which entail and evolve through multiple layers of signification. Considering the complexity of such significations, theatre experience is understood predominantly in terms of the acts of synthesis characterising the phases of cognition and perception. Although it is fused also with components of immediate experience, these components become assimilated, and receive less attention especially in view of the audience. Hence while approached in two theoretical frameworks whose primary subject would be the study of bodies in space, and discussed in the context of two distinct notions—the theatrical work and the monument, space occupies the foreground of these studies in terms of correlations which are intentional and presentational, as well as interpretative and hermeneutic in nature. Therefore, the overview of these two theoretical frameworks offers ample evidence of how in discourse on space, the representational and (visually) perceived features would tend to attain precedence and govern its interpretation, assimilating more fleeting experiential layers and come to stand for the totality of spatial effects. In spite of the fact that research in both of these fields yields an insight into various experiential aspects borne in the immediacy of the correlations, in the final account these ultimately become blended and submerged. Instead, priority is given to the complexities of the presentational, through which the layers of meanings are produced, mediated and perceived, the explanation of which comes to occupy the core of research on theatre. This sustains the diverging terms in which the experience of the two groups involved in the theatrical situation—performers and audience—are being interpreted, bears on the registers of consciousness these entail. Delineated in these terms, the theorization of the theatrical as aesthetic experience revolves around theatrical contents and the correlation with space emerges in its predominantly hermeneutic nature.

Deviating from both of these frameworks, this approach proposes to concretise the setting itself as physical space and explore theatre space as an experiential field in terms of its un-mediated non-mediating effects. In this, re-conceptualising physical space as a *mode* of spatial organisation, allows attending to the formulation of spatial elements, features, and properties as empirical phenomena, and disclosing, analytically, the mechanisms through which they constitute and operate. Theatre space is established and addressed as a distinct material presence prior to artistic and architectural particularizations. Yet this lifting of these particularly 'theatrical' overlays does not imply that inquiry is entirely detached from theatre and the processes it entails. Rather, by addressing the correlation of space with the performance and the event at a deeper level, this inquiry would seek to render a less-examined layer of experience—that which evolves in corporeal terms and due to space. The methodological propositions of the approach will be specified with respect to this particular modality of spatial organisation, adjusted and concretised so as to trace out the ways in which this layer of immediate experience correlates with the theatrical. Ultimately, this approach to space would enable disclosing this layer of experience as it coheres with the experience of the theatrical: embedded in the physical context of the event and the form of actualization of the performance, it vitalizes the particular blend of the aesthetic, ontological and social, pertinent to theatrical experience, at the deep corporeal level of its very formation.

Approaching theatre space in terms of the *mode* allows reconstituting it as a wholesome material presence. It is brought forth as a distinct entity characterised by its resilient spatial form, experientially charged, and working through its inherent properties and principal un-mediated effects. This allows addressing spatial form, analytically, on two levels: it can be examined with respect to its overall operations as the physical setting of the performance, as well as in terms of the specificity of concrete spatial circumstance with which discreet bodily experience evolves. The analysis of overall spatial formation helps disclose its correspondences with the structure of the performance event, and, reciprocally, the dependence of the performance on specified spatial effects. The analysis of these effects at the micro-level with respect to the situated agent posits such effects as essential generic conditions pertinent to this spatial form. It allows exploring their experiential charge as conditions shared by all participants involved. Hence in terms of the mode, analysis of space spans from its capacities with respect to the performance—such as to present, configure, or focus, through to its aptitudes with respect to the body—such as to affect (fear, pleasure), trigger awareness (vulnerability, equality), suggest (relations)—i.e., open up alternative paths of acquisition, and cultivate sensibilities enabling social togetherness. The conception of the mode, thus, is employed as a methodological tool, which on the one hand helps render space as a structured entity in coherence with the principal structure of the performance event, while, at the same time, rendering immediate experience explicit.

Approaching space in the proposed terms allows complementing mainstream perspectives which focus on the artistic expression of the stage and posit space in its mediating 'functions'—always both physical and fictional, with an analysis of the operations of the whole site conducted at an empirical level. It posits theatre space as a wholesome material framework that includes the auditorium along with the stage into analysis, and attends to the properties of this framework with equal precision and sensitivity to spatial detail. Thus it prepares grounds to articulate, in full, the principal characteristics of that physical context in which theatre experience as an aesthetic issue has been embedded all along. In addition to interpretations of theatre experience in the context of the processes of production and reception which emphasise essential distinctions between performer and audience or play and witnessing, this analysis accesses an experiential layer which evolves on unified grounds. It proceeds from within the setting as shared spatial framework, through the specificity of corporeal circumstances and conditions as these open up to experience, and discloses a cluster of discreet processes through which physical space comes to be affective, and productive in analogous terms for all participants involved.

This account of space offers grounds to extend the role of space in explicating certain aspects of theatre experience, the theatrical event as lived process, and the socio-cultural and ontological import of theatre by way of probing into the corporeal constructions of space-to-body correlations as alternative paths of being and acquisition. It brings to the foreground a relatively under-explored layer of discreet immediate experience which is embedded in a zone of direct contact with the corporeal circumstance of the situation, evolves in terms of non-contemplative, pre-conscious processes, and formulates the foundational texture nourishing and qualifying experience. This subtle layer of the lived presents precisely that, which might come to be partially included in every other depiction of experience, but would not come fully forth in either. It needs to be recognised and opened up for inquiry on its own terms in order to be re-constructed, and involved in understanding experience as a whole. Construing of experience within its spatial dimension offers an opportunity to explore certain alternative ways in which theatre partakes in the constitution of agency and the collective, and to render the embodied paths of affect and knowing that are acquired and actualized in pre-contemplative practice.

Inquiry into theatre space in terms of *mode of spatial organization* offers a different perspective on this spatial form not only in that it brings theatre forth as an articulate experiential field. Theatre is a special case also in that it presents one of the most resilient spatial forms—a model, which has been handed down and incorporated in diverse modification throughout its historical recurrence. Its rendition as *mode* comes to highlight spatial continuities and resemblances amongst varying actualizations, rather than aspects of change in form as means in the evolution of theatre culture. Furthermore, approaching theatre space in these terms allows construing of the spatial logic underlying its workings, which can be recognized not only in all three major theatre forms (the end-stage, thrust stage and arena). It also presents a prototype for a range of analogous social spaces with diverse appointed functions: assembly halls, courtrooms, religious ritual, as well as spontaneous collective configurations.

Construing of theatre space in terms of *mode* allows addressing the origins of this spatial form in social and ritual practice, and examining it in correlation with the distinct patterns of collective activities for and through which it has come about. This allows acknowledging this spatial form as an artefact proper and product of material culture. As such it allows construing of the possibility that certain aspects inherited from ritual social practice might have solidified in spatial form, and that these could be traced in terms of affective capacities and operations of physical space. All of these provide a different perspective on issues of socio-spatial reciprocities allow particularising the practices of formulating and inhabiting space, and seeking an explanation for the persistence of this spatial form not in design, but rather in the spatial materialisations of these practices. This spatial form, then, can be opened up for a different reading: it could be seen in terms of some few but fundamental principles that govern this kind of ritual and social organization, as these are reproduced in spatial terms as essential existential conditions. An analysis of this spatial form as an experiential field, then, would help infer such fundamental principles from their material constructions, and offer insight into the discreet experiential processes through which they might be internalized in the context of performance.

Space and its 'theatrical' problems: site and scene in discourse and practice

Linking up performance, experience and space is an intricate undertaking. One of the major difficulties in establishing the role of space in this context lies in the controversy between theatre and architecture, which, from the perspective of space, lack an immediate and univocal relation (Breton, 1998, 4-5). Theatre is an ephemeral art, where space is created for the instant of the performance, may not necessitate an architectural setting, and even when placed within such a setting, transcends architecture as it projects into the diffuse space of imagination. In turn, built space is about permanency, and conceptions of theatre architecture go beyond consideration of theatre production and theatrical design to establish the building as an urban monument. The complexities of these correlations, then, come to reflect on the framework through which the socio-cultural role of theatre and theatre experience in particular are theorized and understood.

The issue of theatre experience forms the common grounds for both theatre studies, and the corresponding branch of architecture. It is seen as evolving within the particular processes of the production, expression and mediation of theatrical contents and the formulation of theatrical meanings, to which the aesthetic, ontological and socio-cultural import of that experience, and of theatre as a cultural phenomenon are tightly tied. Hence although theorization of theatre experience, and its spatial correlate, evolve in the context of two distinct notions—the *theatrical work* and *the monument,* in both, despite of the respective shifts of emphasis, the role of space is indexed exclusively to the particularly theatrical. The role of space is seen and sought in its functioning as a major tool in the construction and mediation of theatrical expressions—i.e., space comes to be interpreted in terms of its essentially representational functions. Central to the constitution of the socio-cultural significance of theatre—experience, process and praxis, space is approached in terms of the dichotomy of 'space as a medium of representation' and 'space as physical place' (McAuley 1999). While inherent in discourse on space in general, this dichotomy becomes utterly explicit in the dramatized context of theatre space, as does the priority given to its mediating functions and representation.

The prime concern with physical space entails the 'divided yet unitary' entity of 'theatre space', which, following McAuley's (1999: 255-277) definitions, entails the stage and the auditorium. Theatre space is studied in its capacity of constituting the physical context and configuring the relations between the stage (practitioner space), and the auditorium (audience space) as the core correlation of the experience of theatre. In McAuley's perspective, as a physical place theatre space 'situates' and 'establishes relations', presenting an 'apparatus of looks'—it is posited in ways that allow acknowledging the diversity of these relations in keeping with the prioritization of the ocular implicated in the 'theatron'.

In architecture, these two spatial components are explored as permanent configurations, which are realized differently in each theatre building. In theatre studies, these two spatial components gain importance with regard to the possible temporary re-definitions they allow for, and which are constructed for the duration of each respective play. Yet in both theoretical contexts these two spatial components—stage and auditorium are seen in terms of their differences with respect to their contribution to the performance. In accordance with the different roles they play in the constitution of the theatrical processes, they are approached—studied and designed with rather different objectives. As it is the theatrical work which is construed as central to theatre experience, its actualization at and through the stage channels attention towards the effects of stage, leaving the experiential import of the larger site (auditorium) largely unattended. For both of these frameworks, then, it is the stage space, which forms the unitary focus—and the prime platform for sharing and communication. Hence while the two groups—performers and participants, in spite of their different roles in the process, are seen to be equally involved in the theatrical situation and the formulation of meanings this proposes, their very positioning would already indicate that both their experience, and their immediate spatial situation would be characterized in explicitly diverging terms.

Space 'in' performance: the theatrical work
In theatre studies, it is the theatrical work—a unique form of art and instance of cultural production which presents the prime subject over which insight is sought. This grounds inquiry into theatre experience within two distinct processes: that which entails the production and presentation of the performance, and that which concerns its mediation and perception. While these conjointly formulate the socio-cultural significance of theatrical praxis, their fundamental distinction as processes of a different nature, also leads to the diverging terms in which the experience of the two groups involved in the theatrical situation come to be interpreted. With respect to space this presupposes a particular way of conceptualizing its role in view of these processes—it is posited as 'space *in* performance'. As comprehensive overviews on theoretical thought from within theatre and performance studies reveal, this role of space is seen in tight reference with theatrical practices and theatre experience—i.e., it is indexed to and analyzed in its

correspondence to processes of production and communication of theatrical meaning.

<u>Theatrical functions of space</u>
Since Aristotle's *Poetics* the discourse on theatre experience as an aesthetic issue is being pursued as embedded in the content of the work, the plot, the character and the performance as prime cathartic instruments (1985), while the site and setting as its larger physical context receives less attention. The brief review of approaches and issues characterising the growing recognition of the role of space presented here, is based on three key studies, each discussing diverse perspectives on theatre within the specificity of its theoretical perspective: McAuley's (1999: 1-35) study on space in performance, Sauter's (2000: 1-72) theorisation of the theatrical event, and Wiles's (2003: 1-22, 240-66) inquiry into the multitude of presentational practices throughout history. From these it emerges that only more recently research into the processes of production and reception has begun involving space as one of the explicit elements of presentation, in its capacities to support and augment the performance. In established conceptions of 'theatre as a composite work of art', an inquiry into the effects of the stage would include the literary text and the complexities of the spatial structures contained within the play-text. Textual references such as place names, depiction of geographical location, descriptions of space and place, reference to objects and indications on proxemic relationships, would come to bear expression not only through the spatial definitions on stage, but also through aspects like bodily positions and kinetics, or gestures, and complement expressions in set and costume design, sound, music and acting. This notion is extended by that of 'theatre as system', which focuses on the construction of meaning via the production, distribution and consumption of signs. Further on, with the distinct shift towards theorizations that reflect the nature of actualization of the performance —namely as live participatory collective event, the role of space is being rethought in keeping with a more inclusive conception of 'theatre as communicative event' (Sauter 2000). Deviating from the closed system of interpreting space favoured by models of figuration and abstraction as stable objects, this framework offers grounds for acknowledging its inherent spatiality. It marks a shift in understanding of the aesthetic as a particular type of experience stimulated by the performance, at the

basis of an inquiry that would lead to disclosing how all participants would attain their ultimate aspiration in the consensus of the theatrical situation.

However, these differences in interpretation do not so much concern its principal supporting functions as 'space *in* performance' (McAuley 1999: 17), but rather reflect the diverging terms in which the production and reception of the 'theatrical work', theatre experience, and theatrical practices it supports, would be understood in different frameworks. Hence in the context of the practices pertinent to theatrical production, the striving to affect through space is necessarily conferred upon the construction of stage space. Through the conventions of dramaturgy, directorship and scenography, this takes the form of temporary manipulations through which 'dramatic space' is moulded and cast upon the physicality of the scene. This is to say that effects of space are produced in reference to, and for the duration, of a particular performance. In theory the interpretation of such effects is sought through extensive taxonomies of spatial functions, which open up towards a diverse range of suggestions about the experience of the theatrical, and reveal the complexities in conceptualizing the interference between fictional and physical realities. Hence, as related in McAuley's discussion of different taxonomies, Ubersfeld's system proposes an explanation through the series of stage space, scenic place, theatrical space, theatre space, and dramatic space. Re-integrating the latter three notions, Jansen's classification entails stage space, scenic place, surrounding space and referred space, while Issacharoff's system highlights components of play in mimetic space, diegetic space, scenic space and extra-scenic space. McAuley's emphasis is on the co-presence of the social reality and fictional reality, and the dualities among physical space and fictional place, on location and fiction in textual space and the functioning of space at the thematic level.

Ultimately, space in performance is construed in terms of the particularly theatrical blend of artistic and actual, physical and fictional dimensions. It is in this capacity, that theorizations of other essential functions—such as the expressions of the theatrical at its interface with architectural realities, come to complement the effects emanating from the stage. Thus, while the account of space with respect to both of these processes converges towards the formulation of 'theatrical space' that is moulded upon the physicality of the scene, it is the broader notion of 'theatrical space' that provides a 'context of inter-pretation for performers and spectators alike', where the architectural presence of the auditorium is but one further aspect in the complex interplay.

<u>Theatre experience—mediated and immediate</u>
This re-orientation towards account of the physical aspects of space coincides with the re-discovery of the body, and the shift in philosophy towards 'lived' experience, where the former emphasis on semiotic 'reading' is superseded with a paradigm centred on the 'live-ness' of performance-as-event. This entails theorizing experience of the theatrical by seeking an account of the constructive involvement of the audience, which is stimulated and activated via the relations among participants: performer-audience, performer-performer and audience-audience. Hence in addition to the functions of space which revolve around the scene as principal place of performance, and are intrinsically entangled with representation, concerns with space come to involve the productive aspects of space in view of how it constructs the theatrical situation itself. In this, the notions of the entire site range from space that 'houses' the experience of the theatrical event in perspectives exploring the various levels of communication involved (Sauter 2000: 1-113), through to space as an 'active agent' 'shaping what goes on within it' (Wiles 2003: 19). This latter notion presents a further shift away from the homogeneity of an 'ocular' space-container which sets the framework for presentation and perception, and towards an account of space as an entity that 'enfolds' the event, the performers and the audience, which is depicted as an immersing tactile and sound reverberating presence. While this depiction of physical properties points to the possibility of including an additional aspect into immediate experience, ultimately, the experience of theatre is located within the dialectical relations of diverse architectural environments with various performance practices. In this way space, analogous to the actors, is to be made to 'perform'- with and in terms of the 'play-as-event' (Wiles 2003: 1-22).

With respect to the depiction of the experience, the 'physicality' and 'lived-ness' of the performance event is interpreted in explicitly diverging terms for the performer-producers and the participants—their experiences are brought forth in keeping with the distinction of their respective roles in the processes of meaning formation. The performing body is seen in its practices: both in its craft to animating the 'content' which it presents, and as a productive path to 'incorporation' and 'embodiment', while the participation of the audience occurs in terms of witnessing and the essentially intellectual mode of perception. This is to say that while space in its immediacy appears increasingly pertinent to the experience of the performer, who works upon and 'energizes' it, the principal characteristic of the experience of the theatrical for the audience emerges in terms of the artificiality borne in the juxtaposition of the physical reality of the stage and the 'fictional'—'dramatic' or metaphoric, which is created in and through the stage space (McAuley: 23).

This distinction pertains also to the productive functions of affect as well. Exemplified in stage fright, a powerful state associated exclusively with the performer, the acting, and the stage space (Aaron, 1986), emotive charge as productive impetus is seen and sought in the modes of performance, which are seen to approximate genuine experience. Thus for instance the possibilities in disrupting and reversing 'the familiar' employed as a strategy inductive of confusion and anxiety, could lead to modes of embodiment where even represented pain comes to be 'incorporated' in performative practice (Solga,2008).

However, for the audience, the mediated nature, artifice and representation at the core of the theatrical experience remain as yet intact: interpretations of productive functions of affect and emotion would appear in a mediated rather than immediate form. For the audience these elements would tend to be associated with allusions of fear allotted to drama. Following Aristotle's profound illumination of the de-stabilizing effect which the discovery of a striking reversal of fortune can produce, the emotive components of the experience of audiences is explicated in terms of that which is conveyed. The explanation of such effects is sought predominantly through the plot, character, and acting as constructive (cathartic) instruments, while spectacle and the larger setting recede into the background, receiving least attention. For the audience emotive components, including powerful feelings such as fear, remain remote, attached to events representing reality and hypothetic characters. As such these are conducted through re-cognition and rely on the more voluntary self-motivated instigative modes of intentionality and imaginational empathy.

Space, then, is assigned the major function in maintaining the double awareness of reality and non-reality (McAuley, 41), while 'present-ness' in the experience of theatre audiences is accounted for as that which is being produced in the actor-audience collaboration based on the performed work (McAuley, 117). The experience for the audience, then, inevitably emanates from the action on stage, and, in perspectives emphasizing 'the act and nature of viewing' as the channel of reception (Bennett, 1990, 72), exploration of effects of space is confined to the visual codes of the scene. While for the performing body the physicality of space and the event-ness of the performance are being acknowledged as sources of attaining aspects of the immediately experiential, on part of participants in the audience, corresponding interest in the immediate and spatial circumstance is not as clearly present.

A major approach to understanding audience experience, then, is through the 'mission' of the theatrical work studied in various reception theories. Hence Bennett's (1990) comprehensive research on reception theories shows that although there is an explicit shift from the text towards diversifying the experiential modality of perception by unconventional staging and performance strategies, audience experience is nevertheless theorized as essentially bound to the mediation of the performance. This would indicate that analogous to the mediated nature of emotive content, the contact with the essentially social nature inherent in the art of theatre retains its indirect character. Social ideas are explored, experimented with, and questioned primarily via realities presented on stage. The fact that performance occurs in the form of a live collective event, too, is subsumed to the theatrical. Hence this event is being conceptualized as constituted by 'actors', 'audience' and 'actants'—i.e., as a specifically 'theatrical mode of community' which is involved in 'theatrical work' (Barr 1998: 10-34). In this way the physical context—theatre space, too, is bound to attain the provisional character special to theatre.

Even in broader perspectives which seek to relate and examine diverse theatre cultures and practices, so as to account for the-play-as-event rooted in bodies and environments, the key issue of inquiry is how space could be made to corroborate with the event. Thus Wiles (2003), relying on Lefebvre's framework, discusses different types of theatre spaces within the Western theatre tradition in conjunction with the respective evolving conceptions of space and self, and highlights these as produced through and for particular socio-spatial practices. With regard to the tripartite history of space, various spatial forms are accounted for in terms of subsequent notions of theatre such as: 'space of emplacement', 'space of extension' and 'the modern site'. While each may contain traces of previous forms, these are affirmed as to the special spatial potential they present in formulating theatrical meanings in keeping with evolving ideas in theatre. In this the last category of modernist space—'the site'—whose spatiality is seen as defined only by its relationships, would best lend itself to function as a 'counter-site' (based on the concept of 'heterotopia'), and so come to speak about 'other' sites that 'represent, contest and invert other spaces in society'. This priority in viewing theatre space, would allow it to emerge as a shared space, and attain explicitly corporeal dimensions (tactile, and acoustic qualities, volume, character). However, ultimately the explication of its effects takes the form of a construction of 'predetermined theatrical' meanings within distinct 'architectural realities'. A vital concern for contemporary theatre is to explore how such 'spatial machines' would partake in the 'unique expressions of cultural statements'—that are formulated as the stage-auditorium interface (Wiles 2003).

'Real' social practices that issue from the live-ness of the performance entail predominantly the 'enacting' of social customs as a practice of theatre-going, extensively documented in McAuley's study on theatre space (1999). Furthermore, the constant 'awareness' of others, as Forsyth (1987) puts forth in his analysis of auditoria, is to be sought as important experiential circumstance enhancing participation. In more recent research, however, the presence of non-mediated feelings on the part of the audience that issue from the corporeality of theatre-as-event and would be taken to correspond to the phenomenon of stage fright, emerge as particular kinds of emotions in 'embarrassment' and 'shame', and productive occurrences like 'collective laughter', 'corpsing', or 'fiasco'. In Ridout's (2006) insightful analysis of contemporary theatre, these are investigated as conditions of discomfort and associated with the performer-audience encounter. Drawing philosophical thought and theatre criticism around the concept of 'theatricality', such phenomena are theorized in the context of theatre in modernity, emphasizing especially those social, economic and political powers pertinent to capitalist growth, which shape the urban condition and mentality, as well as theatre in terms of the pervasive division of work and leisure. Hence these phenomena, though bearing a situational dimension, are explicated rather in terms of the ethics and politics of performance. In Ridout's perspective such 'discomforts' are identified as modern phenomena, characterizing the contemporary theatre situation through practices and attitudes determined by socio-economic circumstances, and seen to belong to theatre to 'underpin' and 'undermine' its functioning as a mode of ethical and political communication. Actualized as psychological events arising at those moments of slippage during a play when performance goes 'wrong' to breach codes and conventions, these offer insight into operations of theatre-as-event, presenting 'constitutive' possibilities within its 'fail-ures'. While highlighting socially significant aspects in the operations of theatre, all of these ultimately depend on the theatrical work to begin.

Space 'for' performance: the theatre monument
<u>Building for the performing arts</u>
In keeping with these priorities, the question of performance space in the architectural field takes the form of 'space *for* performance'—i.e., it is examined in the context of designing and building for the per-forming arts. In studies of theatre architecture, the theatre building is seen as the permanent manifestation of the culturally defined ideas on the institution, on theatre, and on architecture—i.e., it is posited and approached in terms of a monument. Hence the monument—built space proper—is examined in view of a different specifically architec-tural problematic. It highlights areas of special architectural attention: the exterior of the theatre building which asserts it within the broader urban context, and the formulation of its 'protected core' comprised of stage and auditorium (Breton 1989: 4-14). Accordingly, the theatre building is approached in rather diverging terms: while its outward appearance is to be sought as distinctive architectural presence that establishes theatre as 'social instrument' within its urban context, its inward formation ensures the spatial framework for performance, and is to house and enable the temporary theatrical expressions for each production.

Imbued with such three-fold expressivity, the theatre monument as built architectural space presents a paramount concretization of what Lefebvre (1991) conceptualizes as 'representational' space. In order to understand its socio-cultural import, studies of theatre archi-tecture, such as Breton (1989), Mackintosh (1993), Carlson (1989), and Wiles (2003), examine historical examples with regard to subsequent aesthetic ideas and conceptions of theatrical production. More or less explicitly aligning with Lefebvre's perspective on socio-spatial correspondences, these help explicate the variety of theatre forms in the Western tradition, linked with the time and place specific terms in which the monument is socially set. In spite of the distinction between the ways in which exterior appearance and interior constitution are being problematized, discourse on theatre architecture offers a perfect example in showing the power of concerns with representation, allowing to understand how experiential components that are raised in the course of study, would tend come to be assimilated into the phase of 'perception'. Mainstream perspectives would tend to adopt a notion of experience corresponding to that phase of perception, which as a conscious later phase appears to relate the whole process. In this way experience of space comes to denote the broader hermeneutic correlation, and space comes to be construed in predominantly visual and representational terms. This precedence of the visual and representational applies especially to the understanding of architectural space in terms of its expressive powers. The expressive capacities of the monument, then, are studied around the core issues of location, volumetric composition and correlation with other urban elements, the character and style of structural elements, ornamentation and decorative detail. Research in these terms is oriented towards deriving the meanings from these expressions—by way of interpreting perception. Hence in the context of architectural space, too, the notion of theatre experience attains a less 'experiential' and more 'perceptual' character, denoting a correlation which is understood as an essentially mediated one. This prevails in evaluations of the monument based on interpretation of its (visual) appearance as cultural manifestation and a 'text to be deciphered' in semiotic perspectives to theatre architecture (Carlson 1989). It also influences more analytical approaches that aim to establish how an authentically theatrical experience would be supported through architectural means (Breton 1989, Mackintosh 1993).

One particularly practice-oriented line of investigation engages in the questions of design and construction, establishing guidelines based on technical and pragmatic requirements. Such studies, as for instance that of Appleton (1996), examine theatre as a building typology, substantiate technical (audio-visual) and spatial requirements for the essential functional components (performers' spaces, audience spaces, back-stage, services, lobby), in connection with prevailing activity patters and desired correlations. These requirements are refined by taking into account the kind of performance (dance, drama, cabaret), the scale of enterprise (institutional, private, local, communal). The discussion of spatial form in such perspectives is based on arrangement and geometry, and aims to identify the potential of different configuration types of stage and auditorium, such as arena, thrust stage or proscenium, as set within horse shoe, elliptical polygonal or square layouts.

More experience-oriented studies on the 'protected core'—stage and auditorium—focus on architectural space with the concern that it 'houses' the presentation of the performance, while also structuring the principal relations relevant to the experience of theatre. This implies that while attention is allotted to the formation of these two components, architectural definitiveness is to be moderated intentionally. From the perspective of theatrical production, then, the character which architectural space has to assume is one of a relatively neutral background that is to remain open for the constitution of various kinds of performances and diverse theatrical expressions (Breton 1989: 20-21).

This particularly architectural conflation of experiential and perceptual properties, then, shows on the concrete example of theatre, how the prioritization of affordance and appearance of space limits theorization to its capacity to 'convey' socio-cultural meanings. Built architectural space is construed as 'open' insofar as it may accommodate the construction of theatrical meanings, support the theatre experience, and, in architectural terms—insofar as the experience of the theatre building—largely visual—is given to interpretation. Studies of architectural space come to concern predominantly those aspects of built space that are essentially representational. Another important aspect of such emphasis is that it prioritises change and evolution as expressed in the monument, through which the 'social production' of the theatre building is firmly located within the practice of design. As elucidated in Lefebvre's framework, these 'designed' implementations, then, would inevitably entail and enhance components of the dominant ideologies and relations of production, where design presents one of the major means and tools of conveying such ideological components into actualisation. Hence the perspective on theatre as monument would maintain the notion of built spatial form as a means to elicit desired effects and represent and transmit intended messages.

The theatre building would come forth as a vehicle to impress the culture of a society, and reproduce or alter the various established forms of theatre-going.

Theatre as spatial type

That theatre space might become prone to manipulation through design is brought forth with special acuteness in Madge's (2007) discussion on theatre as a *type*. This perspective places the issues of continuity and change of this building form in critical proximity with in broader ideological processes and examines its transition from the spatial actualization of ritual and drama in Antiquity, through to its materialization of the rise of spectacle and entertainment.

Established as a ritual site for the cult of Dionysus, the theatre type is identified by an original 'armature' of five invariant constitutive elements: the megaron shrine, the open space with altar and its enclosure, and the banked seating bounding the site on the other side. In this perspective, the theatre type is brought forth in the light of three distinct evolutionary histories, all of which utilize the potential of the original armature grounded on changing notions of 'essence' in theatre. Hence emphasis is respectively given to the figure of seating, to the cavea—the space of theatrical action (orchestra/stage), or to the shrine (the 'miracle' box stage) where behind the proscenium arch, space is 'lavishly furnished' to animate performance. These modifications through time, then, are examined in correlation with the practices of design, discussing successive variants as to their possible social impact. Resounding with Foucault's power argument, this perspective draws attention to order, as well as to the ocular mechanisms inherent in theatre, as the prime architectural features liable to misuse. It raises critical concerns about the respective ideological contexts and their designed projections in architectural form. Hence although systematic positioning of participants would show a potential to convey, 'diagrammatically', the 'sense of equality', this sense is coupled with and dominated by a sense of subjection, through which the type is asserted as an 'apparatus' manifesting the fixed, requisite relations—and enforcing these for being a relentlessly observable space. With major effects defined in these terms, not only theatres, but also other functional places based on this spatial typology, would be seen as places intentionally perfected for fostering attention and concentration, as tools for exerting 'discipline' and 'control', and hence 'behaviour'

(Madge 2007: 1-35). In a similar vein, Markus (1993) in his comprehensive survey of socio-spatial typologies discusses this spatial organisation in the context of the lecture theatres. Construing built space as close correlate of power, he highlights the spatial organization as hierarchical, and fit for purporting conditions of 'instruction' as well as of 'spatial and social stratification', a trait that, when paired with the mechanisms of observation, could be taken to the extreme of outright surveillance.

<u>Architectural means: enhancing theatre experience</u>
The framework of the architectural monument posits theatre in terms of its complex and layered 'object' presence, focuses on its appearance and affordance, upholds the emphasis on its representational functions, and links its constitution firmly within the practice of design. Hence mainstream research on theatre architecture would tend to emphasize the transformations and changes which it undergoes as linked to the process of perfecting the culture of theatre production. This preoccupation with representation and the role of design in this, precludes exploration of other possibilities in understanding the persistent reproduction of this spatial form, such as those that concern aspects of socio-spatial practice and cultural continuity embedded in this spatial form at a deeper level. It screens off the fact of constitution of this spatial formation for and through social and ritual practice, and its role as model preceding and underlying design – i.e., its role as a physical remnant from former spatial cultures persistently handed down and presenting a corporeal means of cultural continuity. The priority assigned to the visual framework of representation and perception would also tend to overlook a range of socio-spatial reciprocities evolving at a more immediate corporeal level, both in terms of the practices of formulating space, and those of inhabiting it. In this way the third of Lefebvre's conceptions—'lived space'—that involves the physical and phenomenal correlations with space and its appropriation into 'lived experience', comes to be employed only partially. This is linked with the fact that the experiential features of architectural space are seen exclusively in terms of the theatre experience. This emphasis pertains also to the few perspectives which engage explicitly on the experiential aspects of spatial features (as distinct from style and detail) and examine the particularly architectural means through which theatre experience may be enhanced.

In this respect Breton's (1989) study into experiential features of space, takes the form of a concise analysis of major models of the Western tradition as formalizations of distinct theatre practices. It focuses on the special ways in which the spatial relations between actor and audience are sustained in each case, and to what experiential ends. The analysis of historical prototypes extends to encompass several prominent contemporary realizations in terms of special qualities achieved by conceptual design, examining various architectural concepts (such as 'successive enclosures', 'the exterior as interior', and 'extended stage') are employed as guiding principles. These examples would come to suggest that there are further ways in which specifically articulated architectural space can come to influence theatre experience.

The issue of how architectural presence might best support the authenticity of theatrical experience is approached by Mackintosh (1993) by way of deriving 'recurring family characteristics' which diverse examples share. This enhances awareness of the architectural nature of distinctly theatrical traits of experience—such as its intensity, and arrives at the playhouse as a prototype of theatre space where 'density of space', and 'character and sense of place' imbue the relations with special quality. Hence from his perspective, physical space is brought forth as a valid source for the actor's prospect for response, and the audiences' prospect for mutual influence, demonstrating the import of architectural space (form, sectional treatment, boundary articulation and proximity) in this.

Both of these approaches to analysis of theatre space bring forth the capacities of spatial configuration to intensify the relations (among the two groups of participants) and nourish involvement and response (to that which is presented). They point to the validity of analytical means of understanding the workings of physical space, and open up possibilities to acknowledge architectural space in terms of effects that are both authentically pertinent to theatre, and experientially charged.

Recovering experiential charge
This survey brings forth that both of these notions—the theatrical work and the architectural monument are bound to the designed processes of perfecting the culture of theatre production. The significance of space is seen in that it formulates, for each specific performance, the shared framework through which theatrical meanings are produced

and mediated. Space is being understood in terms of a complex system of functions, which merges physical and fictional, material and symbolic, and in this way maintains the conscious awareness of the two-fold reality in theatre. Theatre experience, then, is understood to evolve in an essentially hermeneutic (interpretative) correlation with the architectural and theatrical that is presented to perception, on stage and in space. Both of these frameworks, thus, entail a mode of analysis into the aesthetic, which addresses its formulation through its ties with mediated theatrical content. Yet acknowledging the 'lived' and immediately experiential in its phase of generation, might allow following the kind of movement (in experience) that is prior to representation and still evolves in coherence with the work, meaning, and context.

It is precisely the possibility of positing theatre experience on the grounds of immediate corporeal experience as well which this current approach seeks to establish. This possibility is construed as a potent means to show how physical space would open up to that experience and the micro events of becoming, and allow exploring experience in its constitution as belonging to both the event, and its space. Implementing the framework of inquiry into physical space in terms of a *mode of spatial organization*, intended as an incision into the direct links among space and experience, then, would yield certain essential ways in which this spatial form supports, triggers, and reverberates with the fundamental conditions of the experience in question. It would allow tracing out the experiential as a movement and opening towards emergence within the materiality of space, and in this way rendering the logic of that experience tangible.

Diverging from the above approaches to experience and space, that would tend to ascribe the entire productive potential (experiential, ontological, and aesthetic) of theatre and space to that which is mediated and represented, this current approach seeks to explore such potential by way of bringing into account the fact that this productive potential of theatre has been, all along, also firmly situated in shared physical space of its site. Extending on the premise that this situatedness is far from accidental, and that neither the socio-cultural significance, nor the generative potential of theatre are entirely elucidated in the above terms, this study ventures into the intimate inherent links among lived experience and material space. It will seek to highlight that experience as a distinct area of inquiry, holding that it productively partakes in the amalgam of complex processes through which theatre evolves. By 'lifting' of the representational layers of architectural and scenic particularizations from physical space, this approach evades certain 'theatrical' effects associated with technologies of manipulation of perception, along with their outright suspect traits of exaggeration, lavish detail and artificiality. Instead it seeks to delve, analytically, further into the corporeal properties of the spatial structure of the site itself, disclose a more foundational level at which this spatial form would cohere with the structure of the performance, the lived event, the nature of social and ritual practice, and, ultimately, theatre experience.

Ritual practice and sites of affect
The affective in theatre is rarely put forth in terms of corporeal experience. In correlation with the spatial context, the few experientially-oriented perspectives bring forth such potential in terms of the overall 'sense of place', which is rooted in the density and intensity of requisite correlations. Besides the phenomenon of stage fright, which is linked to the experience of the performer, and the occasional 'embarrassments' for audiences, the emotive in theatre experience—pity, fear, or pleasure—is firmly attached to the represented realities of the theatrical work and bound to evolve via the reflective modes of recognition, the intentional identification, imagination and volitional empathy. The tendency for interpreting emotive components as rooted in the engagement with the theatrical work come forth both in frameworks based on the Aristotelian model, and in frameworks corresponding to the models of 'conversational communities' of postmodern social thought. While the former model would offer unifying grounds via 'empathy' with a protagonist, the latter proposes to find, in the theatrical work, the foundation accommodating plurality, and promoting the conscious and critical stance which communication at this level entails. There meaning formulation is stimulated by a 'communal dynamics' based on diversity, enabled by the live event, the participatory nature of performance—a communal dynamics, which is provisionally 'enacted'. For both of these models the understanding of emotive vigour and transformative potential of theatre experience relies ultimately on the analysis of the respective theatrical work.

Yet the fact that the very possibility of this unique and transformative experience would find us within the shared space of theatre suggests that there is more to be understood both about the experience and about the role of the shared setting in its constitution. Theatre experience as an aesthetic issue does actualise firmly emplaced within this spatial form. Considering that this spatial form is inherited from its distant origins which conjoin the artistic with social and ritual practice, this site can be understood as a physical context which has persistently formalised, hence rendered aspects of these practices tangible, explicit and affective. As material setting of the experience in question, it would support the generation of 'embodied' forms of feeling and knowing as much—i.e., engender the actualization of affect in terms of directly lived experiential components. An analysis in terms of the spatial modality as physical space would offer insight into the corporeal constructions of experiential ingredients that pertain to the aesthetic as well as to the ritual. This would point to the possibility of seeking, within the concreteness of spatial circumstance, understanding of the corporeal means in which aspects of the ontological and social operations of ritual would be instantiated.

As altered and inarticulate such ritual components might have become under the sweeping processes of urbanisation and secularisation, their principal productive functions are still being located within organised collective activities, and at the pre-conscious level of practice. Among the multiple functions of ritual practice, the embodied ways in which the potential in approaching 'liminal' states (Turner, 1982), and abilities of dealing with crisis (Schechner, 1993) have been sought out as especially productive, as well as embedded in contexts akin to theatre. In this way it becomes possible to construe that theatre space might actually hold more affinities with the 'spatiality' of ritual than currently acknowledged—i.e., it might still embed residues of the spatial conditions apt to mobilize forms of knowledge that are acquired and implemented in practice.

Analysis of space in its corporeal generic properties, then, would help render explicit how such aspects might be reproduced in the subtle operations of physical space. It does open up the possibility to attend, analytically, to such aspects, in their rudimentary yet embodied actualisation, and address the internal specificities in which physical space enables and supports their instantiation. It holds that the affective triggered through the body at the site of performance might prove akin to much of the emotive import pertinent to and characterizing the aesthetic context of theatre, as well as that of ritual, and help ascertain the layer of lived experience as their unifying corporeal grounds.

Reasons to seek confirmation of such links and implications and extend on these with respect to space, can be derived from Schechner's (1993) analysis of ritual components in performance. One of the prime issues in his analysis is to re-trace various contemporary mass-events as to their ritual-based origins, and show how they function as major socio-cultural contexts characterising modern urban life which, in the absence of ritual proper, still perform one of its major functions: the harnessing of violence and fear. Hence the function of dealing with anxiety and fear is denoted as an issue, which is to be achieved collectively, and also performatively.

For the context of theatre, though, such corporeal aspects of emotion and fear are explicated and confined to the practice of performers. Still, these would offer grounds to perceive, and pursue the possibility of analogous formations of affect and emotion, in terms of their spatial constitution of the entire site, involving and affecting all participants in the theatrical situation. This would ground a further productive aspect of theatre within space as well—namely the issue of its capacity to cultivate abilities in dealing with the conditions and challenges of existence, in confronting crisis, anxiety and fear, via corporeal acquaintance with that condition. Hence aspects that undermine the univocal definition of the self, and render it labile and open, those that acquaint with vulnerability, and open up the paths of compassion—i.e., aspects that cultivate ontological and social capacities, could be traced in their corporeal constitution. The layer of lived experience and enacted practices, then, emerges as integral to theatre experience, while the affective comes to constitute some special, sensate and bodily registers of consciousness pertinent to the site.

This is to say that at the site, emotion, compassion, or fear would include those measured and mediated forms deriving from the theatrical work, and be complemented with lived emotive components borne by the unscheduled events that accompany live performance. Yet these emotive components would be augmented ultimately, or perhaps inaugurated by way of the affective, which is mobilised in and through conditions of a distinctly spatial nature. As subtle as such circumstances might be, as latent their effects might remain with respect to awareness, these are also presented in their physical phenomenal immediacy and direct affect—they rely on corporeal engagement that short-circuits volition and proceed within a space-body-mind continuum.

Re-tracing affect through space
The affective potential of architectural space and its capacities to elicit emotive response emerges more explicitly in certain perspectives outside the discourse on theatre. Significantly, the most powerful arguments on this issue concern the context of sacred architecture. Hence Jones (2000) in his cross-cultural study on 'built ritual contexts', engages with a comprehensive comparative examination of sacred space. He explores the close correspondence of the architectural monument to ritual functions, explicating this correspondence in terms of a holistic appreciation of spatial features. Employing a hermeneutic approach, his analysis includes both experiential and perceptual aspects in interpreting the operations of built architectural space.

This perspective is revealing in several respects. Based on a potent conceptualization of space as a 'ritual-architectural event', the study presents a compelling argument on affective capacities of space. But one among various other modalities, the 'theatrical' is affirmed as one of the most powerful spatial modalities in staging religious ritual, and hence, in exerting influence over dispositions. However, as methodological framework, this approach is not immediately relevant to the current study, in that it links the productivity of space to a range of 'theatre-like' 'presentation techniques' in staging and organizing ritual events, and assigns major weight to the 'spatial strategies' of designed manipulation. Furthermore, these are completed with the 'impressive tools' of the 'theatrical' expressivity which is put to play at all levels, including in the lavish rendition of architectural detail. Hence while it confirms affective capacities of space in 'alluring', 'persuading' and involving participants in the occasion, space is still seen to fulfil these by way of an inherent dual 'mediation'—to 'engage' and 'enliven'. In this way its potential is linked to the form of intended designed instigation.

As designed architectural object expressive of the sacred, the monument is construed and actualized as a physical manifestation of the sublime, and therefore works through extraordinary features. Design proceeds by employing excessive and rather unique spatial effects and provocative exaggerations of particular features, such as sheer size, highly formalized hierarchical order, peculiar articulation of volumetric form, or architectural components and ornamentation. Its power is seen in actualising special effects, the affective import of which would verge frequently on anxiety: space would shock, crush, engender awe, intimidate, and evoke the sense of inferiority, inadequacy, or confusion (Jones 2000: 129-152). In so far as such space-generated affects retain a moderate form, they would challenge and stimulate through elements of 'productive anxiety' (90-94). Yet in their full force, these techniques, for being grounded on the exceptional, would also tend to trigger the acts of contemplative engagement with space occupying experience in full and diverting attention from the ritual context itself (213-233).

Another form of the affective, which would come closer to the 'distracted' mode of experiencing spatial circumstance, is explored in Vidler's (1992) conception of the 'uncanny'. This conception is explicated, based on an in-depth theorization of architecture and architectural practices in the context of critical theories on modern estrangement. Certain actualizations of architectural space are revealed to manifest intentionally, both literally and metaphorically, the 'un-homely', through which design practice comes to express an aesthetic sensibility derived from the negative dialectics of the modernist avant-garde.

For this present study, which focuses on capacities of physical space with respect to immediate experience and the phenomena of direct contact, rather than on the cumulative effects that would acknowledge the architectural object-building or the urban in their totality, it is the notion of the 'uncanny', which is especially informative. This notion depicts a special kind of experiencing fear midway between potential and actualization. It allows construing of affect as the experiential dimension of a mental state of projection, which could, potentially arise within any architectural space. The particularly spatial provision on which this state depends is the staging and allowance of a slippage 'between what seems entirely homely and what is definitely un-homely', a slippage 'between waking and dreaming' (Vidler 1992: 11), where the boundaries between real and unreal are eroded. This perspective discloses a different aspect of space-related fear, which is located within an unsettling quality, strategically embedded in contemporary architecture. Actualised in design practices relying on subtle deception of visual perception such architectural objects work by way of generating illusionary spaces, blurring boundaries, mirroring, or artful manipulation of light. This points to aspects of the aesthetic—as strategies and affects—which ingrain fear-related components evolving in spatial contexts of 'fragmented forms mimetic of dismembered bodies', buildings 'lost in mirror reflection', 'seeing walls' simulating transparency (Vidler 1992: ix-xv)—i.e., at the level of the architectural object and the urban.

The affective inherent in space can be traced even outside the discourse on space, in studies on anxiety from psychiatric and psychological perspectives, such as that of Hallam (1985), or in terms of sociological inquiry into existential conditions in the modern metropolis, such as in the work of Simmel (1971). Hence for instance the distinct affective conditions in cases of claustrophobia and agoraphobia exemplify connections between powerful affective content in the form of anxiety with the effects of specific extreme or excessive spatial factors hard to tolerate: tight enclosure for the former, vast and uncontrollable space and crowdedness for the latter.

Yet, in bringing forth more particular implications as to the aesthetic, it is in Burke's (1987) philosophical thought where the 'sublime' appears in a striking bond with the 'terrifying' and the 'terrible'. The encounter with the 'sublime' is located within and explicated in correlation with utmost dramatic conditions—'solitude', 'silence', 'vacuity' and 'darkness' (129-160). The experience of each of these conditions entails an explicit extreme spatial quality integral to it. Each of these can be construed as experiential possibility to be invoked in the spatial context of theatre.

While neither of these above perspectives offers a ready methodology, or an affective state directly applicable to the current analysis of theatre space, each offers insight into affect in its space-related constitution. It can be construed how each of these kinds of affects coheres with the theatre context in special and suggestive ways. These perspectives have helped set a whole range of space-induced affects and emotion (fear) in the context of their specified generation and correlation with spatial circumstance, both with respect to architecture in general, and with respect to the built contexts of ritual and the sacred in particular. Experience of architectural space has been associated with the notion of the 'uncanny'. This notion has indicated an especially evocative and disconcerting state that mobilizes through the real-imagined duality—i.e., affect has been linked to spatial ambiguity as a means of staging a 'slippage' into apprehension. In the context of sacred architecture, the 'theatrical modality' has been established as a distinct form of organizing, conducting and presenting ritual which is particularly affective and engaging, asserting these qualities in correlation with articulation of spatial circumstance. The aesthetic—in the form of the encounter with the 'sublime', has been rendered explicit by way of showing how aspects of that experience depend on features of a distinctly spatial nature as pre-conditions of its attainment. All of these ascertain space in its affective capacities, indicating these capacities in their productive role to activate and mobilise. Furthermore, such capacities have been linked up with the passage into alternative and explicitly experiential modes of being, and have pointed to the affective force as a means of enabling ritual practice, and as a way towards the 'sublime'.

For this current study, such links are of special importance, because they support the premise that inquiry into theatre as spatial form at the proposed foundational level, would not only provide access to the explicitly experiential embedded in space. It might also offer insight into the traces, which this spatial form holds from its distant origin. Hence the explanation of this spatial form could be linked also with the character of social ritual practice—reproducing the preconditions apt to insinuate affect and fear in physical circumstance and resonating with a spatialized form of ritual practice. Inquiry into theatre space at this fundamental level and in correlation with the context of its social emergence, would offer an insight into aspects of the corporeal constructions of socio-spatial practices both in terms of constitution, and in terms of inhabitation. Analysis of theatre as spatial form in its principal properties, then, would help render such possible traces legible, in that it discloses how material space induces and carries these affects through.

The theatre mode of spatial organization: an analytical framework

Conceptualising theatre space as an experiential field

Approaching the analysis of theatre space in terms of *mode of spatial organization* actualises the principal methodological shifts proposed in the general framework: it allows receding, temporarily, the function of presentation and perception of the performance to a context, while also lifting off the representational layers of space. The first move brings into focus the setting as physical space and allows examining it as the source and constituent of immediate experience in its own right. The second allows re-constructing theatre space in its concrete material presence, in this way opening it up for empirical analysis.

The conceptualisation of physical space in terms of *mode* facilitates a shift away from space-as-object-in-itself, and towards an inquiry into its operations as an experiential field—i.e., it is construed as the corporeal setting, characterising the fundamental zone of contact of the self with the material world. As such it allows exploring that correlation in terms of the concreteness and specificity of spatial circumstance, and accessing the discreet experiential processes generating therein. In this conceptualisation of physical space, spatial form issues as an actualisation of the constituting principles of the mode. Hence it includes the conventional core of theatre—the spaces of the stage and the auditorium, and can be concretised in terms of their principal elements and features, and prevailing properties and effects. Yet this spatial form is also brought forth as a distinct, resilient and monolithic entity, which entails both spatial and solid components and works through the features of both. It allows attending to the formulation of effects in the specificity of properties issuing from its concrete material presence as empirical phenomena, and disclosing, analytically, the mechanisms through which these phenomena constitute and operate. Thus this spatial formation can be examined as a shared corporeal framework, and understood in terms of its un-mediated non-mediating effects—i.e., as the tangible and qualifying extension of the correlation.

The conceptualisation of the site/setting as physical space allows understanding various aspects of the operations of space through its capacities to configure, re-configure spatial effects which emerge in and out of distinctiveness, and exert affects – it influences, and qualifies, it mobilises. Hence physical space emerges as a dynamic source. Neither deterministic, nor purely phenomenological, it is rendered as it presents both the actual and the potential—as it opens up to experience: it proposes, suggests, and insinuates, it presents experiential possibilities. This allows exploring the corporeal correlation by rendering the zone of contact tangible, and probing into the affective and phenomenal generating therein. It allows inferring, through analysis of space, discreet experience as it takes form—as an event founded on encounter with concrete spatial circumstance. It allows arriving at that which is felt (as distinct from the visual) and lived through (as distinct from the perceived) as productive aspects of the experience of situatedness within concrete physical space.

Analysis of this spatial framework, then, spans from the capacities of the site/setting with respect to the performance—focusing on how physical space embeds and facilitates the performance as a specific occurrence, through to its capacities with respect to the body— focusing on the potentials for experience that generate when spatial effects at various levels configure into distinct conditions.

Three concepts: *isolation, exposure* and *collective containment* are instituted and employed as means to particularise such principal properties and effects. Construed in their three-fold functions as concepts, as spatial terms, and as conditions, these present potent analytical tools that help re-articulate physical space in its operations. All three concepts are understood and asserted as properties, which issue from within the very formulation of the spatial modality, and hence generic to it—i.e., they reoccur within each concrete actualization of this spatial formation. As spatial terms they are extended beyond the connotation of a mere circumstance, single feature, or specification of a location, and come to augment features and aspects pertinent to the whole site, span over and qualify the entire space as an experiential field. They are brought forth, explored and acknowledged as those properties of this spatial form that are inherent and imminent at the same time, allowing to probe into the latent possibilities in terms of their experiential charge.

The analytical potential of these concepts lies in that they operate both as spatial terms and as conditions. As spatial terms impressed upon the site, they economically re-describe the physical elements of architectural space in keeping with the fundamental functions of the site: to define and establish the performance as distinct occurrence, to facilitate the presentation/perception framework of the performance, and to configure the collective. Each of these concepts emerges as a distinct actualization of a set of elements, specific circumstances and mechanisms which, separately and conjointly, support the unfolding of the performance. Hence the analysis in terms of these concepts helps articulate and understand spatial form as it is structured by, and coheres with the performance as a structured event: entailing the processes of production, presentation and encounter with the theatrical work. At the level of the site, this analysis allows rendering explicit how the overall constitution of this spatial entity is characterized by, and reproduces that principal structure of the performance event. In this way it allows construing one further essential manner in which space as principal form integrally correlates with the performance. It also suggests the reciprocal dependence of the performance on specified spatial effects, such as rendered legible in the aptitude of isolation to define and protect, of exposure—to facilitate the presentation and perception of an act, and of collective containment—to accommodate and organize.

Yet, in their function as conditions, they present further analytical and explanatory capacity in that they link up spatial circumstance with experiential content. In this way these concepts allow examining the experiential potential of physical space both at the overall level of the site, and within each specific condition. Each of these conditions partakes in the formulation of the cumulative effects of the site. Yet each also diversifies these effects: each emerges to phenomenal presence by way of re-composing spatial features, and mobilising its specific internal mechanisms. Hence within each of these conditions, spatial features attain distinctiveness as circumstances and effects with different experiential bearing. It is through the intricacies of the corroboration of these conditions, through which physical space vitalizes the possibility of becoming drawn into the irretrievable modality of experience: it presents a qualified matter which, reverberating with the body, invites exploration, and entails active appropriation. Surrounding and affective, it proposes engagement, suggests relations, evokes dispositions, induces feelings, and summons latent abilities. Within each of these conditions the correlation takes on a distinct experiential form. It is in terms of such diverse experiential possibilities, brought into concrete material presence, that the situated agent would come to grasp both aspects of the situation, and aspects of the self as set in this concrete socio-spatial reality.

What renders built space interesting for inquiry at this level is that it is generative with respect to experience in various ways—its qualifying features and properties are is constantly in the making. While governed by an underlying spatial logic, this logic does not cause or pre-suppose an outcome. Rather, by bringing into concrete presence both the actual and the possible, it is the logic of choice, ambiguity, diverse affective charge, and suggestiveness. This renders physical space essentially open: it mobilizes the self towards the modes of active engagement, and of going through change, acquisition and transformation.

In terms of the mode, theatre space is established as an empirical experiential field—a physical framework. It can be examined in its un-mediated effects, specified at the various levels at which they formulate, and explicated in terms of their specific internal mechanisms—a framework that is qualified, affective and permanently open to appropriation. The proposed analysis of architectural space thus prepares grounds to capture, analytically, the passage from space through sense to sensibility. This is enabled by extending architectural analysis of physical space with a (speculative) inquiry into the experiential possibilities embedded in it. This inquiry arrives at a rendition of a cluster of discreet processes and practices that actualize in the grey zone of that which is felt, pre-contemplative non-intentional. Proposing but one particular way of rearticulating theatre space in its physical presence, this analysis brings forth a layer of immediate experience, which, though evolving relatively autonomously from theatrical content, coheres with the structure of the performance event and is integral to its space.

Corporeal correlates: the aesthetic as ontological interruption
This current inquiry into theatre space as corporeal context does bear various suggestions as to the concerns with space in the context of performance, in that it opens up further aspects of the experience of the performance event as to its nature as immediately lived, and the experiential contents this immediacy generates. Yet, with focus on the very constitution of the experiential in the texture of space-body encounter, this inquiry also offers potential in addressing the rudimentary corporeal correlates of the genetic structure of experience. Such potential derives from the possibility to posit the theatrical, in the form of the performance event on the grounds of immediate experience as well, and explore the performance experience through the intrinsic structural mechanisms and experiential instances that can be specified at the level of the corporeal, in spatial terms. The underlying expectation in this is that analysis of these corporeal constructions would help highlight certain essential ways in which this spatial form supports, triggers, and reverberates with the fundamental conditions of the experience in question. By establishing physical space as dynamic constit-

uent with respect to immediate experience, it becomes possible to construe that there would be spatial correlates to the principal structure which experience in general, the aesthetic and its theatrical counterpart share.

Grounds for intuiting such a homology can be found in diverse perspectives on experience as these converge over concerns with the conditions for change and transformation embedded in the experiential process. In terms of these generative principles, Gadamer's insight that the aesthetic is to be construed not as a different kind, but rather representing experience *per se*, does charge the aesthetic with the logic of experience *per se* (1996: 55-70). Essential links to the theatrical emerge in that the fundamentals of the aesthetic experience are contained in the dramatic experience, and, further, in the conceptualization of the dramatic through the performance event. Actually, in this way the foundations for acknowledging the spatiality of the performance event, and the experience, are already laid, yet would remain oriented exclusively towards the mediating functions of space.

Within the confines of this present account of the generative potential of physical space, it becomes possible to suggest that this logic, could be grasped in terms of space—both in view of its centrality to theatre, and in its capacities to articulate the conditions of sensation proper. Such a structure would appear in its most manifest form in the context of the performance event, and can be rendered legible through its still more tangible component—space.

The implications of this present inquiry into the immediate would lie in that it might yield insight into one further way—this time generative—in which space would support the actualization of these genetic principles of experience. That the generative is embedded in the immediacy of direct contact emerges in Agamben's (1999a: 94-104) compelling inquiry into the structure of the aesthetic experience. In this analysis, the aesthetic issues from within the moment of encounter—i.e., these genetic principles are rendered apparent, when the aesthetic as experience is construed to be located not precisely *in* the work of art. Rather, they are actualized in the moving force of the interruption brought about by the encounter with the work. Examining this instance, Agamben argues, does reveal it as an opening up of linear time: it interrupts the routine and habitual flow. Thus this encounter mobilizes interruption as a fundamental mechanism, the potential of which is both aesthetic and ontological. It actualizes as a 'present-ness', as a condition when one is arrested 'before' something, which is at the same time also an 'outside'—'*ek-stasis*'—from the stability of the habitual self, and works as an essential extension outward. As such it enables a slippage into some more essential dimension of existence. Thus, by attaining one's proper mode of being, and reclaiming one's creative capacities, the appropriation of the work becomes also an appropriation of the self.

This mechanism—expressed in the movement of passing into the experiential modality, though perhaps most profound in the compelling presence of an artwork, is in operation also in other contexts such as those of 'ritual and festival' (101), which enable the slippage out of the habitual. Seen from this perspective, theatre presents a rather unique case and context to explore. Entailing and evolving through an amalgam of multivalent processes, theatre can be understood as it would reproduce this mechanism at several levels, and propose and actualize analogous interruptive potential in several different terms. Hence this interruption can be realized in the theatrical, where mundane concerns and routines are suspended to be replaced by engagement that entails the theatrical work. It is also enabled by the performance as the live event context of this encounter. Yet, that encounter is thus also already thoroughly inscribed in space. It is, then, this inscribed-ness of the performance event into a distinct spatial form—which allows construing of and setting the possibilities of this interruption within its spatial links. The proposed re-articulation of architectural space brings it forth as a corporeal context that is qualified and affective, as well as structured by distinct experiential conditions and hence structuring the layer of immediate experience. It in this way would help conceive of and render these structuring instances as physical conditions vital in triggering and actualizing such interruption at the level of the corporeal. That is to say that theatre space can be understood in terms of its capacities to articulate, in its materiality, conditions whose operations are akin to that mechanism. These are staged in space and reproduced through the body in the form of tension among firm situatedness and the impetus of dynamic spatial forces, in the hesitancy over phenomenal ambivalences, in the disconcerting apprehension of experientially inverse situations, all of which effectively undermine the sense of self as stable entity. The analysis of theatre space in the proposed terms, then, would help particularise such instances in their generative functions both as to their experiential charge, and in their intricate internal mechanisms, and further understanding of their corporeal constructions.

Exploring space in these proposed terms might ultimately allow extracting the logic underlying the experience of the performance event—in terms of certain instances (stabilization, de-stabilization and re-stabilization) partaking in the cycle of experience—as corporeal conditions consistent with the formative instance of interruption.

Chapter Four

From space to sense—to sensibility

The generative potential of the corporeal: physical space—a dynamic locus of the actual and the possible

There are many ways in which thought about the public realm and theories on theatre intersect and converge towards shared models. Along with inquiries that link up the changing conceptions of community to the larger social processes of passage and transformation of ritual into theatre (Turner 1982), or those examining these transformations through the provisional construction of collective contexts characterising and expressing the increasingly performance based operations of the public realm (Schechner 1993), such correspondences can be identified in terms of two powerful models. One focuses on denoting the public as a sphere of collective discussion, deliberation and action by which solidarity is reiterated, a position underlying the thought of Habermas (1990), Weintraub (1997), or Jacobs (1995). The other, discussed in post-modern approaches such as by Certeau (1984), or Joung (1995), emphasises the public as a realm which thrives on and acknowledges diversity and supports co-existence by maintaining grounds for conversation, and communication. Correspondingly, the models of how the collective is established and works in the context of theatre span from the Aristotelian—unifying via pity and fear as cathartic instruments, or the 'conversational'—offering a field of possible connection via the celebration of multiplicity and diversity. For all of these the prime power of the context is seen to lie exclusively with the mediating function of the theatrical work.

In approaches which account of theatre as setting and context of social relations and practices, too, theatre proves a potent tool of inquiry into societal phenomena. Interpretations of theatre as a social institution may follow the Foucauldian strict line—highlighting the social setting and spatial context as a technology in instilling behaviour via control and discipline (Markus 1993, Madge 2007), or focus on the constitutive potential of the social encounter in light of Levinas', or Kleist's critical thought, as pursued in Ridout's analysis (2006). While these perspectives may diverge as to the nature of the processes—consensus, or potential communication, their prime concern is to establish the possibilities embedded in theatre in achieving grounds for collectivity. They present inquiries into the socio-cultural role of the context—theatrical, social, and public—as a realm of corresponding practices that support the constitution and observance of the social/public self.

Yet, the persistence with which theatre would come to be posited as an epitome of the public, would offer grounds to pursue a further line of inquiry, asserting, that the context of practices of 'collective questioning' focused on theatrical work may be productively extended to include also the potential of the performance site as physical space and as a locus of the collective. In this regard, instead of interpretations of representational aspects and correspondences, this current approach to space proposes to address, analytically, its unmediated effects and disclose embodied constructions of affect and practice at the discreet level of the corporeal. This would open up the possibility of involving the spatial as a dimension in understanding the readiness with which theatre comes to be employed metaphorically, as well as paradigmatically, as an epitome of the public. Based on the specificity of this current analysis, it would allow for a glimpse on such notions of the public also through the perspective of lived immediate experience.

There are several ways in which the proposed analytical framework opens up to such suggestion. Construed as mode of organization, theatre emerges as one of the most distinct spatial formations embedding the principal organisational forms of collective social practice. It instates a spatial form of utterly legible and powerful identity and proposes straightforward resources of order. Its overall spatial constitution is governed by the prime principle of centring, through which it tightly corresponds to and enables the collective activities in the context of performance. It is this principle, which consolidates spatial elements and components and crystallizes into a figure easily recognised and reproduced.

In this capacity—as mode of spatial organization this form presents one of the most resilient spatial entities still in use since its origins. It has come to be handed down and incorporated, modified for the diverse purposes in the changing theatre culture, persistently employed for the performance contexts of drama encoded in official productions, experimental studio performances, ritual enactments, through to productions of entertainment and spectacle. All three 'fundamental theatre forms' in the Western tradition—the deep proscenium theatre, the open thrust stage arrangements, the full arena—theatre in the round (Wiles, 2003), would appear to reproduce this same spatial logic of the mode. This logic can be traced within the variety of geometric shapes (horse shoe, box, round and elliptical, square) and sectional formation types (playhouse, amphitheatre and flat). Hence while each particular theatre space in its entirety might come forth as a unique amalgam of effects that are produced in the commingling of features of any one of these theatre forms with the traits of the respective architectural space within which they are actualized, its major principal properties nevertheless reproduce the underlying spatial logic of the theatre mode. Each different space, then, along with its specificities, can be analysed and understood through the operations of this underlying spatial logic.

This mode of spatial organisation, along with its prime structuring principles and generic effects would be legible, and operational in each case: in theatres constructed within a uniform prismatic volume (such as the workshop, studio, laboratory and 'black box'), as well as in those where the relations of stage and auditorium are structured in composite spaces (such as the Italian prototype, its French adaptation, the English variants and the Elizabethan court-based schemes, down to Modernist examples of homogenous convertible arrangements). In all these cases, the principal operation of space with regard to 'performance as presentation' and the processes of encounter with the theatrical work, can be examined in terms of the mode, and their experiential properties—explicated in terms of its specified direct effects generating in non-representational physical space. This analytical framework, then, allows approaching the considerable diversity of theatres in which contemporary performance practices take place, on a level they hold in common. Hence, though theatre spaces emerge within their specific historical time, constructed through and expressive of specific socio-cultural relations and incorporating different principles of theatre production, in terms of their principal spatial constitution they reproduce the generic properties, principles, and relations embedded in the theatre mode of spatial organization.

Yet the implementation of this modality for collective purposes is not confined to theatre: it is employed and adapted to rather different social functions as well. It can be recognized as governing the formulation of a range of analogous sites with diverse appointed functions and operating at various levels of institutionalization—such as lecture rooms, assembly halls, places of worship, courtrooms, leisure and entertainment places, through to open-air urban forms (plazas). It is legible also in the spontaneous instantiations of everyday life that generate collective activity—in the occasions and occurrences such as meetings or the gathering around street performances and other incidences.

All of these varieties and actualisations render this modality of organization not only one of the most clearly formalized, but also as one of the most resilient spatial forms, broadly used, frequented and lived with, for ample duration. The theatre mode, in this way, offers a figure, both mental image and spatial construct—that can be understood as integral to the physical constitution of the collective. It emerges in its capacity to organize, embody and manifest the most intense kinds of social sites—aspects which render its analysis in the spatial terms of experience relevant to the understanding of the operations of these sites as social/public space.

There is still another reason for special interest with this spatial form, which has not been illuminated sufficiently—namely, that this spatial form has proven most enduring—it presents perhaps the oldest spatial form still in use. In its principal morphological features it has remained fairly firm—from its distant origin in ritual practice through to its current presences in the secularised pragmatic city life. It has, as a mode of organization, survived developments in socio-cultural practice—marked by the gradual shift away from ritual to secular content both in the context of theatrical performance, and in the diversification of societal functions and organizations in the broader context of the social/public realm. Yet, as emerges in the works of Turner (1982) and Schechner (1993) certain collective practices and mass events along with theatrical performance itself are still seen as vehicles maintaining elements and functions linked to ritual. In analogy, the site as a physical setting and space, too, may be construed in close corroboration with such practices, and examined for possible traces of these origins. Such analogy would be supported by the very nature of this current analysis, which addresses a layer of experience comprised by non-contemplative discreet processes and embodied practice—a layer which enhances the possibilities of constructing such links.

By highlighting spatial continuities, space would come forth as an actualisation, which might have preserved intact qualities and principles pertinent to such social-ritual purpose in its materiality. Hence analysis of physical space in its origins, might offer in a rudimentary form, clues to a few but fundamental principles embedded by way of the material practices of constructing this spatial formation. Its analysis as lived space might offer clues to such principles in terms of the experiential bearing of its generic conditions. It would help disclose a layer of discreet experience involving the socio-spatial practices of inhabitation—through which such fundamental principles and realities of the social world are grasped and internalized.

This inquiry then would open up for exploration one further subtle, yet also vital dimension and include this into the explanation of aspects pertinent to the socio-cultural role of theatre—a dimension of experience that is explicitly corporeal. Physical space can be seen in its capacity as spatial construct that coheres with and materialises the structuring enabling the highly complex forms of socio-cultural activity actualized in theatre—the encounter with the performance. Yet it is in the bodily ways in which it affects—in terms of the immediate encounter with the ambiguities and complexities embedded in physical space—which vitalize the very principles and structuring instances pertinent to the logic of the experiential modality itself.

Artefact: origins in social practice
Locating the study of this spatial modality in the specific case of theatre is especially revealing, because it is as theatre that this spatial form has been founded. It can be re-traced in its historical emergence linked to its social constitution for and through distinct patterns of collective activity, and acknowledged as an artefact proper—a product of material culture. This opens up an opportunity to construe this spatial form as an original prototype and a model preceding design. By way of taking inquiry to the level of material practices, it offers an insight into the corporeal constructions of physical space through material social practice. This allows construing the possibility that certain principles governing this kind of social organization might have come to be solidified within the mode. This, then would allow arriving at an alternative explanation of its principal generic properties, and disclose

its productive capacities beyond its functions to house the social. Examined as an experiential field, it emerges as a physical framework apt to affect and engender embodied practical knowledge, enable social togetherness, and cultivate sensibilities pertinent to the constitution of the collective—capacities that can be taken to account for the persistent re-production of this spatial form.

Furthermore, it is in the case of theatre where such materializations come forth in their most articulate—expressed in distinct spatial conditions. The analysis of theatre-as-lived-space, then, would help re-construct a stratum of phenomena that pertain to the spatial practices of inhabiting—offering insight into the discreet processes through which such fundamental principles might be internalized. This kind of rendition thus would allow addressing and involving further aspects of socio-spatial reciprocity in explaining the inherent properties of this spatial modality, and help disclose physical space in this concrete spatial form as a means of cultural continuity.

The re-conceptualization of built space in terms of the mode of spatial organization, allows pursuing the affinity which theatre bears with other cultural entities examined in sociological frameworks, and drawing on notions of socio-spatial correspondences at the close-up of material practice. Both as organized collective event, and as structured space for social activity, theatre emerges in its compelling resemblance to other cultural entities—art objects, occasions (festivals), physical structures (houses, religious/ritual sites). Hence it becomes possible to seek analogies with studies of such entities from a sociological perspective, which are examined in terms of the socio-spatial correlations in the context of practices, and as subjects relevant to the understanding of the socio-cultural realm, such as for instance in the work of Bourdieu (1977). Points of comparison can be derived from Sissons's (2007) study on the cases of churches and marae in that these present large spatial entities for social activity depicted with ample spatial detail. Following Bourdieu's foundational work, he studies these structures as entities relevant to the understanding of 'spatial references' in their socio-cultural role. Establishing the theatre mode as an artefact allows drawing propositions from sociological and anthropological perspectives into the account of built architectural space: it can be rendered as to its capacities in constituting and expressing the social in view of 'embodied' socio-spatial reciprocities and material practices.

The theatre mode, then, can be examined as a 'structured space' for collective activity and 'materialization of social relations', and thus as a site where the 'grounds for agency are formed and transformed'. It thus would help identify those principal features of tangible material form in and through which a set of fundamental ideas on collective organization, notions of the nature of social relations and the public and hence values integral to these are 'conceptualized', put to practice and 'mediated'.

However, methodologically, this current approach takes a different path in exploring such socio-spatial correspondences. It deviates from the emphasis assigned to the referential capacities of material elements in space and the interpretative methods associating effects in terms of 'spatial clues'—such as 'post' and 'pillar', which in Sissons's framework are studied in their intricate signifying functions. Instead, it seeks to render correspondence in terms of the spatial modality itself taking form—structured in keeping with the respective patterns of activity, and expressing the situation of the social bodies involved. This offers an opportunity to identify major qualities and properties of space in their 'operational' necessity—as mechanisms and circumstances which support and enable those activities within the spatial economy of the theatre site.

Theatre's legible spatial form and its persistent re-production in subsequent modifications is more fully understood when set within its origins in socio-spatial practices: it comes about in the process of conjoining two vital social traditions. As established in historical evidence, such as in Sienkewicz's (1991) study of the genesis of urban life and forms, the first permanent theatre sites are formed by blending the setting of gathering in the oral tradition with that which enables the presentation of religious ritual to public observation. Theatre as physical space, then, can be acknowledged as having evolved not only for a particular social function, but also through socio-spatial practices. It is a spatial form that has been actualized, tested and refined in collective endeavour—a thoroughly physical expression (as distinct from symbolic signification) and entirely social material product—a great artefact proper.

Considered within the very processes of its formation, the physical constitution of this spatial entity can be accounted for in terms of spatial practices both in terms of the activity pattern, and at the level of the body. Hence what gradually solidifies within this spatial form can be construed as entailing and expressing the almost spontaneous efficacy of corporeal correspondences: material space expresses and actualizes the specificities of directional bodies at work in this pattern of collective activity. It formulates the very physical pre-conditions—alignment, adjacency, proximity and orientation necessitated by the functional purpose, establishing correlations with utmost practical precision and in this way enabling collaboration for this context and activity. The principles of structuring and ordering that are brought about through this pattern, materialize in few but powerful physical features: the regular and uniform compact organization, the orientation of social bodies around and towards a distinct core. While these first actualizations would vary in view of the extent of their constructedness—some merely utilizing naturally curved slopes, others achieving this amphitheatrical arrangement by shaping banked seating rows in semblance, these sites are nevertheless already set up in terms of and through these practices. The spatial form has come to incorporate these principal properties as intrinsic conditions, and potently imminent possibilities.

As a social site this spatial form is founded within its larger surrounds by way of differentiation (such as expressed in the density of occupied space), and exclusion (bodies turned/averted towards an inside). In this it actualises the condition of isolation in its aptitude to delimit and define. It assumes its characteristic, frequently concentric structure and arrangement around its core—relying on the circumstance of exposure in its aptitude to present and relate. In this way the spatial form is established also as a place of destination, and becomes expressive of its gravitational power. It invites growth and accretion without losing its principal formal and structured character—i.e., it works also through the aptitude of collective containment to assimilate, accommodate, and organize.

While in its constructedness through and for social practice the theatre-artefact is akin to a communal site, there are also important distinctions that need to be acknowledged. Hence a conventional 'communal site' proper would be seen to work as a 'specified social field' which expresses the shared values and 'collective consciousness' of a particular formulated group (Sissons 2007). In this way such a site would highlight correspondences that are both tightly adjusted to the specific community in terms of the rules and relations established by and for the respective formulated group, and are also corroborated—allowing spatial expression to follow a continuous cycle or sequential development in keeping with these specifics.

In contrast the theatre site has been constructed by diverse communal groups, actualised as practice at a different scale of collaboration, and would therefore entail and express not specifics of a communal group, but the special preconditions for such collaboration. The theatre-artefact would differ quite radically in terms of its scale and role and consequently, the nature of its socio-cultural influence and in these respects presents a physical entity of special status. In contrast to a conventional communal site, theatre materializes a social site that works as a unifying entity at the scale of the city. As material space it embeds a distinct form, blending the structures of artistic, social and ritual practices. It is formed as a place that incorporates and enables the observing of the religious Dionysian cults, the secular drama, festivals and other public occasions and events. Hence, as Sienkewicz (1991: 182-202) puts forth, it occupies, symbolically as well as physically (location), the intersection between different realms of the tripartite polis: the sacred (acropolis), the mundane (agora) and the collective (theatre).

Theatre-as-physical-space would need to be seen in its capacity to actualize and promote the constitution of practices, values and understandings which pertain to the *communal per se*. It belongs to the modes of constructing and nourishing cross-communal togetherness. What could be derived by analysis of the concrete spatial circumstances of the theatre mode, then, would concern the affective experiential charge of these principal features. Such analysis would be disclosing certain essential preconditions that enable the coexistence and collaboration of members of diverse groups or communities—conditions which are relevant to the understanding of principles in the cultural tradition of cross-communal togetherness.

In this regard, acknowledging the possible embeddedness of ritual components in its principal circumstances would help bring forth space in terms of a rather suggestive charge. This would allow pursuing certain implications, which surface in studies where theatre and ritual are more explicitly linked: in terms of liminal states (Turner), fear components accompanying performance events (Schechner), as well as the interruptive potential of festival (Agamben). The current analysis would allow extending on the corporeal terms in which analogous states might come to be induced—by circumstances of a distinctly spatial nature. Special attention in the analysis of space-as-lived would be allotted to possibilities and conditions that provide a path of direct encounter with and immersion of the self (ego) into something larger.

In pursuing links with ritual components, this current perspective relies on two further frameworks addressing the ritual context in its primary functions. In Nietzsche's (1968: 1-144) interpretation of rite (Dionysian art), the impulse to immerse would be construed as enchanting and, and, by allowing to 'let go', help blend with that which exceeds man. In keeping with Mauss's (2002) analysis of ritual a further expectation as to the experiential charge of space concerns its capacities to support and engender those mechanisms, which establish its social and socializing power in practice and act. He elucidates the social repercussions of ritual in terms the following aspects: the actualization and formation of collectivity as it evolves together with the formation of awareness of responsibility and participation in it, the nature of collective states where consciousness is absorbed by togetherness, as well as the generation of collective forces.

Conceived in these terms, the workings of ritual and rite would come temptingly close to the principal conditions of experience in general, and the aesthetic in particular, such as brought forth in the frameworks of Gadamer, Agamben, and Deleuze noted above. Yet such conditions, when taken within the context of the experience of the aesthetic would activate acquisition, while within a rite, they are oriented towards the attainment and affirmation of a collectivity. Acknowledging the ritual root in the origins of the theatre mode would entail the assertion that aspects of the intriguing and productive states issuing in ritual practice and rite, are both commenced and recuperated by these same circumstances pertinent to the site.

Lived space: a constituent of self and the collective
This detour into the origins of the spatial form helps ascertain its pertinence to social and ritual practice. This offers an additional aspect in explicating its experiential charge and understanding its role as enduring model, handed down and incorporated not only for the context of theatrical performance, but also in a range of analogous collective spaces of diverse appointed functions. Thus inquiry in terms of the mode of spatial organisation comes to highlight resemblances among differing actualizations as socio-cultural continuities, and articulates

physical space as a means of sustaining these. This perspective bears potential both in that it allows concretizing less-charted aspects of socio-spatial reciprocities in the constitution of these collective sites, and in that it discloses these sites through their shared physical and social qualities, and affective charge. Re-traced in its social origins—a model preceding design, this spatial form can be examined as an arte-fact that is produced for and through material social practices. It al-lows construing space as it embeds and solidifies certain fundamental principles pertinent to the collective. It emerges as a material presence imbued with experiential charge—social, ritual and aesthetic. Its anal-ysis in terms of immediate experience as lived space, then, would allow deriving such principles from within their spatial expressions as experiential conditions, along with the stratum of discreet processes through which such principles might be grasped.

Theatre emerges as a structured spatial form, with capacities to reproduce the conditions embedding conjointly the social, the ritualis-tic, and the aesthetic. An analysis of physical space would offer a fur-ther dimension in understanding its capacities to mobilise that layer of experience evolving due to space. It would offer grounds to acknowledge immediate experience as a vital layer in the operations of theatre as socio-cultural context—cultivating the self and the col-lective, enabling coexistence and collaboration, and nourishing the cultural tradition of cross-communal togetherness.

The generative potential of the corporeal: emerging spatial forms as forms of emergence

Theatre presents a concrete case which is both challenging and inter-esting for analysis in terms of experience. It materialises one of the most distinct and monolithic spatial entities, proposing a powerful utterly legible identity and straightforward resources of order. Gov-erned by the prime principle of centring, it is structured by, corre-sponds to, and enables the collective activities in the context of the performance event. This principle consolidates all spatial elements and components, through which the theatre mode crystallises into a spatial figure easily recognised and reproduced. However, when ex-amined within and in further detail, it emerges as a deeply ambiguous and intense experiential field, charged with controversial forces and impulses.

Each of the generic conditions—isolation, exposure and collective containment—partake in the constitution of the overall operations of the spatial form, enhancing the processes and relations intrinsic to the unfolding of the performance by way of their specified effects. Yet within, they also contradict each other, undermine the univocal bearing of the overall effects and diversify the experiential charge of physical space. Each of these conditions emerges into and out of distinctiveness by way of composing and re-composing spatial elements and features in particular ways. While distinct, each renders tangible certain special aspects of spatial circumstance, activates specific internal mechanisms, and in this way triggers different experiential bearing. It is through the intricacies within, and the corroboration of these conditions—i.e., through their capacity in bringing forth both the actual and the possible, whereby this spatial modality works: a qualified affective and controversial matter which invites exploration and entails active appropriation. As physical space theatre vitalises the possibilities of direct bodily engagement and reverberation, suggesting relations, invoking dispositions, inducing feelings, and summoning latent abilities. Surrounding, material and concrete, physical space brings the specifics of situatedness in this context, into explicit phenomenal presence. It mobilises those alternative paths of knowing and becoming that evolve in entirely corporeal terms. As experiential bearing these concern the sense of self, of belonging and participation, of the complexities of membership, the grasp of a notion of what it takes and what it means to partake in that larger reality—space supports the processes of attaining the intuition over certain essential principles underlying and enabling this form of social assembly.

Methodologically, this analysis into concrete physical space from the perspective of the bodily and immediately experiential does open up possibilities to further understanding of built architectural space. The proposed concepts—isolation, exposure and collective containment, employed as analytical tools in their dual functions as spatial terms and as conditions, link up spatial circumstance with experiential contents. Hence this approach allows examining the very formulation of spatial effects at multiple levels, and addressing their corporeal constructions as distinct experiential possibilities. It allows probing into their experiential charge and tracing the productive passage from spatial condition to sense and sensibility—i.e., it proposes but one particular means to attend to discreet immediate experience in its corporeal mode of generation, along with the affective and cognitive registers of consciousness this entails.

Isolation
<u>Conceptual implications</u>
Isolation as a spatial term is taken to confer the requisite condition of the performance event with respect to the general flow of life. In this regard, it is acknowledged as part of the functions of the theatre building, marking the separation of the theatrical from the everyday by 'framing' the prime activity (presentation/perception) in certain ways, transforming actions from 'unmarked' to 'marked', and in this way eliciting corresponding behaviours (McAuley, 1999, 39). However, in this current approach, isolation is construed in rather different capacities. It is posited as a term which exceeds its connotations of a demarcation of the event. Taken beyond the notion of margin, it comes to include the definition of the site as distinct from an outside, while at the same time instituting, within, essential and experientially consequential conditions for all participants, which are legible both among the groups, and as relations among individuals with respect to each other.

As a concept, isolation describes the condition of being set apart, placed alone, separated and distinct from others. With reference to its etymological roots (*isle*—a piece of land within sea), isolation also signifies this condition through the principal means by which it is accomplished: it denotes the state of 'being (al)one' while simultaneously being aware of the larger surrounds. This would suggest a particular way of occupying space—namely, within the perception of a special sort of correlation to something else. In this sense—being set within a different medium—isolation becomes effective only in a more extensive context. Distinction is achieved and maintained by means of a threshold around that which is isolated. Isolation, then, indicates the circumstance of being surrounded, hence bounded, and detached from anything else: it can be construed as a condition instigating a sense of centring.

<u>Corporeal constructions</u>
As one of the conditions that generate within the very actualization of the theatre mode, isolation articulates the capacities of the mode to define the entire site as an entity with respect to its larger physical

context. This requisite condition becomes expressed in a special way: it involves the perception of the medium in which the site is set, and relies on its depiction through a negative correlation with this medium. One feature, by which this definition is achieved, is its enclosure that differentiates by way of delimiting the site, allowing it to be recognized as a distinct entity and occurrence. In built space, the sense of disconnecting from an outside is rendered tangible in the special treatment of the transitions and thresholds around its core—where deep doorways, curtains, and void as distance emphasise the crossing towards the inside. Yet this sense of detachment is frequently enhanced in the passage through a number of spaces (foyers, couloirs and backstage) that circumscribe the core (comprised by stage and auditorium). While originally such spatial organization aims at the appropriate functional relations among main and supporting spaces in the operation of the theatre building, in terms of experience it actually facilitates the gradual construction of the sense of the condition of isolation, through which the process of disconnection acquires an almost ritualistic quality.

While for the different groups partaking in the event this particular experiential sequence evolves in dissimilar ways, the very processes of detachment from an outside do characterise the experience of all parties involved. For the performer, isolation from everyday life is achieved by way of an approach through tightly inter-woven, densely organised utility spaces. Yet the backstage, comprised by the informal and secluded spaces of preparation (rehearsal, make-up, storage and technical equipment and maintenance) not only acts as a complex boundary, but comes to contain in its own terms. This way the backstage space procures the isolation of the stage, and enhances the effect of segregation from the actual performance area. Access to the stage comes to actualise an instance of rupture in experience—a trespass into the highly formalised spaces of the stage and auditorium. Construed in terms of the mechanisms of isolation, the stage begins to act as an autonomous hinge, a focal area distinct from both the backstage and the auditorium. Decisively disconnected from backstage, it assumes the status of a destination, a centre. The isolation of the stage from the auditorium, is subtly but instantly established through the distance in-between and the special spatial arrangement of each of these spatial components, but is also subject to refinement and articulation in other ways, such as through the proscenium arch or the curtain, as well as the spacing of an orchestra pit.

In the case of the participant, too, isolation initiates as much as frames the experience of the actual performance. On arrival, the participant also traverses a sequence of spaces that augment the disconnection, and seal off the performance from the outside—such as the lobby that receives and mediates procession to the core space. While all of these spatial components contain various socialising episodes as constituents of the 'social function' of theatre (McAuley, 1999, 40-44), and formalise the occasional and at times ceremonial character of the event, they also verify the transition towards a different realm. Following this sequence, the approach to that different realm culminates in the arrival in the auditorium. Hence, in contrast to the unobstructed lobby and directional urge of the corridors, the auditorium, too, comes to be experienced as a destination. In built space this quality is tangibly articulate: the auditorium is instated as an entirely encapsulated space, decisively centred on the stage and characterised by a frequently fixed order. Yet the sense of isolation and its correlates of centring and arrival is supported even at less elaborate sites, where the formation of the performance event, too, depends on the exclusion of an outside. The sense of detachment simply derives from focusing on a centre within—where spectators avert from a larger context to surround the performance act, and the provisional stage takes the form of a void.

Along with the boundaries and elements that emphasise demarcations and thresholds—both material and as spacing, a further spatial means in constructing this condition is orientation. It not only instates the presence of a core, but at the same time also articulates the motion towards that centre: it mobilizes the dynamic impetus of focusing, which comes to characterise the operation of this spatial modality as a whole and throughout. This spatial mechanism applies even to events that are 'open' organizations (such as processions), or those that emerge spontaneously (such as street performances).

In the context of the condition of isolation these spatial elements and mechanisms help articulate how the site attains the quality of a place of destination: stable in its reliance on a single spatial principle, sedimentary in its nature, and protected—qualities which contribute to the feeling of embeddedness, rootedness, as well as to that of belonging to an entity that is distinct.

While less univocal and palpable within, the spatial circum-stance of isolation figures in the divisions between spatial components (stage-auditorium), which take the form of elements that both distin-guish and connect (such as the proscenium arch), as well as the dis-tance that takes the form of a more or less explicit void. Yet, however subtly, isolation becomes effective also at the very minute scale with respect to individual participants, where discreet means of segregation are at work: the balconies, the box-like lodges, the small-scale ele-ments like steps and railings, down to the specific seats assigned to each participant, which further the sense of isolation by dispersing. In that respect even orientation works as a mechanism of dispersal, felt in the regular ordered positioning where alignment and orientation of bodies towards a common external point of attention, would counter-act apparent physical proximity and prevent direct contact among neighbouring others.

Isolation as a form of experience
The experience of this condition, then, derives from the sense of boundedness which facilitates a temporary detachment from other possible occurrences. It also disconnects, invoking the sense of being apart and distinct. However, unlike its effects in other contexts, where isolation might connote seclusion from the other as for instance the privacy and protection actualized in a hospital, or severs correlations as through the restrictive means in a prison, in the context of this so-cial assembly the discernment of one's own position is inherently dependent on the apprehension of others. It actualizes as the move-ment away from the other and towards that inward centre.

It can be perceived how this condition would trigger an aware-ness of one's situation and self as an affective process, which is both alerting and, in a way, self-contained. In this regard the experience of the condition of isolation—i.e., of being held fixed in space, as well as short of relation, mobilizes two internal mechanisms both of which stimulate the processes of concentration: it invokes a centring, and enables absorption in the immediate instant. This allows construing how concentration as focused attention would comprise more than involvement with the presented work. In terms of the corporeal expe-rience of the condition of isolation, this state can be construed as one of suspense—in which one might become aware of being decisively located among others, while also being self-absorbed—held short of a relation. Hence it is a condition apt to trigger an intense state of being, and perhaps even awareness of that, and in this way prepares the possibility of actualizing total presence.

In terms of the condition as experiential instance these internal experiential mechanisms can be understood as setting off a process of accumulation, which works as a re-activation of that which is centred. Yet precisely thus this form of experience is revealed to be not quite as straightforward. The process of self-awareness as activated self-containment can be construed as one which, unexpectedly and paradoxically also prepares the grounds for de-stabilization: it emerges as a crucial pre-condition of the possibility of departing from the 'habitual' and moving towards more intensified states. Hence isolation as a structural instance of experience augments the possibility of change to come forth as a more resolute outgrowing of the self. Hence it would involve a series of mechanisms, through which, in addition to the engagement with the self, other engagements can be contrived and anticipated. While the sense over the condition of isolation would lead to a consciousness of being a separate entity, it is also a condition that can be construed as it becomes conductive of awareness of further aspects of the self. It would help ground acceptance and involvement with the roles presupposed by the site, entailing both the performance activity and the social assembly. Yet it would also aid the grasp and embodiment of essential aspects of membership, and contain the grains of bond relationships. This subtle ambiguity of isolation as form of experience, which derives from the perception of one's own position and relies on the apprehension of and negative differentiation from others, then, is both augmented, and countered and undermined by the workings of the other principal condition of the site—exposure. Their controversial effects gain dynamic impetus in that exposure relies on the same principal features, yet reconfigures these towards quite different effects.

Exposure
Conceptual implications versus scopic conventions

In conventional use, *exposure* is employed as a spatial term firmly attached to the condition of a performer, an act of presenting something to an audience, and, by extension—the space of the stage. The fact that theatre provides the principal setting for one of its meanings, namely 'frequent appearance before the public', prompts its use within the limits of this appointed sense, and supports the preconception that exposure exclusively applies to the situation of the performer. As presentation relies on placing that-which-is-performed in a way that facilitates its observation by a large number of onlookers, exposure is broadly taken to describe the situatedness of the stage with regards to the auditorium, and account for the spatial circumstance of openness as lack of obstruction and visibility.

It comes to be used in the sense of an experientially consequential condition only as linked to the experience of the performer in the phenomenon of 'stage fright', such as brought forth in the studies of Aaron (1986) and Ridout (2006). In Aaron's (1986) psychoanalytical approach this state is connected with the major effect of exposure in that the actor performs 'standing alone in front of a thousand of strangers' (65)—i.e., in terms of the explicit circumstance of visibility on stage. This is to say that the capacity of exposure to affect is recognized in that it enhances the actor's fear of unmasking—of the audience seeing 'something it is not supposed to see, namely, his fear' (59). Such effects of exposure are fore-grounded by the mental strain over the role that the actor assumes, and interpreted with reference to the performative act. Examined in terms of the distinctions between 'signal' and 'traumatic' anxiety, the emotive impact of stage fright is associated more tightly with the latter. This points to the psychic origins of its destructive effects in the inner suppression of defence mechanisms, and assigns the circumstance of exposure the status of but one of various factors that enhance this notorious state.

In Ridout's exploration (2006: 35-69), the phenomenon of stage fright is rendered as the anxiety integral to the profession of the actor, which has come to be characterized by tough competitiveness, and explicated with reference to certain exploitative technologies of the theatre industry. Reflecting the general socio-cultural conditions of modernity that blur the distinctions amongst realms of existence and purport radical individualism in the practicing of 'privacy in public', these modern theatrical technologies entail a special expectation which enhances the anxiety of the performer: that in order to 'move' entertainment consumers, the art of acting would rely on and make use of the performer's private experiences.

While beyond visibility spatial aspects are not a central issue in these accounts of stage fright, they do provide grounds to infer certain links between circumstances and symptoms of the condition of exposure. Extensive documentary material is made available especially in the former source, while the latter links up with a range of social perspectives on encounter, such as Levinas', shedding light also on its social implications.

For this current analysis, in contrast, it is the condition of exposure that is conceived to trigger such states of anxiety in the first place. Furthermore, the condition of exposure is not confined to the tight correlation with the stage but is construed and rendered as a as a property generic to the theatre mode and a prolific and utterly affective condition characterizing the entire site. Its operations are diverse and explicated in terms of various spatial and internal mechanisms, which allows rendering its deeply disturbing bearings consequential for all participants involved.

Similarly to isolation, exposure presents a potent concept for the present inquiry, in its aptness to designate distinct conditions of a spatial nature, and reveal these in terms of experiential connotations and emotive charge. Like isolation, exposure as a concept denotes a distinct way of occupying space and comes to signify this condition in terms of the principal means and the specific spatial mechanisms, through which it is achieved. It, moreover, characterizes a way of being in space, namely, within the acute perception of a correlation to something else.

Along with these, and even with regard to its most straightforward meanings, exposure also qualifies this 'way of being' as a condition not entirely innocuous, where uncertainty or even risk as fear-related ingredients, inevitably intertwine. Hence while it is taken to describe a location with regard to some major powers (the elements, forces and onlookers/observers), it comes to suggest a possibly harmful influence. When it designates a situation that 'allows one to be seen', it implies that this situation is enforced in a way so as to 'exhibit' and 'display'—subject to a gaze.

Yet, the kind of accessibility conveyed by the term also goes way beyond visibility: it implicates operations through more profoundly physical, as well as more deeply affective mechanisms. This suggests that it would be essentially the feeling of being prone to some special manipulation through space, and under the effects of relations of a certain kind, which would account for its 'uncanny' charges. Exposure entails a 'laying open' that is carried out in such a way as to invoke submission, stirring up a sense of 'being in an unprotected place', a potential 'subject to influence or action', hazardously disclosed and palpably bare. It imparts a sense of lack of all sorts: lack of obstruction, of protection, or defence. This sense of lack then builds up to the extent of insinuating the possibility of intrusion: inspection, judgment, ridicule, attack. It in this way renders vulnerable with regard to something in excess, overwhelming, or unpredictable.

Further reference to the constitution of the word, especially the pre-fix *ex-* and the word *pose,* help detect some more intricate implications, which translate into physical terms as dynamic impulses or shifts, and are, moreover, paired with compulsion. The prefix *ex-* itself upholds two suggestions: in the sense of 'without' it denotes stasis, while in the sense of 'out of' and 'free of', it indicates motion—direction away from, and change with respect to a condition previously held. In turn, *pose* as 'placement' conveys constraint in that one is being firmly situated within specific circumstances and relations. Thus in the 'presenting of one to another', exposure is actualized as a putting forth and out of position. Pertaining to both a placement (being kept, held, at rest, arrested), and a displacement (a forceful alteration of a former, accustomed, protected circumstance), exposure can be conceived as a physical condition essentially ambivalent, and hence labile.

Exposure bears still more deeply affective ambiguities that point to apprehension, and even components of fear ingrained in the experience of this condition, throughout. This is so because the 'presenting of one to the other' in this modality of spatial organisation does not implicate any direction. The assertion that this spatial form actually ensures a 'reverse' presentation to someone occupying the focal point, can be supported by calling to mind how persistently theatre has been employed as a figure of the knowledge presented to the mind, receiving its physical expression in the memory theatre of Giulio Camillo (Yates, 1969: 135-174). Thus, while in special cases the relations between the parties might be controlled, the spatial situation of exposure itself does not hold any 'direction' appointing 'the exposed': the 'presenting' in question is bound to turn out inevitably, and decisively reciprocal. The repercussions of exposure, then, lie in that it collapses distinctions between observer and observed, intruder and intruded, active and passive. It subjects participants in that relation to the possibility of a perpetual, and haphazard oscillation between two polar opposites—two experientially inverse conditions.

As this sense appears to build up primarily on the distinction of the location of the 'exposed' with respect to its immediate environs, it becomes apparent that it would be possible to instigate the sense of 'being exposed' even without a 'visible' counterpart. Such distinction, explicitly executed, would suffice to invoke an 'other' to which a particular location appears in correlation. This comes to articulate certain 'internal' mechanisms at work, such as the liability of conflating perception with apprehension. Exposure exerts its most vicious aspects under circumstances that impair control, or vision: circumstances of expanse of space, blurring, concealing, or manipulation of light that is blinding either in its brightness, or in its absence. In relation to this latter circumstance it is possible to perceive aspects of the sense of exposure ingrained in the experience of darkness, though with regard to vision they appear as contrary circumstances. Ultimately it is precisely thus: by insinuating something that is felt-but-unknown, exposure subjects to a dual deprivation—that of perceiving an actual relation, and that of conceiving of a meaningful response.

<u>Corporeal constructions</u>
By marking the essential distinctions between the circumstance of 'being visible' and the conditions of 'being exposed', the conceptualization of exposure has helped re-constructed exposure as an analytical tool which renders explicit the most prolific and deeply controversial effects of the theatre mode with respect to immediate experience. It attains the capacity to reveal a set of inherent and disconcerting ambiguities which span the whole site, and come to qualify the minute situations of all participants involved. Exposure is 'sensed', viscerally felt, constructed through properties of physical space that are also tactile, even haptic in nature, and proceeds, as much, through and in terms of the body. This allows anticipating that not only the bodies of performers, but also those of members of the audience would assume an alerted and active status, registering the specifics of their circumstances, and acknowledging their condition.

This rendition of the theatre mode opens up the opportunity to complement interpretations conferring a variety of experiential characteristics pertinent to the theatrical situation (communication of theatrical meanings, intensity of performer-audience relation and complicity) with one that augments reverberations among spatial circumstances, experiential components, and structures of fear. 'Dramatized' through exposure, the site emerges as an engaging material substance charged with and operating through dynamic impulses and tensions. The feel of being prone to some special manipulation through space and under the effects of intense relations, is made palpable, inscribed in architectural form at various levels: engendered through the dynamics borne in the spatial constitution of stage and auditorium, through the constriction of emplacement, through the subjection to, at times unexpected, encounter, all building up to its destabilizing and even artfully disconcerting—'uncanny' effects.

In spite of the fact that exposure is spatially constructed relying on the same principal features effective in the constitution of the condition of isolation, it emerges to phenomenal presence in terms of a set of specific and rather dynamic mechanisms, and articulates tension and polarization. Hence for instance at the level of the site-event correlation, the mechanism of focusing on the place of action is already actualized as the condition of isolation in that the site, and the space of the stage are defined and delimited. However, the impetus of focusing is both enhanced and diversified in the operations and circumstances special to exposure through which it articulates the spatial mechanisms facilitating the conditions of the presentation. These special manipulations entail the animating mechanisms of putting forth and out of position, both spatially and perceptually, and become instrumental to the construction of exposure as a condition.

The prime place for such articulation in built form is the stage, and its effects can be understood in terms of the spatial operations of exposure. Hence the stage is not only set apart from its surrounds (isolation), but is also forcefully augmented in ways that set in motion spatial forces and animate the space throughout. It is presented dynamically, put forth as an active pole—by way of extending its physical space and enlarging its field of influence. When it is instated as a node that configures the rows of seats in tight correlation, it is forces of attraction that are being rendered in physical form. These effects are perceivable even when the stage is set within spaces with flat floor (a staging form frequently employed in smaller scale studio theatres with less equipment). They become most express in the case of the full arena type surrounded by seating, where the scene acts as the physical and geometrical centre of such forces, and appears univocally amplified, and the whole site works devoid of conflicting forces.

Even the simplest means of sectional distinction of the stage regarding the auditorium enhance the sense of exposure by producing specific dynamic impact. The articulation of the stage through a sinking move that would submit the stage to observation, then, dynamically enhances the principal focusing dynamics, and achieves tactile rendition of centripetal forces especially when conjoined with amphitheatrical sectional treatment of the auditorium. In contrast, the cases where the stage is disclosed by an elevating push, and imbued with the power to impress the act into space as an emitting pole, the principal 'gravitational' dynamic of the theatre mode (focusing), is rendered controversial in that both impulses are maintained explicitly in physical space.

The proscenium theatre form, too, presents a special case of mobilizing ambiguous spatial conditions. In theatre practice, as Wiles observes, this theatre form that has been rejected as outmoded, is recently being rediscovered as the most 'theatrical' space available, in that it resists transformation of the performance into mere spectacle, and also in that the frame itself offers a tool to 'problematize' relations between viewing and viewed (2003: 238). Yet there are also dynamic aspects of this form that amplify its affective operations at the level of the corporeal. The circumstance that the box stage offers only one interface with the auditorium and in this way would restrict certain aspects of exposure is enhanced also by the decisive separation instated by the proscenium arch. However this tendency of partially secluding and embedding is also counteracted: this spatial construction of the stage actualizes it as an absorbing void, a funnel coaching attention that is, moreover, framed.

In contrast the actualizations of the thrust stage make exposure palpable through the forces of a launching motion forward towards the auditorium as a vigorous intrusion into it. Another set of means in altering the dynamic impact of the stage concerns the formal and sectional constitution of the stage itself. Thus for instance the raked or modular thrust stage would tend to generate a dynamic impetus akin to that of an amphitheatre, but is mobilized in a counter motion, and, working in the opposite direction, shifts and compresses space towards the auditorium.

Such rendition can be extended to involve in more detail various possible modifications of these principal forms and point to their specific effects: such as for instance the effect of an apron stage that projects forward and re-asserts it also as a node within the auditorium, while an orchestra pit—a spatial interruption—would emphasize the singling out as a means of presenting on the stage. Nevertheless, even limited to such principal cases, this perspective not only explicates the role of space in constituting 'performance as presentation' through various mechanisms and specified effects of exposure. It also allows recognizing the essentially animating impact of these mechanisms throughout, charging space and mediating the sense of tension between actual situatedness and experienced volatility.

However, these spatial constructions are not reserved solely for the purpose of 'presenting' an act on stage. Formulations of the auditorium are, as much, specific actualizations of the mechanisms and circumstances of exposure, and as such do amplify its affective operations, along with enhancing the dynamic character of the site. In this, more intricate means of destabilization and ambiguity are formulated, spatial uncertainty is constructed, rendering the overall effects of the mode controversial, and augmenting the tensions between decisive placement and the sense of being subject to special spatial manipulation.

Even a simple straight row flat floor face-to-face arrangement actually ensures that the auditorium confronts the stage and is analogously displayed. In terms of configuration of the rows of seats, the cases where the auditorium converges towards the place of action becomes experientially effective in that it univocally expresses the power of attraction and gravitation of the centre. In the arena stage form, this configuration makes tangible the very force of focusing, while in the case of a thrust stage it marks the confrontation palpable by counteracting the force of convergence with the horizontal impact of the thrust stage. A different set of forces is mobilized through sectional treatment: in cases where the auditorium is manifestly presented by way of a steep incline, by the jutting out of the balconies (as frequently employed in contemporary theatres), or through the vertical drive of tiers (gallery or box systems). The uprooting momentum of these spatial forms is, then, enforced by the sweep of the tout confinement of a boundary that presses in. The effects of these spatial constructions interact, or interfere with the effects of different configurations, mediating the sense of exposure as a physically ambivalent condition.

Furthermore, the affective nature of circumstances of exposure derives from the fact that its principles are executed in strict geometrical discipline: legible, frequently primary form, axial alignment and symmetry. In this, adjusting the spatial components in tight, formatted interdependence emerges as one explicit physical manifestation of the compulsory traits of exposure. These help explicate the peculiar intensity, with which the principal relations—those between performers on stage and participants in the auditorium, are perceived. Hence while the case of the full thrust stage set within the playhouse type is seen to materialize these relations at their most 'direct' (Mackintosh, 1993, 9-25), the affective power of this spatial form can be understood in that it also is paradigmatic of exposure between the two parties involved.

Among these manifold actualizations, the amphitheatre—evocative of the austere space of the steep and confined hemicycle of the Ancient Greek model, would come forth as paradigmatic of the more controversial and ambiguous aspects of exposure. There several of its mechanisms operate with acute precision and economy through the curved slope, which sets the semi-circular or polygonal seating, but also forms and almost encloses the space. Yet, while this spatial formation marks the stage in the vortex of focusing forces, the amphitheatrical fan-like spread around it embodies the decisive reciprocity of exposure. Furthermore, in augmenting spatial continuity with the stage and within the auditorium, amphitheatrical configurations enforce awareness of all participants involved in the situation, and undermine the possibility of safe repose or detachment—it spatially compels to engagement.

Strictly configured through the circumstances of exposure, the relations between performers and audience, along with their appointed purpose to increase attention to the action on stage, have the effect of charging the 'in between' and experientially contracting space. They not only consolidate the uprooting effects of the site, but are also resolutely reciprocal. Thus in the operations of exposure at the site, along with its more obvious effects, one can conceive of the actualization of those rather intricate and profuse conditions implicated in the concept that trigger disquieting, unsettling, even alarming effects. It bears on a fundamentally unstable and ambiguous stature, such as that one is an observer and observed at the same time.

This sense becomes still more complex, as exposure operates also within the two distinct spatial components, diversifying the contingent relations among the two groups of participants with still another set of relations among and within these groups. For a performer, accustomed to relations among fellow performers within the space of the scene, such dual stature would appear as but one dimension of his condition, a part of the craft. Yet, paradoxically, for a participant in the auditorium such ambiguity might surface quite unexpectedly.

That the members of the audience, too, actually tend to rely on preconceptions associating exposure as a circumstance of the performer, emerges in that the fact of 'being observed' would be reported by participants as cause of distinct discomfort (Bennett 1990: 97). This discomfort is triggered not only in being observed by fellow members of the audience, but applies also to case where undue contact is made through a gaze, gesture or direct address, as utilized in certain performance strategies (Purcell 2005). While the experience of the condition of exposure is a shared condition for both parties, there are differences as to the awareness of this. For the actor, bound to occupy the vortex of its major spatial mechanisms and forces, exposure would underlie and account for the intensity of the notorious state of stage fright. Yet for the participant in the auditorium, this condition is actualized at its most dubious. Its disconcerting momentum is partially concealed, due to the foreground circumstances such the ensuring view-hence-power-over the event, the side-by-side alignment with fellow participants, the stability of the seat down to its backrest. These would account for the subdued form of emergence to phenomenal presence—or its delayed recognition in encounter. In this respect it is interesting to note the resemblance, between the 'framing' operations of the proscenium arch, and the frame of the deep box or loggia space as actualised in the Italian model, where the framing, in both cases, does render the sense of safe embeddedness in a protected pocket of space, disconcertingly ambiguous.

The sense of exposure is more apt to surface to awareness under the workings of rather explicit circumstances, or manipulations that undermine apparent accommodation in space, such as when participants are set within a steeper slope, perched on edge, less protected, laid open to the influence of subtle but turbulent spatial forces and impulses, and in constant awareness of others. Exposure actualizes with special intensity in cases where the stage is inserted into the field of the spectators (horse shoe, theatre-in-the-round), through which the conventional set of relations (participant-performer) is diversified and comes to involve the direct relations among participants with analogous intensity. Furthermore, these configurations dramatically enhance the sense of exposure for the participants in the audience, by decisively placing them as a background to adjacent action on stage— a situation which renders them strikingly liable, prone to observation in the very same way as the performer. Finding oneself placed as part of the action on stage turns out as a disconcerting discovery, as would any construction of direct relations beyond established codes and conventions by means of reversing and displacements, strategies frequently underlying experimental performance practices.

<u>Exposure as a form of experience</u>
With respect to a singular agent, exposure enhances the mechanisms of focusing and centring, magnifying the effects of isolation as to the awareness of oneself. Yet in contrast to the context of isolation, where the sense of being singled-out-from something else works in favour of stability and actualises detachment and self-contained re-activation, under the circumstances of exposure the sense of self becomes rather vigorous and animated. The agent is not only activated by being thrust forth, but compelled to assume an active status, as the experience of exposure takes form in terms of acute polarization. Bearing manifold implications and mechanisms, the condition of exposure triggers the discord amongst acute discernment of one's situation and self reverberating with the disconcerting effects of the mechanisms of presenting, and an utterly active and outward orientation actualizing its relational impetus. The sense of polarity and tension is engendered at various levels, such as through the conflict between being immersed in the midst of diverse spatial forces and mechanisms with their dislodging effects, yet also being firmly emplaced. The sense of tension and apprehension generates from within the spatial circumstances that linger between the comfortable and disconcerting, the reassuring and unnerving.

Exposure as a condition builds up and thrives on the affective charge of apprehension at the verge of anxiety. It alerts and mobilizes. For the actor on stage this transforms into the 'elated states' underlying the vigour of artistic performance (Aaron 1986: 125). Analogously, exposure would present the productive force to propel participants out of repose, and out of the habitual that would preclude the possibility for genuine experience, and render them essentially open to engage and go through change in the course of the event, so as to become as much producers as products of the experience in question.

Exposure is a form of experience where the acute sense of self derives from minute critical or crisis conditions. It is rooted, as much, in the bodily sense of becoming an object of intense inspection, while engaged in the act of observation. Hence the condition renders explicit the collapse of the distinctions among observer and observed, among active and passive, among and subverted and intervening. It insinuates a corresponding polarity within, and can be construed in terms of the perpetual oscillation amongst these experientially inverse conditions. It is imparted by an entanglement with uncertainty—the encounter with the lack of, or still more uncannily—with the deterioration of the possibility for attaining safe and univocal foothold of self and consciousness. Stirring elemental fears, these circumstances actualize a semi-physical, semi-apprehending condition—the interval where anxiety is at its most intense.

The spatial constructions of exposure and its internal mechanisms cohere with and in a way reproduce conditions that trigger analogous symptoms and aspects of fear and anxiety discussed in various frameworks. Hence Freud's (1949: 13-45) profound inquiry links fear with the subconscious, Kast's (1994) study discloses the interface and mutual nourishment between fascination and fear as possibilities for personal development, Hallam's (1985) discussion of the generalized anxiety syndrome points to its roots in ambiguity and confusion, while Burke's (1987) seminal work on the modes to the attainment of the sublime and the aesthetic shows how these are entangled with dimensions of fear. Though generated as subtle pre-conscious bodily reverberations with spatial conditions and circumstances, the fear components of exposure do derive directly from the setting, and are affective rather than mediated. Rooted in immediate experience they therefore bear the vigour of the lived which renders them utterly productive. The impetus of fear-related affect not only upsets habitual patterns, but is also conducive of creative improvisation, and, hence, emerges as a state rather potent, as well as unpredictable.

It is in such affective terms that exposure vitalizes acute awareness of one's liabilities—it acquaints with vulnerability through the body. Yet this acquaintance by way of corporeal circumstance also discloses the inherent polarity and ambiguity of vulnerability. It does support attaining awareness of the fact that liability and risk are invoked for both the passive and the active poles: such as that of the 'exposed' that is readily associated with lack (of vitality, strength and ability to resist), as well as, paradoxically that of the active 'intruding' pole—for being oriented outwards and concerned with its act of intrusion. Hence the condition of exposure triggers the complex processes of conceiving and accepting of the liability to reciprocal reversals, and the coexistence, within, of these controversial aspects. It presents bodily ways of acquaintance and discovery of vulnerability as a prolific and shared condition inherent to the social.

Yet it is these same circumstances and mechanisms of relating and presenting which also instigate the keen awareness of others, the condition of exposure incites and enables a realization of these others as they are being captured in the same unsettled and vulnerable state. In this regard the intuition of one's potential liability—the sense of vulnerability—could be construed as enabling possibilities of passing from the self-contained states and positions of mere co-presence, towards the modes of engagement, involvement and exchange—i.e., it is these same unsettling circumstances that further capacities to construct connection, as a potential to institute change by relating, and expanding and incorporating that towards which one extends. In the context of dialogue, possibilities of construing vulnerability in its liberating potential is asserted in Jenkins's (2002) analysis, arguing that in contrast to tolerance, vulnerability renders identity open to transformation with respect to its capacities of receptivity, permeability and generosity.

In the context of the corporeality of the site, the experience of the condition of exposure, then, emerges as an utterly productive instance of potential openness and acquisition. It can be construed as an experiential condition which is apt to compel participants to acquire a bodily knowledge of the liabilities and strengths of vulnerability. Still further, it allows agents to intuit this vulnerability as a profound dimension of the practice of membership which generates and entails the force to expand and acknowledge. It is through the experience of these 'darker' sides of the social and spatial reality that would alter established notions, such as that of exposure as the submission of the performer to the mercy of a distant spectator. The bodily experience of the condition of exposure, and vulnerability, then, would nurture deeper levels of sharing and of equality at the basis of bond relations. It is thus that the experience of the condition of exposure might ground the possibility of grasping a different principle of power: that of generosity and the power to be affected. Within the extending-and-contracting logic of this spatial form, this alternative principle would be suggested as a force to expand and encompass and acknowledge the other. As an experiential condition, exposure in this way eases the paths of compassion, and engenders what can be conceived as a bodily practice of empathy.

Collective containment
<u>Conceptual connotations</u>
Collective containment depicts the operations of the theatre mode by emphasising its capacities to express and establish the performance site as a shared space. As physical space it houses and enables the various processes of engagement with that which is shared, and through which the possibilities of constituting a collectivity would be supported. In denoting the site, collective containment conjures two mutually enhancing spatial conditions. The term 'collective' accounts for effects of space which facilitate assembling—so as to unite and conjoin, and reception—so as to accommodate a variety of agents and components. It comes to designate not only that a whole is formed by gathering that comes to characterise a group, but also that the individuals and components act and work together in a common enterprise. Collective containment thus comes to suggest that there is a process by which a whole is gained or acquired—members collect gradually from various places or sources, they amass and accumulate. In its more personal underpinnings too, the term connotes some subtle processes of regaining control (of oneself and of one's wits) and summoning up (one's faculties or powers).

'Containment', in turn, relates togetherness (*com*) of parts or fractions, emphasising a capacity to hold (*tenere*) these together by way of enclosing and including, or restraining within fixed limits. As a conceptual construct, collective containment comes to denote conditions, which not only bring diverse parts close to each other. Moreover it comes to imply togetherness in terms of processes by which the 'common' is kindled and evolves, such that its possible expansion or influences require, in a way, keeping within, or protection.

<u>Corporeal constructions</u>
The spatial constructions of collective containment encompass the mode itself in its totality. At this point of the study it can be understood that the conditions of isolation and exposure come forth, analytically, as two distinct conditions through which the mode as collective space actually works. Collective containment builds on, incorporates and amalgamates the mechanisms of exposure and isolation into the operations of the site as an entity. Its power to assimilate and amalgamate into a larger totality can be identified as the mechanism specific to this experiential condition. In spatial terms collective containment connotes the capacity of the site to accommodate larger groups of people, as well as propose their involvement in a common occasion. As such it not only balances various technical and practical concerns with physical space such as sightlines and acoustics, or seating comfort. It also actualizes the primary and socially consequential properties of the site. Thus visual and physical openness are enhanced in ways that actualize the entity as unifying field: it accentuates admission, accommodation and inclusiveness. While these would be features that depict the character of many of the supporting spaces (lobbies, halls, refreshment bars, rehearsals, green rooms, etc.), they are rendered most explicit in the spatial constitution of the core site itself—the stage and auditorium.

Composite by nature, the articulation of the site as a unifying spatial entity is expressed in the principles of order through which its two constituents—stage and auditorium—are established as mutually complementary parts that form a larger whole, while also preserving their respective identities and definition. At elaborate sites, the mutual completion of stage and auditorium is rendered both by their orientation with respect to each other, and through their tightly interdependent positions. The sense of the whole site as an entity is maintained through the effects of coordination, and derives from the constructions of their spatial relations. These relations may entail their positioning as mutually supporting units, such as actualized in the close adjacency and attachment of stage and auditorium in end-stage and proscenium formats. It may be rendered tangible also by way of their more resolute integration in interlocking, such as the protrusion of the thrust stage, or the total inclusion in the form of the arena type formats.

Hence in spite of the inherent structuring, the overall identity of the mode is rather one of balance, coherence or spatial continuity. It relies as much on the stage comprising a focus, as it depends on the pronounced spatial precedence of the auditorium expressed in its larger scale and frequently sedimentary arrangement and articulation. This entity is perceivable even in variants, where components are rather strongly differentiated, such as in the Italian type, where the proscenium is quite distinguished from the auditorium, which itself features flat 'parterre', and rows of boxes.

The spatial integration procured in terms of such unifying effects of collective containment, not only assists the processes of identification with, and belonging to a place that is distinct. It also formalizes accommodation within, and together. This sense of belonging, the awareness of the collective nature of the site, and hence the sense of sharing and participation are bound to be still more intensified in the monolithic space of amphitheatre configurations, reminiscent of the stern prototypes of Antiquity, where bodies are held in the steep curved slope to form and envelope its core.

In the spatial constructions of collective containment, the major mechanism of focusing takes on a special expressivity. While this mechanism in the context of the condition of isolation would articulate the centre as a destination and support the sense of arrival, and procure the core as tool of presentation under the circumstances of exposure, within the workings of collective containment it becomes articulate as the prevailing principle of centralization governing the whole site.

This principle actualizes two essential qualities characterizing this spatial modality. One concerns the gravitational forces of the spatial form: although delimited, this form allows and invites growth without losing its character as structured space. As such it generates the powerful quality of the site in its extending-contracting dynamics, which comes to materialise the process of assembling itself. This dynamics can even be observed at sites which lack the tout definition of an enclosing boundary—expressed in the corresponding pulsation of tightly aligned collective bodies, where the site is comprised as a common achievement.

The other quality marks the compulsory traits of this collective pattern in spatial form, enhanced by the strict geometrical formatting of the spatial components. This would derive from the single sweep of the enclosure frequently taking a primary geometric shape, the axial composition, or the regularity of an arrangement of rows of seats. Yet in interpreting the sense over these compulsory traits of the site, this current analysis would deviate from views that take such features as designed for their disciplining repercussions, procuring spatial segregation and hierarchy, and hence instigating control and behaviour. Rather, it would assert that along with these above effects, the proposed spatial order also highlights homogenizing and unifying effects. The current analysis of the spatial constructions of collective containment allows construing how these would build up to the sense of belonging, equality, and identification and propose a sense of membership grounded on sharing. While each agent is assigned a place for ample duration, it is a place within a space that is encompassing, integrating and highlighting likeness and consonance. These become tangible in the capacity of the whole to assimilate, without eradicating, all kinds of spatial differentiation, and propose coalescence and sharing instead. Furthermore, as its origins in social practice would confirm, this order actually inherently coheres with the nature of the body and the structure of the collective activity pattern—it corresponds to the collaborations in the assembly. The order of physical space therefore, would come to be felt, acknowledged, and embodied as a constructive necessity. As indispensable in facilitating the operation of the collective site, as it is in positing of agency as observance, this sense (of order) would, in this way, point to experiential effects that ease the transition towards involvement—where participation is implicated beyond mere appreciation (as relatively passive viewing), to suggest rather the processes of active engagement and acquisition.

Hence exceeding the notion of common presence, collective containment formalises accommodation within, and together, so as to incite the sense of belonging. It builds up and stimulates engagement not only with each other (already triggered by exposure), but suggests participation in the common occasion. In this regard collective containment receives and builds on isolation and exposure, while also reconfigures them both as productive ingredients. That is—it overcomes the separation of the solitary self-contained centres, and makes tolerable the extremities of exposure, while appropriating their energies and impulses into a confluent field. Such a notion of energies being part of the experience is validated with respect to the 'intangible' flow of energies amongst actor and audience, as well as among the audience, brought forth as speculative finding in Mackintosh's (1993) comparative study of theatre spaces as 'intensity'. This notion can be extended to explicate the homogenizing potential of the spatial form as a whole, a quality which would support the transformation of the states respective to isolation and exposure into a common endeavour. This common endeavour develops at several levels and involves a variety of processes, each proposing a different dimension to collective containment as a form of experience.

<u>Collective containment as a form of experience</u>
These effects of collective containment are sustained in view of the body/agent as well. Under the condition of collective containment, the solitary centres procured by isolation (as dispersal and self-centring) and still upheld by exposure (as alerted self-awareness and their viable correlation), are permeated by a unifying larger field, releasing and suspending their self-centring effects. Collective containment as a condition, then, involves a two-fold awareness: that of being distinct (individuality) and that of being immersed and part of something larger (assembly), assisting the engagement with the roles and relations proposed by the site. These equalizing effects of the space enhance the sense of simultaneous presence in space and occasion as aspects of direct sharing, and the common attention to the presented work—as indirect sharing. This allows sharing in terms of association and kinship to evolve, upon which conceiving of a collectivity beyond sum and accretion becomes possible. That, which evolves as collective activity, then, entails both active participation in the construction of the performance itself, and engagement with collectivity at different levels.

The performance site as a social space and occasion allows depicting and exploring such levels in terms of various mechanisms through which the encounter with, and the constitution of the collective occur. This relates not only to the diverse social practices that pertain to social conduct and entail the enacting of formal and ceremonial motifs—social practices, which reaffirm social relations, conventions and contracts. It pertains to the special 'form of questioning' (Breton, 1989, 4) which, as venture, is instituted and accomplished at the site, and hints at its socio-political potentials.

Yet, experientially, the circumstances formalized by collective containment appear most consequential in their capacity to render tangible conditions akin to ritual and rite—to the extent of enabling observance in the form of organized communal practice, constraining conduct and attitude, and, bearing on the sense of solidarity. The affective forces of the immediately experiential can be construed as conducive to attaining states of an ultimate opening up of the self, and in this way being rendered susceptible to the experiential modality of becoming. This would enable an entirely different – lived grounds on which the encounter with, participation, and association with collectivity evolves, as it actualises, in bodily ways, aspects of the fusion of actor-ship and spectatorship exemplified in the Greek model, where such fusion is enacted by the chorus.

This spatial form as a site where diverse social practices are enacted, allows glimpses on the notions of the public—ranging from a sphere of collective discussion, deliberation and action by which solidarity is re-iterated, to a realm which thrives and acknowledges diversity. Whichever the model, through the perspective of the suggested forms of experience, a range of discreet conditions and processes come forth in terms of the possibilities these open up, not only as being conducing, but also as engendering affect and practice that enable cross-communal togetherness.

With respect to such dimensions and the opportunities they open up, this spatial mode emerges in its generative potential. This potential lies not only with its function to facilitate observance and consensus, which, in the thought of Habermas (1990), would be denoted as the agreement over that which is. It comes about through the capacities of space to enable departure from the passive states (entertainment, distraction), and towards those active states that allow awareness of responsibility and participation to evolve into an affirmation of collectivity as an active exploration of possibilities.

The generative potential of this spatial mode builds up through the spatial constructions and workings of all three inherent conditions. Utterly fertile and fluid, these trigger possibilities for actualization, which entail the intense yet pre-contemplative bodily processes of becoming as a venture into acquisition. However, it also offers, in the act of witnessing, the possibility of more proper conscious appropriation. Instantiated and sustained as an articulate corporeal experience for the agents on and before the stage, witnessing comes to be embodied as an act and practice inherent in this kind of assembly. Hence, by actualizing witnessing, this mode of spatial organization lends validity to the experience undergone, in that this experience is set within the physical references of this shared space, occurs simultaneously, and hence as observed in the collective presence of this assembly. Spatially constructed, witnessing operates through the productive oscillation among polarities (observer/observed, active/passive)—aspects that can be construed as building up to a discernment of the process of becoming both producer and product of the experience in question.

Quite distinct from 'seeing', witnessing is an act and practice where one is simultaneously participant observer and observed. It is constructed through exposure and facilitated best in places that sustain a constant awareness of all the other fellow participants. This state, on the one hand, requires observance and responsibility, and hence amounts to becoming conscious over ones diverse roles in a common endeavour. On the other hand, it works towards confirming the reality of anything undergone at the site by way of having discerned one's own, as well everyone else's presence in space. This allows associating intangibles (affective states, feelings, insights) in to the immediate physical framework—i.e., imposing a form on that which would otherwise remain only a period of time, and attaining awareness of occurrences as articulate experiential ingredients. Hence the act of witnessing stabilizes, in that it allows the simply phenomenal to solidify into structures of memory: it allows a safe recuperation by way of the assimilation of change. Based on the awareness of the presence of others, it 'objectifies' by lending credibility to a private feeling, a state, or an act. It thus articulates an essential quality of the mode—to enable grasping and committing to memory that which has been experienced, a phase of actualizing processes of conscious appropriations.

The spatial intricacies of bodily knowing and becoming
The approach to analysis in terms of mode of spatial organization and by way of the articulation of its generic conditions has helped render space as it becomes available to the bodily ways and appropriation in experience. Physical space has come forth as a vital vibrant matter posing challenges, mobilizing through a range of controversial charges deeply entrenched in its materiality, bringing conditions into tangible presence as possibilities for the actualizations of the situated body. Validating the absorbing qualities of the immediately experiential, these conditions are viscerally felt. They present as much a potential for response to sensibles, as they are a pathway to awareness, especially while, acknowledged by the body they would condense in the fairly stable clusters of discreet occurrences and processes that consti-

tute *forms of experience.* With respect to the particular experiential bearing of the mode these conditions help construe, infer, and bring to the foreground certain fundamental principles of the collective—as an especially affective blend of the social, ritual and aesthetic. These allow intuiting how space becomes conductive of those alternative paths of embodied feelings and practices through which realities of the social are grasped, and sensibilities enabling social togetherness—internalized.

With respect to experience in general, these conditions come forth in their capacity to augment and vitalize the very possibility of becoming drawn into the unique, authentic and irretrievable experiential modality of becoming. Experience has been brought to the foreground in terms of discreet processes that belong to the vicinity of the corporeal space-body correlations, and begin in terms of the 'feeling' phase as a possible response—reverberations that are spontaneous, explorative, pre-conscious, non-contemplative, and suffused with affect. Triggered in and through spatial circumstance, this layer of discreet experiential processes helps confirm the constitutive capacities of physical space characterising the zone of contact, and highlight that which is corporeal and affective in its passage towards and assimilation into complex mental events of more properly autogenic nature, through which the function of conscious incorporation would actualize. With respect to understanding how this modality of experiential becoming evolves at the micro-level, each of these conditions in their distinct operations allows construing particular internal mechanisms and occurrences. Hence these conditions emerge in their capacity to reproduce, in physical space, the instances or phases of 'stabilization', 'destabilization' and 're-stabilization' analogous perhaps to those of experience *per se*—i.e., they help render explicit how space both commences and recuperates the experience in question. Space can be construed as it actualizes its generative capacities: triggering the experience by framing and engendering these instances simultaneously, as a perpetual choice, and opportunity.

Chapter Five

Discussion

Methodological constructions: the spatial dimension as analytical and explanatory tool
This study has focused on establishing physical space, theoretically and methodologically, as integral and constitutive component in the experience of the situated body. It has proposed an approach, which examines the narrow incision of direct correlations among material circumstance and discreet experience, holding that analysis in these terms would further understanding of the generative potential of built space with respect to emergent consciousness. It has traced out an analytical framework, grounded, theoretically, a series of methodological propositions, and specified the conceptual tools that enable a reconstruction of material space as empirical entity and inquiry into its operations as it opens up to corporeal appropriation. It has posited the area of space-to-body correlations as a distinct area for research, and ascertained the cluster of processes that evolve through and with spatial circumstance as integral to immediate experience.

The implementation of this approach to the concrete case of theatre space, has demonstrated its capacity in disclosing novel aspects pertinent to the understanding of the materiality of space, the situated body, and discreet experience, along with the affective, cognitive and ethical embedded in the intimate and immediate correlations with space. The proposed conceptualisation of the corporeal as the realm of space-to-body correlations has allowed examining space as the extension of the correlation, and as a dimension characterising and qualifying the events of contact—capturing, analytically, the passage from space to sense to sensibility.

The approach is developed specifically for this narrow section of direct correlations. It entails a particularisation of experience-in-the-terms-of-space, and, thus, addresses aspects of the operations of space neglected on other accounts. Spanning from analysis of concrete physical space, through the discreet experiential processes of correlating, to aspects of mentality, its framework is necessarily hybrid. It begins with analysis of space, which relies on techniques and precision in attending to spatial detail characteristic of architectural field. However, this analysis deviates from established architectural priorities and the interpretative schemes of perception, and arrives at a radically altered conceptualisation of spatial form in its generative potential in view of processes of emergence. The methodological principles and propositions, which support this conceptualisation and allow extending inquiry further into the experiential processes and their contents, are informed by diverse perspectives and conceptions engaging in the notions of space and experience.

The shift away from interpretations of representational priorities and towards an examination of the productive embedded in the material presence of space at the experiential level, aligns with the shift towards the lived. With respect to space, this shift entails the insight that lived experience is to be understood as a spatialized form of existence and as such provides the base of possibilities for any acquisition—insights which are shared by thinkers of different lineages such as Husserl, Gadamer, Merleau-Ponty, Lefebvre, and Massey. Each in their own terms, these argue for the importance of recognizing the import of the physical presence of space, which actualizes existence in a concreteness that need be taken into account in explicating lived experience, subjectivity, and the larger socio-cultural processes of co-existence.

Building up on the readings of space in spatial theory (Lefevbre, Massey), where the productive potential of space emerges in its open, porous, fluid and relational nature, this current study focuses on the space of built form as an area relatively neglected in these theorisations. By way of approaching built space, analytically, at the experiential level, it brings to foreground a range of aspects—affects, processes and practices—that in their own terms do pertain to the manifold and essentially open-ended experiential correlations with space. In attending to the materiality of the space-to-body relations, and examining this as a special zone of discreet phenomena of contact, it establishes that built physical space at this level is equally open and productive, engendering, from within that zone of contact, alternative ways of bodily becoming and cognition.

In this way, this approach arrives at a rendition of the productive capacities of material space. This exceeds the 'negative' productivity associated with built architectural space, where its presence is posited as possibly deterministic, and serves to offset the relative autonomy of agency in the activities of resisting, formulating and re-formulating space. Instead, construed, conceptualised, and approached analytically with respect to the situated agent, built space is brought forth as a physical framework of unmediated and non-mediating effects. The rendition of its presence at this level offers an opportunity to examine the ways in which material space works, disclosing a whole range of discreet processes that are equally productive, as well as intimately involved with other aspects of that which is lived. The explanatory potential of the proposed conceptualisation with respect to the productive capacities of the space of form is confirmed in the course of detailed analysis of the concrete case. Its findings establish that this account of built space does not contradict the principles on which inquiry into 'lived' space is based, but, rather, augments the productive role of material space in the modality of lived experience.

This approach proposes but one particular way of restoring the continuity in the account of the physical presence of built space—with respect to experience. It concurs with the call for the recognition of physical space at that level, a recognition which, as put forth by Strohmayer (1998: 105-121), can help overcome established notions of architectural space as constituted framework and index of meanings shared in perception, and open up understanding of alternative modes of meaning formation, to be attained in experience.

In re-constructing physical space with respect to experience, this approach is based on the systematic conceptualisation of space as the corporeal realm of the correlation—co-extensive with the fundamental relatedness of the body/self with its immediate surrounds. The area which becomes available to analytical inquiry, then, is the area of effects of physical space, actual and potential, as these qualify the zone of contact. The inquiry into these contact phenomena as possibilities helps infer experiential content and disclose the experience with space as a source of meaning formation in its own right. Thus, by re-articulating physical space in the vicinity of body, this approach enables drawing the spatial dimension out of its indicative implicit form and self-evident state in frameworks of emergence and becoming, and into its explicit corporeal presence—a precondition of disclosing how its materiality qualifies experience taking form.

Inquiry into this narrow section of corporeal correlations particularizes discreet experience as a phase that is prior to the conscious constructions of agency, yet also intimately and integrally correlated, and relevant to the understanding of these constructions. It captures certain aspects of the discreet that can be addressed only as set within a concrete spatial context and at the very minute level of the corporeal. Some of the paths of exploration that can be pursued from within this narrow incision pertain to the ways in which discreet experience would open up to the specific circumstances in which it is set, and with which it evolves. This type of inquiry, then, helps understand events within concrete spatial detail, and would explicate their tendency towards certain actualizations. Or, in thinking 'that which is also possible' (Dewsbury 2003), it offers an insight in terms of experiential content, where affective, ethical and cognitive components are elicited from within a particularization of the physical circumstances of the experiential event. Inquiry into the events in this zone of contact by way of physical space allows probing into what concrete spatial conditions might suggest and bring into presence in the instance of grasping of the vitality of the world—i.e., how would these characterize the ontological and social realities that come to be known in this process.

In this rendition, physical space attains explanatory potential; it offers an insight into certain specific aspects of the corporeal which is in keeping with the understanding of the body as a social construct. The crucial importance of bringing into account the specificities of the social and material world is being unequivocally brought forth as a precondition in understanding the body as both the 'locus' and the 'measure' of that world. This argument is central to Harvey's profound concise analysis of discourse on the body (1998: 401-421), where he explicates why the return to the body and its study as irreducible basis for all understanding, would need to be grounded on real spatio-temporal relations between material practices, representations, imaginations, institutions, social relations, and the prevailing structures of political-economic power. Understanding the body, then, would need to take into account the fact that the performative activities available to the body are dependent on the social and economic environment—through which the issue of direct perception and experience is to be ascertained as more than the presentation of immediacy (Harvey 1998: 403).

Although addressing rather narrow section of specific aspects of the correlations, this approach, in linking up experience and space directly, has made material space available to analysis, and employed it as a means for concretising the experience in question. This allows foregrounding the experiential layer of becoming 'with' and 'due' to space—in the form of aspects of emergent consciousness which generate 'from without'. These derive from, and highlight the ways in which space brings the circumstances of social and spatial realities into concrete presence, and, possibly, to awareness. The processes that generate therein are non-contemplative, as well as removed from intentionality and action. They would tend to remain at the preconscious level, receive no expression as such, and could, therefore, only be inferred, derived circumstantially through analytical account of spatial detail. Yet these are also aspects that are pertinent to the understanding of immediate experience, and of the workings of space with respect to it. In terms of experiential bearing, the cluster of discreet processes that can be accessed, offer insight into the constitution of alternative paths of acquisition embedded in lived corporeal experience. These processes belong to space integrally, as well as present legitimate constituents of the sensate basis of the shifting dialectics of mentality. They further understanding of the ways in which physical space would concretise existential conditions as the conditions of situatedness, as well as on the capacities of the self grasping the realities of this situatedness – they approach the generative potential of contact phenomena.

The method for this type of inquiry is based on the systematic conceptualisation of physical space as the extension of the relation, and as part of the realm of the corporeal which space and body intimately share. The re-articulation of space in its corporeal presence and its operations with respect to the situated body relies on, and particularises a range of concepts—encounter, reverberation, becoming, emergent, feeling, sense in the course of establishing the nature and mechanisms at work at this level of discreet experience.

This theorization and re-articulation of space enables a decisive shift away from image and representation (the monument as expression of aesthetic ideas through physical appearance in detail and style) and signification (spatial clues as expression and reference of a social field). Instead it arrives at a rendition of material space as grounds for a complementary inquiry into its role in constituting agency and the collective, exploring it as a charged experiential field. Opening up physical space to analytical inquiry entails re-articulating spatial form as empirical entity, examining the physical construction of possible unmediated effects in terms of specific spatial mechanisms, forces and relations. A major methodological proposition is to posit architectural space at a potent mid-level and in this way foreground that layer of experience which evolves in the terms of space itself—the stratum of phenomena of feeling-with which characterises the zone of contact.

Instituting the conception of 'mode' of spatial organization allows lifting off layers of representation and rendering space in terms of its direct effects with respect to immediate experience—i.e., it allows addressing a layer of experience prior to, and different from the layers of activities taking place in space. Instead, built space can be brought forth as physical presence, examined in terms of principal features and generic properties, and, in this way, captured in its operational modality. The logic of its operations which can be disclosed at this level, lies in its perpetual constitution: effects emerge into and out of distinctiveness, building up through concrete spatial forms—conditions—that are, in this way understood as both immanent, and imminent. By drawing analysis to the level of the corporeal, this approach helps render the workings of space with special precision. It allows insight into, and explication of the very ways in which spatial phenomena and conditions formulate: they come forth as emergent forms, bringing into presence the actual as well as the potential embedded in physical space. This approach helps particularize the structuring mechanisms underlying such operations as belonging to both space and the processes of the very formation of experience. This, in turn, prepares grounds for a deeper understanding of spatial operations with respect to the unfolding of the immediately experiential.

However, in order to arrive at the bearings of such possible effects, the approach conjoins spatial analysis, with a speculative inquiry into the minute innate potentialities of the spatial at the level of the body—identifying space-body correlations in terms of processes of immediate experience. In this respect this study, while maintaining its spatial specificity in construing of experience, approximates the modes of empirical analysis characterizing non-representational theory. By bringing into account distinct aspects of the phenomenal presence of the encountered reality, this analysis begins to disclose essential existential condition for all experience—a 'becoming' which is triggered and qualified through the very contact with the materiality of circumstance with which experience evolves. It allows obtaining more detail in understanding these processes, and include that which 'reverberation'—the sensate path of correlating—'extracts' form a given condition, into account of immediate experience. Physical space can be understood as a locus of the possible concrete and shared sites of emergence.

This approach opens up built architectural space for an analytical inquiry, which articulates the potentialities embedded in the correlations in terms of the reciprocal passage—from space to sense to sensibility, addressing processes of constitution (of agency) that evolve at a minute corporeal level, and can only be inferred, circumstantially. It establishes that, construed at this level—in its empirical corporeal presence to experience, built space is always open to the productive appropriation of the situated body.

Inquiry into the workings of space as dynamic constituent of experience relies on a conceptualization of physical space as an extension of the relation—the corporeal being understood as the realm which space and body share. The proposition to examine the material construction of prevalent effects, rather than of single features, is an important methodological tool in evading slippage into determinism, as well as into the purely phenomenological, both of which bear explanatory difficulties, epistemologically and ontologically. Instead, this approach ensures that contact phenomena are depicted and addressed in terms of a complexity (experiential condition, its possible emergence to phenomenal distinctiveness), which might suggest direction (form of experience), but excludes any pre-determination. Hence although space works through that which is bodily, physical and sensual, what is elicited from its analysis emerges in terms of possibilities for corresponding experience—i.e., analysis foregrounds how material circumstance makes essential existential conditions available to awareness. Reciprocally, detailed examination of physical circumstance provides a fresh vantage point on the co-relation, and a tool for exploring, particularizing and understanding immediate experience. These are disclosed in terms of the specificity of underlying mechanisms and relations that come about from within that zone of contact and reverberation. Analytical work at this level allows perceiving and establishing space, empirically, as genuinely productive in multiple ways—it is brought forth as an entirely corporeal framework through and in terms of which aspects of becoming are actualized.

The spatial dimension, thus, becomes explanatory not only in that it discloses the subtle mechanisms through which the self grasps its own presence within these conditions. Furthermore it provides a rendition of the specificities characterizing the nature of the situation—it allows inferring what may be intuited in the course of this contact. This grounds the theorization of physical space within the productive layer of discreet occurrences of reverberation, and allows probing into what concrete experiential effects and ingredients might issue from within the texture of contact phenomena.

The approach allows establishing that at this empirical level physical space is inevitably 'open', and always productive. It extends on aspects of the 'lived' in that it derives a range of experiential ingredients generated in and through space that are not addressed elsewhere, or explicated at this level of concreteness. Yet furthermore, it also renders explicit more intricate structural mechanisms pertinent to the generation and constitution of lived immediate experience through its most tangible component—space.

Discreet experience in the constructions of self and the collective as aspects of the authentically theatrical

The implementation of this framework to the specific case of theatre has helped particularize the methodological propositions, so as to facilitate analysis of a concrete spatial form. It confirms that inquiry into the corporeal can yield new findings and explanatory schemes with respect to discreet experience, and the registers of consciousness pertinent to it. The analysis of theatre space in the proposed terms complements established perspectives where space is seen in its relatively experientially neutral functions to house and stage the performance. Rather, it focuses on the potentiality of space to 'do', recognising its capacities to be suggestive of experience.

The layer of experience disclosed in this analysis, is important in several respects. It brings to the foreground essential aspects of the lived experience, which is a prime characteristic of the very nature of the performance as a life event. In contrast to interpretation of theatre experience in terms of the processes of production and perception of theatrical meanings, this layer is founded in properties of space itself, affective throughout and in equal terms—where physical space as shared corporeal framework provides common grounds for all participants involved. Furthermore, although this layer evolves on its own terms, and can be explored in its relatively autonomous constitution, it, nevertheless, does maintain a productive correlation with the experience of the performance, in multiple ways.

One major way of explicating the generative potential of space at this level entails the analysis of the physical constitution of its properties as generic conditions. From within the specificity of this analysis it can be derived, that such generic conditions are both inherent, and emerging—always under construction. Their articulation in terms of concrete physical features shows how they potentially rely on physical features and elements, compose and recompose these into configurations with differing effects, enhance and reformulate dynamic forces—they emerge in and out of phenomenal distinctiveness. This helps render explicit how physical space works—it presents both the actual and the potential.

The rendition of the experiential workings of the generic properties of this spatial form, then, is enabled by the series of conceptual constructs—isolation, exposure and collective containment. Employed in their capacities as spatial terms, as modes of being in space that define distinct existential conditions, and as forms of experience, these allow detailed analysis and understanding of the intricate workings of the logic of this spatial form. Moreover, they offer insight into the internal mechanisms linking up the experiential sequence from space to sensibility.

By providing links between physical circumstance and experiential content, these constructs assist in rendering space experientially consequential, and in this way allow addressing, analytically, a layer of experience at performance previously unaccounted for. This originates in space, evolves at the level of the corporeal, and bears the affective and cognitive which issues directly from contact with circumstances of spatial situatedness. It helps infer—access, particularize and recover a range of discreet processes, and posit these as affective correlates of the overall experience and productive ingredients on performance.

At a theoretical level, the recognition of this layer of immediate experience, offers a complementary dimension in discussing the intensity, character, and authenticity of the theatrical, as a dimension which does not come forth as an explicit aspect in mainstream research on theatre. In established perspectives, discussion of the site in its entirety is linked to authenticity in so far as particular configurations would define the requisite relations (performer-audience, audience-audience, and actual-artistic) with special intensity. In this the spatial form of the playhouse is seen to constitute the relations among the two groups of participants at their most condensed, and in this way support the prospect for 'mutual influence' and 'response' to the performance (Mackintosh 1993). The other formation with special import to the theatrical is the horseshoe or arena configuration, which, by showing real and fictional in parallel and superimposed on each other, builds up towards the dual awareness of the realities and artifices of the theatrical, and enforces the readiness of audiences for 'complicity' and participation in the 'play' (Purcell 2005: 74-84).

Distinct from these studies in that it addresses lived experience in more general terms, and is, respectively, based on a different set of concepts, this current study nevertheless arrives at an experiential layer inherent in and relevant in understanding theatre experience. This layer articulates legitimate aspects pertaining to the experience of theatre: it issues from the corporeality of the site, engenders a mode of being which entails immersion in the moment, is suffused with feelings, and on its own terms, equal for all, enhances the possibility of turning participators into more properly performing agents. Physical space on its own corporeal terms proposes the passage to activated and intense states of the directly lived. These corporeal terms are there, available to all participants involved and place their distinct experiences of theatrical realities on unifying grounds.

Focusing on theatre as a specific case has offered the opportunity to conduct a special type of inquiry. The conceptualisation of physical space at the level of 'mode of spatial organization' has allowed linking this spatial form to its constitution in social and ritual practice, and provided insight into this spatial form as a means of social and cultural continuity in two respects. One concerns the resilient persistence of this spatial form, and allows understanding it as a model preceding design which has been handed down and incorporated in diverse modifications throughout its historical evolution. As a spatial model it can be recognized within all three major theatre forms in the Western tradition (the proscenium, the thrust stage, and the arena/theatre in the round) implemented within various spatial formations (such as playhouse, amphitheatre, or box). It can also be perceived in the underlying spatial logic which governs the formulation of a range of analogous social sites with diverse appointed functions and operating at various levels of organization: ranging from lecture rooms, assembly halls, places of worship, or courtrooms, through to spaces for entertainment, and even open-air urban forms. The proposed approach, then, along with its findings, bears relevance to all of these and can be employed as part of their analysis. It also points beyond schematic figurative resemblance and towards an altered conception of 'mode' as a 'spatial' type that is characterized by shared physical and social qualities.

Yet furthermore, construing of physical space in the form of mode of spatial organization, helps highlight these shared physical and social qualities in terms of spatial continuities—from its distant origins through to its presence as lived concrete experiential field. It can be employed as an analytical tool, providing access to the possible constitutive operations of space embedded in the corporeal. As such, the conception of mode would show affinity with notions like 'milieu' and 'schema', in that it addresses experiential phenomena which evolve in terms of non-discursive pre-conscious processes and in practice. Analogous to these notions it can be employed as a means of analysis, for the range of discreet processes which defy direct observation and need be deduced and explicated theoretically. However, while both milieu and schema disclose the logic of practice as continuous as well as productive process of acquisition of practical knowledge, they explicate socio-cultural continuity exclusively and tightly linked to the traits and characteristics of the practices themselves (Bourdieu, 1997, Allan, 1993). In this, milieu denotes the setting of activity as pattern of social properties, while the 'schema' functions as a mental structure holding the essentials of how to think, feel and act (Allan, 1993), both dynamically effective in the formulation and re-formulation of practical knowledge, in practice.

Complementary to these notions, analysis in terms of the mode, addresses processes pertinent to the setting that are of explicitly spatial nature. In its spatial continuity—from its origins, through to experiential field—the theatre mode can be construed to function as a kind of corporeal actualization of a schema, that can be taken to render explicit the ways in which space embeds, in its resilient morphology, and vitalizes, as experiential field, a few but foundational principles of the social. In this regard, analysis has disclosed physical space as a tangible experiential field with the capacity to engender paths of acquisition which are attained, implemented and transformed at corporeal level and in terms of the ceaseless activities of embodiment, in practice.

The fact that this spatial modality is rooted in ritual practice, too, can be traced within the operations of space, especially in the intensity with which collective states, and their fear-like correlates, are commenced and recuperated, throughout various actualizations. While actualised perhaps at their most acute in the stern space of the Ancient Greek prototype, such intensity would issue, in analogous form, through the corroboration of all three experiential conditions, making the links with ritual most palpably affective in the spatial constructions of the condition of exposure. This spatial continuity would hint at certain ritual-based strategies underlying the spatial structuring and formation of the theatre mode, which cumulatively build up towards approximation to and perhaps even immersion into analogous states that are deep down inherently intermingled also with fear-related components.

In this respect the current analysis allows extending on accounts on fear in the context of performance by specifying the terms in which fear is insinuated through space, so as to become a prevailing circumstance for all participants, a finding that would suggest that in the overall operations of this spatial form, structures of fear might actually be omnipresent. It allows intuiting the corporeal constructions conducive of fear and anxiety, by rendering the generation, operations, and techniques for its productive transformation and dissolution at the individual level tangible, inscribed in physical space, and stretched in duration. It also points to the potentialities of the site with regard to cultivating our abilities in facing fear. This might include also larger phenomena like 'agoraphobia, alienation, and angst', which can be attended to exclusively at a collective setting and through 'collective strategies' (Kast 1994).

In terms of findings, this study arrives at a re-construction of a stratum of experiential ingredients which generate at pre-contemplative level directly from space, and evolve as discreet bodily processes. These ascertain theatre space as a site through which realities of the social are grasped, and confirm experience in and through space as an authentic path of acquisition of practical knowledge. This approach, then, bears on discourse on theatre in that it complements inquiry into the functions of space in establishing the social and cultural significance of theatre, by rendering one that coheres with, yet also evolves relatively autonomous from theatrical production: to maintain, and constitute sensibilities vital to the collective at the level of corporeal immediate experience.

The significance of this layer lies not only in that it involves dispositions such as concentration, activation, or compassion appropriate to the acts of performance and perception of theatrical content, but also in that it discloses the ontological and social bearing of the site as it supports the constitution of self and the collective. This layer entails the productivity of affect and corporeal engagement as alternative and valid paths in confronting issues of vulnerability, power, and membership to the assembly, all of which appear to be entangled with, and reverberating with structures of apprehension, anxiety and fear. Although such experiential potential might tend to remain at the verge of awareness, it is nevertheless a potential which is integral to the structure of the performance event, and intrinsically embedded in physical space as such. Hence while during a particular performance this potential would be fore-grounded by the play and tend to remain unrecognized, the impetus of the immediately experiential would nevertheless come to augment the particularly theatrical. The affective and cognitive ingredients engendered within space begin as induced mental events which are apt to emerge to consciousness as plausible candidates to participate in, and invigorate the overall experience. The corporeal as part of the theatre experience affirms performance as engagement (distinct from performance as distraction) and augments aesthetic pleasure with the enjoyment that derives from effort invested in undergoing and incorporating change as lived, through space.

Employing the 'mode' as an analytical construct through which to inquire into the discreet processes and mechanisms of constitution and the emergent, ascertains this spatial form as an experiential field, where it capacities by far exceed its signifying functions and affordances. Along with and aside of these functions, physical space is understood as it captures and articulates aspects pertaining the social realm as concrete corporeal situation, and, by way of the bodily encounters with possibilities generating in space, works as a dynamic source in acquiring practical knowledge, and in cultivating and enabling the collective. This approach to space opens up towards a different type of inquiry—one that allows following up the experiential as a path of embodied feeling and understanding. It examines space as a locus of socio-cultural continuities, and its role as such—as one aspect of its productivity.

Space embeds both the concrete and actual in that it materializes physical circumstance, force, mechanism, and the potential and imminent—in that it stages conditions in their viable emergence to phenomenal distinctiveness as experiential possibility. It acts a as a dynamic site through which we grasp aspects of the socio-spatial reality, and acquire insight into the collective, and the self as member of that assembly. It is a material substance which activates and qualifies engagement with self and collectivity: it proposes and orients towards awareness of the nature of social togetherness, the attainment of intuitions over the risks and pleasures of openness, the grasp of alternative paths of being and knowing—all of which come forth rooted, as much, in the corporeal.

The primary bearing of this approach is on the conception of architectural space: it has been oriented towards disclosing and confirming that physical space, even that of this most formalized monument—theatre, is actually, and inevitably, 'open' to productive appropriation when construed at the level of the body. However, within its margins, this study also attends to, and extends on spatial practices and issues of socio-spatial reciprocity. These concern aspects of reciprocal correlations that can be rendered explicit by examining concrete circumstances and specified effects of architectural space—aspects which are less-explored or explicated elsewhere, as are also certain ingredients of the dialectic relationships between the physical and the social self.

The theatre mode exemplifies a very special case, where such reciprocities can be understood as issuing from the very constitution of this spatial form: it has been seen and rendered as an authentic artefact formulated not only for but also through social practices. It in this way points to the possibility of arriving at an alternative explanation of its enduring effects—as a spatial form where fundamental principles pertinent to ritual and social practice are materialized, and which, in its reproduction, manifests and confirms this spatial form (mode) as a means of socio-cultural continuity.

In turn, its analysis as lived physical space, allows re-tracing few but essential principles pertinent to the very foundations of socio-spatial organization within the practices of inhabitation. It offers opportunity to infer and re-construct the processes through which such principles might be intuited, concepts and values grasped, and internalized—incorporated. Among these it is perhaps the bodily knowledge on vulnerability, and the embodied practice of empathy to which it opens up, which emerge as particularly constructive. This is so because as Allan (1993) discloses, empathy in its outward orientation and functions in expanding the foundations of understanding is the sole practice with potential to enrich our very repertoire of practices.

This site, then, can be understood as a corporeal experiential field vitalizing essential preconditions for the coexistence and collaboration of members of diverse groups, and cultivating sensibilities that nourish the operations of the social. Intuited as but one particularization of how our 'thrown-togetherness' might actualize in the context of theatre, it confirms the corporeality of space-body relationships as still another, physical, framework through which we exercise cognitive, creative, and emotive abilities, and ultimately re-think and embody selfhood.

This perspective, ascertaining the capacity of space to formalize, intensify and sustain conditions and thus render experiential ingredients discernible, helps conceive of the site as a socio-cultural context, apt to engender and assist in the construction of the self and its repertoire. It conveys evidence that experience in and through space does frame and support the actualization of such ontological functions not only within the aesthetic and through the performative event, but also on its own terms, instating the site as corporeal component of theatrical praxis. It offers the opportunity to construe a performative process, which evolves though different modalities of experience, engages different levels of consciousness, and is, productively, embedded in the corporeal.

The modality of discreet experience immediately spatial: the structuring mechanisms of the corporeal

Isolation, exposure and collective containment prove to be potent analytical tools as spatial terms impressed upon the site of performance. They economically re-describe the fundamental functions of the setting, with respect to the performance, in terms of its properties as spatial form—to define and protect, to facilitate the presenting and perception of an act, and to accommodate and organize. In this, they also disclose the intrinsic dependence of these functions, and the performance, on specified effects of space, which involve the aptitude of isolation to centralize, of exposure to relate and present, and of collective containment to equalize and assimilate.

The conceptualization of the spatial mode in its coherence with the performance event through the proposed constructs contributes to deepening understanding of theatre experience, the aesthetic, and experience in general, in several respects. When considered as a dimension complementary to the theatrical, analysis of material space helps reveal how appropriate emotive dispositions—such as compassion, pity, fear, and pleasure—are invoked experientially, come to correspond and connect with the theatrical content and hence, cumulatively, support the encounter with the artistic work. Yet the experiential generated through space exceeds dispositions, and is also quite distinct from interpretations of theatre experience understood as closely correlated with and issuing through the theatrical work. In contrast, the immediate that is being foregrounded by this current analysis of space, need be acknowledged as a modality that is experiential, and rather different from the mode of understanding and re-cognition that any form of mediation would also entail. The magnitude of such a distinction lies in that the content-based framework of theatre experience highlights comprehension of something observed and ultimately external, and thus would presuppose the need for a theatrical work to begin, while this proposed analysis directly relies on experience for probing into certain affective states. This embeddedness in the corporeal ensures that the layer of experience addressed, comes to entail the special impetus and charge of the genuinely affective—it evolves through direct encounter.

Each condition comes about by specific spatial mechanisms, and activates its concrete internal forces, mobilizing in its tangible experiential circumstances, and generating its affective and cognitive contents. In this respect, isolation, exposure and collective containment open up an opportunity to conceptualize the site and the event by conferring forms of experience that resonate with the perception of theatrical content, yet still remain relatively autonomous. It might be the rendition of this experiential layer as explicit component in theatre experience, which would also help account for the rigour of experience at performance, on behalf of all participants involved. The presence and generative potential of this layer would allow construing that if a departure from performance-as-distraction to performance-as-productive-event is possible, this process would be supported and enabled, as much, through the experience of spatial conditions in their own right.

However, considered in its own terms, the rendition of this relatively autonomous layer of experience 'with' space begins to disclose aspects of a more fundamental and vital coherence—that which pertains to the logic of operations of space with respect to that experiential layer. Contemplating this spatial form analytically, thus, helps uncover certain intricate mechanisms as these govern the course of evolvement of the experience in question. By taking the direct correlations with space foreground and identifying the nature of their corporeal constructions, this analysis attends to the experiential aspects of these correlations, and explicates the essential openness of the process. This openness is twofold, entailing the phenomenal emergence of the generic conditions by way of composing and re-composing of spatial features, as well as the generation of the discreet processes taking form, actualizing the possibilities embedded therein. Space in this way is construed in its capacity to materialize both the actual and the potential, and affect through both.

This focus on the minute and corporeal layer of discreet experience helps identify and particularise two distinct phases of the experiential process, and discern each of these as to its predominant nature. This focus is especially revealing with respect to the initial phase of largely neglected micro-events that begin from without. This initial phase belongs to the direct contact, and, for coming about through a fundamental encounter, evolves as spontaneous, pre-intellectual, explorative, and un-determined process—it confirms the constitutive capacities of the corporeal and affective as possibilities open to appropriation. The passage of the mental events that are triggered in this 'contact' phase into feelings and impulses of more properly autogenous nature and their subsequent attainment in witnessing—helps recognize how the function of conscious incorporation is enabled and actualized. This allows construing of the process of actualization of an experiential possibility embedded in space at the micro-level, as it evolves from sense through feeling to sensibility: through initiation/activation in direct contact, presses towards appropriation/assimilation, and might come to be attained. The discreet processes of this 'induced' type, then, resonate with the principal sequential nature of experience, marking instances analogous to those of the experiential process. Hence both on the very minute scale of induced discreet processes, and on the larger scale of experiencing spatial circumstances and effects, the tangible corporeal constructions and workings of the generic conditions, render the course of passage from a relatively stable or habitual state into the active mode of 'destabilization' and 're-stabilization' explicit. They help infer such a structure from the very ways in which space actualizes its constitutive capacities: reproducing the experience by framing and engendering these instances simultaneously, as a perpetual choice, and opportunity.

In this the experience of *isolation,* while ensuring the mobilisation of capacities for concentration and attentiveness, provides the precondition for a breach in the habitual through internal activation and accumulation. *Exposure* renders active and destabilizes by confronting with dramatic polarity, within and without, compels to engagement and releases the impulse to relate and expand, augmenting that impulse through the productive impetus of fear. *Collective containment* sustains the capacity to immerse and reverberate with that which is larger than the self as a potential for acknowledging and incorporation of the encountered, as well as the capacity to affirm the experience and commit it to consciousness, and hence resign from it. It can be perceived how these experiential conditions build up as structuring instances that cohere with the principal phases of the experiential sequence: stabilization, de-stabilization, and re-stabilization.

Their physical constitution relies on the same spatial features—i.e., their potentially simultaneous occurrence renders them immanent—these come forth as spatial formations always in emergence—composing and re-composing into and out of phenomenal distinctiveness. Yet once they attain presence, each of these conditions becomes an affective possibility apt to actualize in a distinct experiential form—in that it articulates particular spatial circumstances and relations, triggers specific internal mechanisms, and incites characteristic states. Hence analysis in terms of these spatial concepts, and in their potential intricate correlations, helps extract the logic behind the immediate experience in question, and, by extension—the experience of the performance event in terms of an underlying structure—by which each condition can be discussed in association with a certain instance partaking in the denoted cycle of experience. Thus, these constructs emerge as analytical tools capacious enough to approach the workings of space in its own right. This enables a shift of concern in understanding the experience in theatre—from the particularities of a theatrical form, to the generic conditions of the experience in the context of performance.

Extracting the spatial logic of experience: performance as encounter—encounters at performance
The notions of performance and experience as customized in theatre studies, and largely adopted in architecture, appear indispensably linked to a 'content'—to the effect of a more or less explicit threefold confluence. Here, the theatrical 'work' (text, process) comes to stand for the performance (as the object), and for the experience itself (as the vehicle)—linking the interpretation of these to a predominantly reflective mode based on recognition. Hence theatre experience understood in such terms, in a way, also relies on the safe distance to that which is acted out, and attains an essentially mediated character—a mediation which extends to characterize also the nature of the emotive and affective elements that this experience contains. Based on intentional identification with a protagonist, the volitional empathy with the dramatic reversal of fortune emplaced in the plot, these emotive components would be of a different category—distinct from actual affective and cognitive ingredients generated in the immediate experience. In contrast, the shift of focus towards the operations of physical space and the recovery of the immediately experiential as under-explored dimension of the performance experience brings this inquiry close to accommodating and particularizing the conception of experience as encounter, at multiple levels, and at the basis of a rendition of the experience of performance in terms of its generic constitution.

Links with various frameworks reflecting on experience as an encounter, can be construed especially with focus on the notion of emergence of something new, in the instance of contact. Hence in Deleuze's thought, the potential to transformation and change in encounter allows for a 'non-epistemic' performative ontology in terms of practical competence, where 'the emergent' is construed to generate in the bodily processes of confronting, acting upon, and being affected by that which exceeds the self—i.e., in terms of the difference and disturbance of the 'other' (Dewsbury 2000). For Levinas (1998), encounter bears on a mode of being which is essentially outward oriented, where the 'I' participates in what exceeds it. The ontological possibilities of encounter are seen in the exchange among two entities as their mutual 'nourishment' and 'enjoyment', which constitute the ultimate event of 'being' itself. These views then can be drawn productively into theatre theory, as in Ridout's critical analysis of the problems of contemporary theatre practice (2006: 1-34, 70-95).

Resonating with the principle notions of these frameworks, this current approach takes up, explores, and establishes these notions in their relevance with respect to the specificity of bodily encounter with the realities brought forth through physical space. It institutes and extends the theorisation of the conception of corporeality as the realm of the correlation, and grounds its validity on concrete empirical analysis of the circumstances of that contact. It arrives, analytically, at a particularisation of the workings of space as it materialises the conditions special to that concrete reality in the form of experiential possibilities, drawing a whole new cluster of phenomena—those that begin as induced—into account, and into the area of discrete immediate experience. It examines the experiential possibilities embedded therein and specifies experiential bearing of and through the proposed conceptual constructs. This analysis allows not only concretising the physical circumstances engendering the elemental conditions of physical encounter in the form of its consummate manifestation in exposure. Furthermore, an analysis of material space through the proposed conceptual constructs does offer grounds to extract the spatial logic underlying the experience of the performance event—as encounter. It specifies encounter within its physical actualization at site: in terms of underlying structuring mechanisms, phases and instances, in the internal processes of generation and operation of affects, and in the constitution of a range of possible occurrences and acquisitions that are, in this way, grasped, at micro level.

In shifting the inquiry into space with respect to experience towards its operations at the level of the corporeal, this analysis is already situated within the most intimate and direct zone of contact. This allows understanding the very nature and mechanisms of space-to-body correlations as founded on encounter, and rendering these explicit as they evolve through a rudimentary, yet also palpably physical form of reverberation. The relation actualizes in terms of the principles of the encounter: it comes about through the direct contact between two entities that is essentially unmediated and sensational, and therefore also spontaneous and pre-intellectual.

Analysis of physical space as the concrete context of the contact, then, allows seeking and explaining the emergence of something new which this contact inevitably entails, in the specificity of spatial circumstance. It allows understanding the role and workings of physical space in view of situatedness, specifying the course of involvement with space. It also allows concretising experiential contents by way of disclosing the ways in which distinct spatial conditions trigger awareness of and bring into presence the circumstances of a corporeal social situation within which one finds oneself placed, captured and directly involved. Space renders aspects of the situation tangible, and in this way qualifies the process of contact—i.e., it allows a glimpse on what may issue in the course of the unpredicted, unexpected, or unknown which contact by nature entails. Engagement with space does entail the alarming force of surprise which renders encounter productive—it stimulates the novel, and resolves in pleasure when bodily integrity is not jeopardized. Within the grey zone of the 'induced', relocated and reformulated in terms of the specificity of space and body reverberating, this encounter would entail the following discreet processes and mechanisms:

> a confrontation/contact with something unexpected— a contact which, as peripheral or distracted as it may be, presupposes the abilities to distinguish and attend to a challenge, as well as a capacity for coherent response—i.e., it involves concentration and accumulative activation—a shift away from the habitual and towards intense modes of being;

> an engagement—which presupposes a capacity to relate and expand, at times perhaps to the point of fusion, and to explore the specifics of the social situation—i.e., in proposing a direction outwards in deploying these energies, it triggers an impulse entailing the temporary suspension of the self/ego, vitalizing an active status, and, in this way, utter openness as a mode of becoming;

> an affirmation of that which is encountered—which presupposes a capacity to acknowledge the other, the situation, and the experience, enabling the mechanisms for its incorporation, as well as a capacity to resign from it.

It is possible to perceive how such mechanisms pertain to and begin to depict a sequential structure though which an encounter evolves. It is also possible to conceive how these resonate with the conceptual constructs that have been posited as the essential conditions formulating the components of the performance experience. While maintaining the essentially unintentional nature of encounter as something the sources of which lie in the outside, this analysis, by addressing these spatial internal mechanisms and explicating these as structural instances in correlation with encounter, offers insight into how certain spatial conditions for its incitement could be engendered. Hence it is through the explicit effects of isolation to arrive at stabilization, that self-containment is instigated via centring and detachment; much as it is through the effects of exposure to initiate de-stabilization, that engagement is achieved via polarization and extension. Correspondingly, it is through the effects of collective containment to finalize de-stabilization and achieve re-stabilization, that the production of that which is shared and the affirmation of that which is new is realized via assembly, assimilation and the conscious registers of witnessing. The corporeal terms and conditions of encounter can be understood through the specificity of the corporeal constructions of these forms of experience, which are brought about and brought to awareness through space.

Analysis through these conceptual constructs shows that the potential of physical space exceeds its complex coherence with and operations in staging the performance, where the encounter with the theatrical work is cumulatively supported. Rather, the constitutive potential of space extends to encompass the ontological and social, the emotive cognitive and ethical, as distinct experiential import. Various encounter types belong to this experiential layer and can be understood within the specified context of each form of experience:

> encounter with the self in terms of an awareness—of oneself as a separate entity, of one's capacity to attain more intense and activated modes, and access alternative paths of knowing;

> encounter with the other in terms of an engagement—augmenting one's capacity for contact, and the ability to expand and enfold the other;

encounter with a collectivity in terms of an acknowledg-
ment—of one's capacity to participate in a common endeavour, as well as one's capacity to assimilate change.

Though coming about through the corroboration of all three experiential conditions, each of these encounter types could also be associated
with the specified mechanisms and circumstances of the conceptual
constructs at work. Along with insinuating the emotive dispositions
appropriate to the perception of theatrical content—such as pity, fear,
pleasure—these conditions are constructive in their own terms. They
enable embodied knowledge of the self in its correlations: disclose
what membership and participation entail, acquaint with vulnerability,
underlie the emergence of alternative notions of openness, generosity,
or power—allow intuiting the practice of compassion and empathy in
their bare urge and necessity. All of these come about in immediate
experience, embedded in direct encounters with a concrete corporeal
situation. Analogous to, but also autonomous from the utmost affect
that the dramatic discovery of the unexpected has upon the individual,
space vitalizes its own prime mechanism: a rudimentary, yet entirely
corporeal and affective, multi-layered and polyvalent encounter,
which interrupts the habitual, intensifies being, renders active, and sets
us on the paths of discovery.

The aesthetic and the ontological
        This current analysis of corporeal experience in the context of
performance allows conceiving of possible links with more specific
accounts of experience, namely that of the aesthetic. Such links issue
both in terms of certain essential dimensions of the aesthetic experience, and in terms of a homology in the structure of experience—
allowing to intuit resonances among the structuring instances, through
which the aesthetic would appear to evolve. Although lacking a univocal conceptualization, diverse perspectives on the aesthetic converge on the issue of the transformative potential of the aesthetic experience. Inquiries seek to establish the fundamental conditions and
principles of the experience—as a basis to explicate its import in recovering the affective, creative and cognitive capacities of the individual. In a genealogical sketch, Shusterman (1999) delineates four
major dimensions of the aesthetic experience as the concept evolves
through pre-modern and modern discourses. The 'evaluative' dimen-

sion refers to the essentially valuable and enjoyable character of the experience, whereas the 'phenomenological' dimension expresses the fact that this experience is vividly felt, affectively absorbing, and focusing attention on the immediately presented. The 'semantic' dimension addresses the attainment of the meaning of the experience, as opposed to mere sensation. The 'definitional' dimension deals with the close identification of the experience with the demarcation of the work of art.

It is possible to perceive that this current inquiry into the spatial as a constitutive dimension of experience, which at this point is specified in the conceptualization of the performance as a spatially structured event, does intersect with some of the concerns articulated by these dimensions of the aesthetic. Its coherence with the first three dimensions in particular is confirmed by the findings of this analysis within each specific condition. It allows asserting that placing the experience, and in this way the performance event, out of an entertainment conception, a model of recognition, and a purely sensational base, would be supported through their material effects:

> the pleasure of involvement and growth as to grasp elements of the new (performance as engagement vs. performance as distraction);

> the absorbing qualities of that which is bodily and unmediated as to trigger an experiential mode (affective vs. cognitive); and

> the function of conscious incorporation as to confirm the experience (meaning formation vs. mere sensation).

Asserting the import of the particularly corporeal and experiential triggered through the circumstances of the site in facilitating the aesthetic, becomes the more justified in the light of inquiries, which establish the essential coherence of features and characteristics among the aesthetic, and experience in general. Hence Csikszentmihalyi (1999) in his analysis of the aesthetic encounter derives major dimensions of these two experiential forms arguing for their confluent nature and identifying the structure of the aesthetic experience in the process of fusion with the flow of the world. This process entails a set of conditions: the focusing and immersion in the moment by limitation of the stimulus field and exclusion of concerns with past and future, the nature of engagement where desire for authority over the situation is released through which action and awareness merge, the loss of self-consciousness and transcendence of individuality as a central condition for the attainment of heightened state of consciousness. All of these are construed as shared features which enable the access of 'flow experience', facilitate the potential fusion with the world, and culminate in intrinsic satisfaction and enjoyment derived from the very involvement and attainment of that heightened state of being as a form of understanding (1-26).

More specifically centred on the constructive potential of the aesthetic experience, inquiries revolve around a transformative moment, which takes specific form in the lexicon of different thinkers. Hence in a hermeneutical perspective, such a moment is seen to actualize in the engagement with something new which triggers a 'negation of former experience'. This moment forms the grounds for 'genuine experience'—i.e., it enables *Erlebnis*—as that which is lived through, as distinct from *Erfahrung*—that which pertains to accumulated knowledge—a conception through which Gadamer (1996: 55-70) conjoins the notions of the aesthetic with that of experience per se. Hence in this perspective, the aesthetic is not seen as a different kind, but rather as a representation of the 'essence of experience per se'—i.e., as expressive of the 'logic of experience' (Gadamer 1996: 70). The fundamental mechanism through which this logic operates is seen in the very condition of interruption of the normal habitual flow, and the change which this calls forth—a moment where 'the whole of life consciousness' is affected and engaged in the processes of constructing and assimilating that which is new. Yet while processes of the contact and incorporation of the new are comprised by the dissolution of elements that have lost validity, they also entail the preservation of relevant ones, through which such assimilation ensures the possibility of continuity within the very course of experiencing (Gadamer 1996: 69).

In explicating the experiential force of the aesthetic through and within the ontological, Agamben's (1999: 94-104) analysis presents a powerful argument. Shifting away from analyses centred on the artwork and its representational content, he proposes inquiry into the aesthetic in terms of the very encounter with the work of art. Thus the experience emerges by a crucial structural instance—i.e., in the moment of interruption of the habitual where the self is displaced—*ek-stasis*—and in this way comes in contact with some more essential capacities. This moment of interruption mobilizes the prime constitutive mechanism as a modality of transformation: it calls forth and reconnects the self with its most creative potential, and facilitates acquisition of both the aesthetic and the ontological in the appropriation of the work of art.

It can be construed how these different frameworks—one pointing to an underlying shared logic of the experience, the other deviating from an aesthetic analysis of the artwork towards the theorization of the aesthetic experience in terms of the very relation with the work of art—concur on the issue of principal resonances and mutual enforcement of the aesthetic and ontological, and validate, within the ontological, the most invigorating and productive effects for both.

The links with these frameworks are subtle and confined to the limitations of this current study, yet they also, analogously, span the theatrical, aesthetic and immediately experiential, in a way evidencing their confluence, as well as the nourishing potential of the corporeal. The analysis of the corporeal constructions of a particularly spatial nature, has provided grounds to conceptualize the performance as encounter at various levels, and identify various forms through which encounter as such actualizes. Whether approached at the level of the overall structure of the performance event, or at the level of minute situation and experiential condition, the analysis discloses the correlation as one of encounter –i.e., a fundamental reverberation with spatial circumstance. In this, the principal conditions which space brings into presence do cohere with the structural instances for both the aesthetic and ontological modalities of experience. In the expanding contracting dynamics of the site, experience can be understood in terms of its intimate initiation by alertness and self-containment (centring/isolation), the expansion achieved through affective identification and engagement (exposure), and an extension finalized in immersion with the collective, and sealed in collective testimony and witnessing. What this exploration in terms of situatedness and experience in conjunction allows for, then, is the possibility it opens up for detailed examination of these experiential conditions through the perspective of immediate experience in its corporeal construction, which helps disclose certain intricate, perhaps even intrinsic, mechanisms of such self-constitutive acts. This study would indicate not only that processes at this level do enable the emergence of productive states and ultimately shifts in the conscious mind as much, but also articulate their intricate and perhaps inherent entanglement with apprehension and fear-components, considering the impetus of exposure. These issue from, and accompany all occurrences within this experiential layer, embedded in the disconcerting effects of polarization and tension among experientially inverse conditions, the bodily grasp of vulnerability as profound and shared condition, and propose the corporeal basis of the embodied practices of empathy and generosity.

In the theatrical context, along with the other principal means of interruption—the encounter with the work, the performative event—it is in the operations of these subtle structuring mechanisms through which physical space reproduces a rudimentary but thoroughly corporeal interruption. Physical space can be construed as it assumes the capacities and the status of a pivot, suggesting, through the body, the possibility of multiple trespassing into a productive mode.

The role of the spatial dimension, then, can be sustained not only in that it triggers the experiential as a modality of becoming by corporeally constructing conditions for experience and presenting these simultaneously as immediate and immanent potential—a perpetual choice and opportunity to enter that experiential mode. Furthermore, analysis of this spatial form also establishes how space participates in constituting the structuring instances which underlie the aesthetic in its tangible and structured theatrical form, and experience in general. It helps construing how this moment of interruption of the habitual flow is not only actualized via the performance event and the encounter with it, but is embedded deeply in the materiality of situatedness. It discloses the spatial dimension in its explanatory potential with respect to the actual and the possible, both at work within the situation, identifying the processes and occurrences of contact at micro-level, in their spatial specificity, and tracing out a special range of aspects, which the corporeal/experiential and the theatrical/aesthetic share—affective and akin.

Beyond theatre—everyday sites

Isolation, exposure and collective containment allow the encounter to be recognized as distinct experience. In the built space of theatre they are spatially staged and supported, they are effective for ample duration, and they are dramatized—imparting states and relations with a ritualistic quality and intensity, at times attaining the weight of symbolic acts and gestures. This might perhaps be the very reason why forms of experience pertinent to the encounter, would attain legibility and engender awareness particularly in the context of the performance event. In built form, these experiential conditions are spatially constructed, which intensifies their effects and renders them as explicit, tangible presence for the situated agent. In their material realization at the site of performance, they could be, theoretically, recognized and acknowledged as pertaining to but one among the manifestations of the structure of experience—aesthetic, theatrical and corporeal.

The utmost productive aspects of theatre as a site of emergence would generate within this three-fold, where the mediated and immediate intersect: the framework of artistic and architectural referentiality overlaying physical space—connoting the represented both in theatrical semiosis and the architectural significations of the monument, and the framework of physical space where immediate lived experience evolves through its corporeal constructions.

However, while examined as generic to the operations of theatre space, where they appear in their most formalized realization, isolation, exposure and collective containment characterize this particular modality of spatial organization and in this way exceed the theatrical context. They are at work as experiential constituents at the many analogous collective sites whose formulation is governed by this same spatial logic. Their experientially consequential effects come to characterize the operations of spatial organizations for diverse appointed functions: secular and sacred spaces of assembly, of learning and celebration, work and entertainment. They exert their subtle influences also otherwise in the broader context of everyday experience in public space. Still legible as spatial organization, this mode is spontaneously reproduced in all the instances and occasions in everyday life that generate collective activity—meetings, gatherings around street performances and other incidences. While spatially less explicit, these configurations nevertheless sustain the conditions of isolation and exposure in palpable form and qualify experience, as this modality is established in the alignment of the participants themselves—as an achievement of collective bodies. It is such spatial homology—the broad variety of collective places reproducing this spatial form along with the principles, qualities and experiential potential embedded in it—which would disclose a range of corporeal aspects of the socio-cultural influence of theatre as a realm and model of the social.

Yet furthermore, the fact is that these conditions actually depict rather generic existential conditions, to be encountered in daily life. In Sennett's (1994) capacious historical inquiry of cities from the perspective of the social body, exposure and isolation do come forth as concepts with deep implications with respect to the experience of the public realm. Both of these concepts are taken up and examined as aspects, the experience of which marks significant differences—they help depict the historically particular ways in which these conditions have been accommodated, and have been made sense of. They are brought forth as aspects characterizing the urban experience, and linked with the sense of self in the respective historical context. Their interpretation is embedded in the evolutionary process of individualization, encompassing issues of control (the spatial strategies of isolating the different), of bearing and dignity (the exposure of the naked body, or its concealment), the strive for comfort (the pleasure principle) expressed in a growing withdrawal and detachment from the physicality of urban space and its condensed spatial and social circumstances. In Sennett's analysis, isolation and exposure come forth as dimensions effective over the sense of self, and present recurring aspects through which to derive the changing ways in which bodies have been experienced, the possible meanings these conditions have been engendered, and the correlations of bodies with space in the context of the urban—designated.

Within its narrow area of inquiry, this current analysis offers a vantage point on these conditions through their spatial constitution at the very minute level. This allows acknowledging the import of these conditions in terms of the logic of their constitutive capacities—foregrounding a phase of the experience in a way prior to the culturally grounded meanings through which they come to specifically affect the historically situated agent/body. This does not imply that they are taken as a-historic or all prevailing, but rather, that for this analytical approach they are employed as tools to disclose the spatial dimension in its productive operations. These concepts are analyzed in spatial terms which, as conditions, actualize in a distinct form—i.e., they are associated with capacities to trigger the experiential as active modality, as well as, in the course of this process, engender awareness of realities of the social, selfhood, and membership in it.

Inquiry into their spatial constitution allows construing how they would also issue as circumstances to be encountered in daily life. In contrast to their constructions in built space—formalized and intensified for the duration of the entire event, in daily experience they would lack formal expression, and their effects would be less articulate and fleeting in nature. Nevertheless, these conditions can be apprehended still as possible constituents of analogous experiential ingredients—and hence as integral to social space, characterising the broader context of everyday experience. It is perhaps in terms of the deep effects of these conditions understood as distinct forms of experience (rather than in terms of the phenomenality of the purely visual), and as part and aspect of the public/social realm, that the productive embedded in the spatial dimension would be rendered at its most profuse.

Detailed account of its spatial constructions and mechanisms specifies isolation as a condition that works though the impetus of centring and becomes productive in two respects, both of which help distinguish and root identities. While it evolves within awareness of simultaneous situatedness, with others, it actualises a way of being in space which brings to presence the self as being self-absorbed and short of a relation. Isolation, then, can be understood as a condition or instance of affective acquisition: based on the discernment of one's situation and self as a separate entity, it entails self-awareness that raises alertness, yet also contains it within. It emerges as a precondition of accumulation towards an intensified mode. Actualizing stabilization as a re-activation of that-which-is-centred, isolation assists the possibility of anticipating, preparing for, and contriving of forms of engagement and, thus, of a more resolute outgrowing of the self. Exposure, in turn, issues from the unsettling sense of displacement and tension between force and impulse, and is intensified through the perpetual oscillation among experientially inverse conditions: active/passive, observer/observed, and subverted/intervening. Hence it emerges as a mode of being that vitalizes the sense of being captured in a potentially vulnerable condition, either way, and in this way prepares grounds for the realization of this vulnerability as a profound shared circumstance. These explain how exposure renders the self not only active, but also open. Exposure imparts bodily knowledge on vulnerability as inherent in the social situation. It augments the self in its potential 'permeability' and 'receptivity', both of which, as Jenkins (2002) reveals in discussing the context of dialogue, would come forth as utterly productive. Embodied vulnerability, too, empowers. The bodily acquaintance with it summons latent capacities for self-composure, it alerts, but also allows grasping certain deep aspects of equality – i.e., it opens up alternative channels for sharing, and eases the ways of compassion and empathy. In the extending-contracting dynamics suggested by its spatial operations, the possibility of grasping altered notions of self, power, and generosity is proposed as an expansion—so as to encompass and incorporate that which is being encountered.

By focusing on the intricate constitutive mechanisms these conditions set in motion and formalised in built space, and explicating these through their corporeal constructions, this analysis brings to the fore a different set of aspects at work in these conditions. These are relevant to the understanding of material space in its capacities to qualify experience, and of the body/self in its capacities to engage with, reverberate and embody the possibilities of a spatial context. This analysis thus arrives at a depiction of certain rudimentary yet also foundational principles in the operations of collective social space. Simultaneous, as well as arising through shared features and elements in their spatial constitution, the affective influences of the conditions in question enforce and interfere with each other, alternate between augmenting and suspending specific effects, calling the self forth both in a mode of self-control, and in a mode of acquisition. Their conjoined experiential charge and impetus as socially significant conditions, then, is oriented: they strengthen the emergence of the social self, and are conductive of the grasp and embodied internalization of the complexities involved in the social reality. Analogous to the aesthetic, yet pressing through the body, they partake in extending the repertoire of practices enabling social togetherness, building up on the immediate experience of these conditions, and tracing out a corporeal trajectory towards altering notions over equality, participation and membership.

Witnessing, too, as an act, practice and condition pertinent to the shared space of the public realm, is disclosed in further specificity through analysis of its spatial constructions and operations. On the one hand, in the act of witnessing, it is the physical framework of space, which supports the potential of conscious appropriation as an assimilation of change undergone linked with the concrete circumstances of the social situation. The facticity of spatial circumstance to witnessing renders everything that evolves in the course of the event valid, legible and mnemonic, and thus allows for a safe reconstruction—stabilization. It 'objectifies' by lending credibility to a private feeling, a state, or an act. These aspects of the operation of human mentality that employ the productive force of capturing fleeting insights through links with physical context are substantiated in Yates (1969) seminal study on memory in the context of consequent theories on the mind and corresponding techniques of enhancing/expanding it. In the light of these insights, and in analogy with the workings of memory, the practice of witnessing can be understood as a process of linking mental components—ideas, concepts, feelings—to properties, qualities, and forms of the physical environment. Corporeal circumstance even at this fundamental bodily level, then, bears capacities as prop and link among various levels of mentality—sense and affect, but also memory and associative imagination.

On the other hand the analysis of corporeal circumstance allows construing in witnessing, the processes embedded in simultaneity and co-presence in space, which goes way beyond the visual, and towards disclosing aspects of their embodied corporeal actualization. Simultaneous presence is an inherent characteristic of the public realm, and a prime feature in its operations. As Arendt (1987, 5-12) asserts, the presence of others seeing and hearing, is by far not a passively perceived feature, but fundamental to the very possibilities of attaining a sense of that realm as safe and shared, and in assuming responsibility and presence within it. Yet further analysis of witnessing in its spatial constructions, helps show how spatial circumstance not only articulates co-presence, but involves forces and internal mechanisms which render that experience utterly tangible. It in this way confirms the possibility of arriving at awareness of a range of further aspects of the realm as shared, and ultimately guides the incorporation of a crucial function of the public—where one is simultaneously aware of the 'other', and aware of oneself—as the 'other'.

Analogous to the formalized operations of space in the context of performance, the presence of these conditions and circumstances in everyday experience of social space, conjointly, actualize a potential towards similar ingredients and forms of experience. As subtle and fleeting these may be in the everyday, they amount to becoming engaged, and becoming agent—both producer and product of the experience in question. Within its limitations, this inquiry helps render further capacities of the body with respect to space, and of the spatial dimension in the constitution of self and agency. Approaching these correlations from a different angle and in terms of the import of corporeality, it arrives at another set of aspects pertinent to the correlations between the physical and social selves. It ascertains the corporeal as experiential ground, which activates alternative paths of being and knowing—i.e., from within which awareness of our essential vulnerabilities, freedoms and capacities to explore and enjoy openness, and the risks this openness entails, are engendered. It attends to the role of space in the constitution of the collective and the operations of the social realm, specifying aspects of socio-spatial reciprocities. It provides glimpses on notions of the public, which can be attained through the perspective of immediate experience, and in terms of the specificity of the underlying spatial mechanisms and structuring potential which this analysis has brought forth and particularized.

Conclusion

This book presents an inquiry into the generative potentialities of material space with respect to emergent consciousness. It has sought to reconstruct, theoretically and methodologically, built architectural space in its physical presence respect to the situated agent—as it opens up to immediate experience. It has argued that analysis into the intricate ways in which space and experience link up, directly, would offer new insights into space, body, and lived experience. Such analysis would, through the vantage point of the corporeal, further understanding of the constitutive capacities of space with respect to experience, along with the affective and cognitive registers of consciousness embedded therein.

The proposed inquiry ventures into the problematic of built architectural space, which is a less-charted area in discourse on the lived, on space, and on immediate experience. Hence, while located at the interstices of various fields, and informed by diverse perspectives, notions, and conceptions, the inquiry traces out a specific approach grounded on a systematic rethinking of built space in terms of experience, and experience in terms of concrete physical space. It conjoins established concepts in novel ways, and in extending them towards analysis of concrete spatial circumstance, opens them up to accommodate further aspects brought forth in this process of concretization.

A major aspect of contribution is the approach itself—instituting the methodological and conceptual tools to enable analytical inquiry into the experiential potential of physical space. Central to the approach, the concept of corporeality is theorized as the realm of intimate reverberation between space and body. The re-articulation of space as an integral component qualifying the zone of contact, allows specifying the possible events of contact. By re-articulating material space as the extension of these correlations, the analysis accesses other, as yet neglected kinds of correlations such as those of situatedness, and involves these in providing an account of the productive capacities of space. The approach enables attending, analytically, to the corporeal constructions of a cluster of experiential phenomena that begin from without as induced discreet pre-contemplative mental processes, and confirm these as authentic paths of becoming and grasping the realities of the social and material situation.

This approach establishes built physical space as a distinct area of research at the experiential level, and the layer of space-to-body-correlations—as a layer of vital processes integral to the lived. Its analysis in the proposed terms ascertains physical space as a generative source with respect to the emergent, and as a dynamic constituent of experience. It is explained in terms of its un-mediated and non-mediating effects—a qualified materiality, which presents both the actual and the potential, and is, at this experiential level, always open to the situated body. This openness is substantiated in several respects. In terms of the concreteness of the corporeal, the operations of physical space are specified not only as to experiential contents, but also in terms of deeper internal structures and mechanisms, both of which offer an explanatory dimension in understanding discreet experience. Examining the effects of concrete spatial form helps understand how physical space comes to embed and mobilise experiential possibilities—it discloses particular properties of the concrete situation as these pass into and out of phenomenal distinctiveness. Configuring through the same physical elements and components these present material conditions that are generic to the spatial formation, yet are also actually emerging to awareness—they are both immanent and imminent. Physical space brings the essential existential conditions of our immediate situatedness in the material world into concrete presence through circumstances and qualities that are always under construction and always open to appropriation. Hence in foregrounding processes of correlation in their corporeal constructions, this approach helps render experience taking form. It discloses the intimate interdependence among spatial circumstances, and experiential bearing and content. Physical space is brought forth in terms of the particular internal mechanisms of diverse conditions, which it mobilises as instances structuring experience—concretely and concurrently these are present in space as a perpetual choice and opportunity.

Capturing the productive passage from space to sense to sensibility, this inquiry helps further understanding of the discreet processes of correlating with material circumstance as paths of change and acquisition—i.e., as these open up towards the ontological, emergent and becoming. Set within physical space, discreet experience emerges not in terms of reaction, reflection, or expression of underlying inherent structures. Rather, inquiry into the specificity of the correlation does allow attending to immediate experience in its corporeal mode of generation, and obtain insight of this in terms of spatial structures and mechanisms. Furthermore, examining material space as concretely present to experience, does ascertain the possibility of sharing, in experience, of actual circumstance. Space can be understood as a shared site of emergence triggering experiential processes which are corporeal and actual, and, while reverberating with spatial circumstance, are at the same time also essentially open, prone to chance and unpredictable. Subtle, non-contemplative, and thoroughly embedded in the corporeal, these processes do not pertain to meaning as tied with mediated content. Rather, they help construe how meaning derives from this very contact: it issues from the potential of the sensate and bodily as a passage towards active and alternative modes being and knowing, as well as from the affective and cognitive charge of the context that is, spatially, brought into concrete presence.

The case of theatre presents the implementation of the approach to a specific modality of spatial formation, and entails a set of particular conceptual constructs. It functions as an exposition and concretisation of its methodological principles and propositions, but also as an attestation to the explanatory potential of inquiry into the spatial as experiential dimension. It confirms the import of this layer of discreet experience in articulating further aspects of that which is authentically theatrical, and of physical space in the constitution of the socio-cultural role of this particular architectural monument—theatre.

The argument presented in this book can be taken to mark but one step towards acknowledging concrete physical space in its productive capacities. Within its limitations, it offers an insight into the construction of a layer of immediate experience, which is productive of meaning both in that it nourishes processes of embodied practice, and in that it vitalizes the disturbance of the habitual, augments the impetus of change, and, in this way, the generation and incorporation of practical knowledge. It renders aspects of the physical and the social self, of socio-spatial reciprocity, and of discreet experience, that can be addressed through and in terms of the corporeal correlations, and inferred from the specifics of the contact—through material space. It provides glimpses on the ontological and socio-cultural operations of social space through the perspective of immediate experience with space—pointing to aspects of its role in the constitution of agency. It confirms material space as grounds for further empirical research into the corporeal and its generative potential - a foundation and issue of the nexus of space, body, experience and consciousness.

Bibliography

Aaron, Stephen. 1986. *Stage Fright: Its Role in Acting*. Chicago and London: University of Chicago Press.

Agamben, Giorgio. 1999a. 'The original structure of the work of art' in *The Man Without Content,* (tr. G. Albert). Stanford, California: Stanford University Press: 94-104.

Agamben, Giorgio. 1999b. *Potentialities: Collected Essays in Philosophy*. Stanford California: Stanford University Press.

Allan, George. 1993. 'Traditions and transitions', in Cook, Patricia (ed.) *Philosophical Imagination and Cultural Memory: Appropriating Historical Tradition*. Durham: Duke University Press: 21-39.

Appleton, Ian. 1996. Buildings for the Performing Arts: A Design and Development Guide. Boston: Butterworth Architecture.

Arendt, Hannah. 1987. 'The Public Realm: The Common', in Glazer, Nathan and Lila, Mark (eds) *The Public Face of Architecture. Civic Culture and Public Spaces*. New York and London: The Free Press: 5-12.

Aristotle. 1985. 'Poetics' in *The Complete Works of Aristotle* (ed. J. Barnes). Princeton, New Jersey: Princeton University Press: 2316-2340.

Atkinson, Tiffany (ed.). 2005. *The Body. Readers in cultural theory*. New York: Palgrave Macmillan.

Bachellard, Gaston. 1969. *the Poetics of Space* (tr. M. Jolas). Boston: Beacon Press.

Ballantyne, Andrew. 2008. *Deleuze and Guattari for Architects*. London and New York: Routledge.

Barr, Richard L. 1998. Rooms with a View. The Stages of Community in the Modern Theatre. Ann Arbor: University of Michigan Press.

Benko, George and Ulf Strohmayer (eds). 1997. *Space and social theory. Interpreting Modernity and Postmodernity*. Oxford and Malden Massachusetts: Blackwell Publishers.

Bennett, Susan. 1990. *Theatre Audiences. A Theory of Production and Reception*. London and New York: Routledge.

Bergson, Henri. 1944. *Creative Evolution* (tr. A. Mitchell). New York: The Modern Library.

Bourdieu, Pierre. 1997. *The Logic of Practice* (tr. R. Nice). Cambridge: Polity Press

Bourdieu, Pierre. 1977. *Outline of a Theory of Practice* (tr. R. Nice). Cambridge: Cambridge University Press.

Breton, Gaelle. 1989. *Theaters*. New York: Princeton Architectural Press.

Brook, Peter. 1990. *The Empty Space*. London and New York: Penguin Books.

Burge, Tyler. 1997. 'Two kinds of consciousness' in Block, Ned, Owen J. Flanagen, and Guven Guzeldere (eds) *The nature of consciousness. Philosophical debates*. Cambridge. Massachusetts, and London: The MIT Press: 427-435.

Burke, Edmund. 1987. *A Philosophical Enquiry into the Origin of our Ideas on the Sublime and the Beautiful*. Oxford: Basil Blackwell.

Butler, Judith. 1979. *Excitable Speech*. London: Routledge.

Carlson, Marvin. 1989. *Places of Performance. The Semiotics of Theatre Architecture*. Ithaka and London: Cornell University Press.

Certeau, Michel. 1984. 'Walking in the city' in *The Practice of Everyday Life* (tr. S. F. Rendall). Berkeley, Los Angeles and London: University of California Press: 91-111.

Crossley, Nick. 2007. 'Researching embodiment by way of body techniques' in Shilling, Chris (ed.) *Embodying sociology: Retrospect, Progress and Prospects* (Theory Culture and Society). Oxford: Blackwell Publishing: 80-94.

Crary, Jonathan and Sanford Kwinter (eds). 1992. *Incorporations, Zone 6*. New York: Urzone, Inc.

Csikszentmihalyi, Mihaly and Rick E. Robinson. 1990. *The Art of Seeing. An Interpretation of the Aesthetic Encounter*. Malibu California: The J Paul Getty Museum and Getty Center for Education in the Arts.

Deleuze, Gilles and Felix Guattari. 1994. 'Percept, affect and concept' in *What is Philosophy?* (tr. H. Tomlinson and G. Burchill). London and New York: Verso: 163-201.

Dewsbury, John-David. 2000. 'Performativity and the event: enacting a philosophy of difference' in *Environment and Planning D: Society and Space* 18: 473-496.

Dewsbury, John-David. 2003. 'Witnessing space: knowledge without contemplation' in *Environment and Planning A* 35: 1907-1932.

Eisenman, Peter. 1992. 'Unfolding Events' in Crary, Jonathan and Sanford Kwinter (eds). *Incorporations, Zone 6*. New York: Urzone, Inc.: 422-427.

Forsyth, Michael. 1987. *Auditoria. Designing for the Performing Arts*. London: Mitchell.

Freud, Siegmund. 1949. *An Outline of Psychoanalysis* (tr. J. Stachey). New York: W W Norton & Company Inc.

Gadamer, Hans Georg. 1996. 'The Aesthetics of Genius and the Concept of Experience' in *Truth and Method* (tr. J. Weinsheimer and D. G. Marshall). New York: Continuum: 55-70.

Gibson, James J. 1983. *The Senses Considered as Perceptual Systems*. Westport: Greenwood Press.

Gibson-Graham, Julie K. 1997. 'Postmodern Becomings: From the space of form to the space of potentiality' in Benko, George and Ulf Strohmayer (eds) *Space and social theory. Interpreting Modernity and Postmodernity*. Oxford and Malden Massachusetts: Blackwell Publishers: 306-323.

Goffman, Erving. 1982. *Interaction ritual: Essays on everyday behavior*. New York: Pantheon Books.

Gregson, Nicky and Gillian Rose. 2000. 'Taking Butler elsewhere: performativities, spatialities and subjectivities' in *Environment and Planning D: Society and Space* 18: 433-452.

Guattari, Felix. 1992. 'Regimes, Pathways, Subjects' in Crary, Jonathan and Sanford Kwinter (eds) *Incorporations, Zone 6*. New York: Urzone, Inc.: 16-36.

Habermas, Jurgen. 1990. *Moral Consciousness and Communicative Action* (tr. C. Lehardt and S. Nicholsen). Cambridge: Polity Press.

Hallam, Richard S. 1985. *Anxiety. Psychological Perspectives on Panic and Agoraphobia*. London and New York: Academic Press.

Harrison, Paul. 2000. 'Making sense: embodiment and the sensibilities of the everyday' in *Environment and Planning D: Society and Space* 18: 497-517.

Harvey, David. 1998. 'The body as an accumulation strategy' in *Environment and Planning D: Society and Space* 16: 401-421.

Jacobs, Jane. 1995. 'The Uses of Sidewalks' in Kasinitz, Philip (ed.) *Metropolis. Centre and Symbol of our Times*. Hampshire and London: Macmillan: 111-129.

Jenkins, Fiona. 2002. 'Plurality, Dialogue and Response: Addressing Vulnerability' in *Contretemps* 3: 85-97.

Jones, Lindsey. 2000. *The Hermeneutics of Sacred Architecture. Volume Two: Hermeneutical Calisthenics*. Cambridge, Massachusetts: Harvard University Press, distributed for the Harvard University Center for the Study of World Religions.

Kasinitz, Philip (ed.). 1995. *Metropolis. Centre and Symbol of our Times*. Hampshire and London: Macmillan.

Kast, Verena. 1994. 'Angst und Faszination. Emozionen in Bezug auf das Fremde'. in Egner, Helga (ed.) *Das Eigene and das Fremde: Angst und Faszination*. Solothurn und Dusseldorf: Walter-Verlag: 214-238.

Kracauer, Siegfied. 1995. 'The hotel lobby' in *The Mass Ornament.Weimar Essays* (tr. and ed. T. Y. Levin). London and Cambridge: Harvard University Press: 173-188.

Lakoff, George and Mark Johnson. 1999. *Philosophy in the Flesh. The Embodied Mind and its Challenge to Western Thought*. NewYork: Basic Books.

Langer, Susanne K. 1988. *Mind: An Essay on Human Feeling*. Baltimore and London: The John Hopkins University Press.

Latham, Alan. 1999. 'The power of distraction: distraction, tactility, and habit in the work of Walter Benjamin' in *Environment and Planning D: Society and Space* 17: 451-473.

Lefebvre, Henri. 1991. *The Production of Space* (tr. D. Nicholson-Smith). Oxford and Cambridge: Blackwell.

Levinas, Emmanuel. 1998. *Totality and Infinity. An Essay on Exteriority* (tr. A. Lingis). Pittsburgh: Duquesne University Press.

Mackintosh, Iain. 1993. *Architecture, Actor and Audience*. Londonand New York: Routledge.

Madge, James. 2007. 'Type at the origin of architectural form' in *The Journal of Architecture* 12(1): 1-35.

Manning, Erin. 2009. *Relationscapes. Movement, Art, Philosophy* (Technologies of Lived Abstraction Series). Cambridge Massachusetts and London: The MIT Press.

Markus, Thomas A. 1993. *Buildings & Power. Freedom and Control in the Origin of Modern Building Types*. London and New York: Routledge.

Massey, Doreen. 2005. *for space*. Los Angeles and London: SAGE.

Mauss, Marcel. 2002. *A General Theory of Magic* (tr. R. Brain). London and New York: Routledge.

McAuley, Gay. 1999. *Space in Performance: Making Meaning in the Theatre*. Ann Arbor: The University of Michigan Press.

Merleau-Ponty, Maurice. 1992. *Phenomenology of Perception* (tr. C. Smith). London and New York: Routledge.

Meyer-Dinkgräfe, Daniel. 2005. *Theatre and Consciousness. Explanatory Scope and Future Potential*. Bristol and Portland: Intellect Books.

Nettleton, Sarah and Jonathan Watson (eds). 1998. *The Body in Everyday Life*. London and New York: Routledge.

Nietzsche Friedrich W. 1968. 'The birth of tragedy' in *Basic Writings of Nietzsche* (tr. W. Kaufman). New York: The Modern Library: 3-144.

Öztürk, Maya Nanitchkova. 2013. 'Cultivating space: Artifact and agency in theatre before and beyond its scenes'. To appear in *Space and Culture*, November 2013.

Öztürk, Maya Nanitchkova. 2010 a. 'An uncanny site/side: On Exposure, Dark space and Structures of Fear in the Context of Performance in *Contemporary Theatre Review* 20(3): 296-315.

Öztürk, Maya Nanitchkova. 2010 b. 'Theatre: From Mental Image to Corporeal Constructions of Community' in Meyer-Dinkgräfe, Daniel (ed.) *Consciousness, Theatre, Literature and the Arts 2009*. Newcastle: Cambridge Scholars Publishing: 109-121.

Öztürk, Maya Nanitchkova. 2007.' Corporeal thresholds to Consciousness: on the effects of Structures of Exposure and Structures of Fear at Performance' in Meyer-Dinkgräfe, Daniel (ed.) *Consciousness, Theatre, literature and the Arts 2007*. Newcastle: Cambridge Scholars Publishing: 101-115.

Öztürk, Maya Nanitchkova. 2006. 'Through the Body: Corporeality and Consciousness at the Performance Site' in Meyer-Dinkgräfe, Daniel (ed.) *Consciousness, Theatre, literature and the Arts*. Newcastle: Cambridge Scholars Press: 143-158.

Pallasmaa, Juhani. 1995. 'Identity, Intimacy and Domicile. Notes on the Phenomenology of Home'. in Benjamin, David N. and David Stea (eds) *The Home: Words, Interpretations, Meanings and Environments*. Aldershot, Brookfield: Avebury: 131-147.

Purcell, Stephen. 2005. 'A Shared Experience: Shakespeare and Popular Theatre' in *Performance Research* 10(3): 74-84.

Ridout, Nicholas. 2006. *Stage Fright, Animals and Other Theatrical Problems*. Cambridge and New York: Cambridge University Press.

Sauter, Willmar. 2000. *The Theatrical Event. Dynamics of Performance and Perception*. Iowa City: University of Iowa Press.

Schechner Richard. 1993. *The Future of Ritual. Writings on Culture and Performance*. London and New York: Routledge.

Shusterman, Richard. 1999. 'The end of aesthetic experience' in *Journal of Aesthetics and Art Criticism* 55: 29-41.

Sennett, Richard. 1994. *Flesh and Stone: The Body and the City in Western Civilization*. New York: W W Norton.

Shilling, Chris (ed.). 2007. *Embodying Sociology. Retrospect, Progress and Prospects* (Theory Culture and Society). Oxford: Blackwell Publishing.

Shilling, Chris. 2007. 'Sociology and the Body: Classical Traditions and new Agendas' in Shilling, Chris (ed.) *Embodying Sociology. Retrospect, Progress and Prospects* (Theory Culture and Society). Oxford: Blackwell Publishing: 1-18.

Shilling, Chris. 1993. *The Body and Social Theory*. London: Sage Publications.

Sienkewicz, Thomas J. 1991. 'The Greeks are Indeed like the Others: Myth and Society in the West African Sujata' in Pozzi, Dora C. and John M. Wickersham (eds) *Myth and the Polis*. Ithaca and London: Cornell University Press: 182-202.

Simmel, Georg. 1971. *On individuality and social forms: Selected writings* (ed. D. N. Levine). Chicago: University of Chicago Press.

Simmel, Georg. 1995. 'The Metropolis and Mental Life' in Kasinitz, Philip (ed.) *Metropolis: Centre and Symbol of our Time*. Hampshire and London: Macmillan: 30-45.

Sissons, Jeffrey. 2007. 'From Post to Pillar. God-houses and Social Fields in Nineteenth-Century Rarotongs' in *Journal of Material Culture* 12(1): 47-62.

Solga, Kim. 2008. 'Body Doubles, Babel's Voices: Katie Mitchell's *Iphigenia at Aulis* and the Theatre of Sacrifice' in *Contemporary Theatre review* 18(2): 146-160.

Strohmayer, Ulf. 1998. 'The event of space: Geographic allusions in the phenomenological tradition' in *Environment and Planning D: Society and Space* 16: 105-121.

Turner, Victor. 1982. *From Ritual to Theatre. The Human Seriousness of Play*. New York: PAJ Publications.

Varela, Francisco J. 1992. 'The Re-enactment of the Concrete' in Crary, Jonathan and Sanford Kwinter (eds) *Incorporations, Zone 6*. New York: Urzone, Inc: 320-338.

Vidler, Antony. 1992. *The Architectural Uncanny. Essays on the Modern Unhomely*. Cambridge and London: The MIT Press.

Weintraub, Jeff. 1997. 'The theory and politics of the public/private distinction' in Weintraub, Jeff, and Krishan Kumar (eds) *Public and Private in Thought and Practice: Perspectives on a Grand Dichotomy*. Chicago: University of Chicago Press: 1-43.

Wiles, David. 2003. *A Short History of Western Performance Space*. Cambridge and New York: Cambridge University Press.

Williams, Simon J. and Gillian Bendelow. 1998. *The Lived Body. Social Themes, Embodied Issues*. London and New York: Routledge.

Yates, Frances A. 1969. *The Art of Memory*. Armondsworth, Ringwood: Penguin Books.

Young, Iris M. 1995. 'City life and difference' in Kasinitz, Philip (ed.) *Metropolis: Centre and Symbol of our Times*. Hampshire and London: Macmillan: pp 250-270.

Index